Canons of Children's Literature

Canons of Children's Literature

Volume I

Edited by

Sunita Sinha

ATLANTIC

PUBLISHERS & DISTRIBUTORS (P) LTD

Published by

ATLANTIC

PUBLISHERS & DISTRIBUTORS (P) LTD

7/22, Ansari Road, Darya Ganj, New Delhi-110002
Phones : +91-11-40775252, 23273880, 23275880, 23280451
Fax : +91-11-23285873
Web : www.atlanticbooks.com
E-mail : orders@atlanticbooks.com

Branch Office
5, Nallathambi Street, Wallajah Road, Chennai-600002
Phones : +91-44-64611085, 32413319
E-mail : chennai@atlanticbooks.com

ISBN 978-81-269-1758-7 (Vol. I)
978-81-269-1760-0 (Set)

Printed in India at Nice Printing Press, A-33/3A, Site-IV,
Industrial Area, Sahibabad, Ghaziabad, U.P.

Dedicated to

Falak, the two-year-old battered baby...

who had been admitted at the premier AIIMS Trauma Centre, New Delhi on 18 Jan 2012 and was battling for survival. Despite all efforts by the doctors to revive her, Falak left the brutal world she had briefly inhabited for, hopefully, a better one, on 16 Mar 2012.

Preface

> When you write for children, don't write FOR children. Write FROM the child in you.
>
> —Charles Ghigna (Father Goose)

> Obedient miniature adult, mischievous free spirit, or mini-consumer—the image of the child in society has changed many times over the past three hundred years.
>
> —Iris R. Snyder

"Children are made readers on the laps of their parents", remarked Emilie Buchwald. Like the concept of childhood, children's literature is very much a cultural construct that continues to evolve over time. K. Hanson appropriately defines children's literature as "...the material created for and widely read, viewed and heard by children, that has an imaginative element...." Though it is one of the most innovative and spellbinding literature written for young people, yet it is only recently that academic study has embraced its range and complexity. The recent years have seen a dramatic change in the status of children's literature—from just being the concern of a few brave individuals, it has become the focus of countless courses, conferences and works of scholarship.

Our first rendezvous with literature transpired in childhood, fed on lullabies and hymns, fairy tales and bedtime stories, and has marched from alphabets and 'how-to' books, jokes and comic strips, to novels of fantasy, science fiction and adventure. The journey which began in childhood and the foundations of literacy laid then, persisted with us as we turned adults engaged in nurturing, educating, and entertaining children. Encompassing a wide range of works, including acknowledged classics of world literature, picture books and easy-to-read stories, fables, folk songs, and other, primarily orally transmitted, materials, children's literature has come to assume immense significance today.

The history of the development of children's literature is laden with the overwhelming urge to impose adult values on children. The Bible was regarded as the only reading material necessary for children (Clyde, 1983), and all early attempts in reading instruction were ultimately directed at understanding this work. The stories of saints and martyrs, and bestiaries or books about exotic animals, were therefore, probably the first printed books available to children. As early as the fourteenth century, children learned to read using horn books consisting of a piece of paper or parchment fit into a recess in a tablet of wood or leather on which the letters of the alphabet, a set of Roman numerals and perhaps the words of the Lord's Prayer were written or printed. As the student learned to read, the simple letters would be replaced by longer sentences. The seventeenth century saw the prevalence of a highly moralistic literature for children, concerned with the right and the wrong, with sin and damnation and almost completely barred humour from the stories. The eighteenth century visualised the translation into English of the classic fairy tales such as Cinderella and Little Red Riding Hood and the commencement of the English novel with *Robinson Crusoe* and *Gulliver's Travels*. Though not written particularly for a young audience, the stories of romance and adventure invoked readers of all ages, both in their original forms and in the many illustrated and simplified editions that followed. In the nineteenth century, works of literary merit, although not specifically aimed at children, were made available but only to children of middle and upper classes. This century has seen the development of literature, specifically for children, catering to their desires and demands. Thus, the Victorian era emerged as a golden period for classic children's books like *Alice in Wonderland, Adventures of Tom Sawyer*, and *Little Women*—and great illustrators—Kate Greenaway, Edward Lear, and Howard Pyle, to mention a few. Books and games for children became plentiful and inexpensive. In the twentieth century, children's literature was distinguished by a heightened multiplicity in both characters and authors and continued as a flourishing publishing industry for young people with adventure stories, series books like the *Hardy Boys* and *Nancy Drew*, science fiction and fantasy. Recent years have brought books tied to movies and commercial products from Disney to Star Wars as well as the psychologically-oriented young adult novel. Most children's literature prior to the twentieth century embodied a white ideology that was reflected in both the text and illustrations. From the 1920s onward, there have been attempts to provide a more multicultural approach to children's literature.

Despite the recent trend of categorizing children's literature by age, an increasing number of adults have begun reading children's books, blurring the boundaries between children's and adult texts. J.K. Rowling's *Harry Potter* series, begun with *Harry Potter and the Sorcerer's Stone* (1997), has been a huge success with both child and adult readers. Francesca Lia Block's postmodern fairy tales, such as *Weetzie Bat* (1989), and the darkly ironic *A Series of Contemporary Children's Literature* continue to be a highly innovative and challenging field. As children's literature has become an increasingly financially profitable business, more successful writers who have first established themselves as writers for adults such as Carl Hiassen (Hoot, 2002) and Michael Chabon (Summerland, 2002), are opting to write for children.

The present anthology, *Canons of Children's Literature* (Vol. I), with around a score of learned papers by scholars from the world over, remains my humble effort, to extricate children's literature from the narrow boundaries of the past and to place it in the foreground of literary scholarship, facing the future.

Joyashri Choudhury's explorative paper, "Truth and Power in the Magical World of Children's Literature" opens the anthology with a precise historical estimate of the enigmatic children's world, right from its origins in The Hornbooks and Chapbooks of the medieval period to the present, discussing quite magnanimously the growth and status of this brave new literature.

In, "Classical Fairy Tales and Greek Children's Literature" George Papantonakis explores the impact of fairy tales on children's literature and focuses on the treatment of Little Red Riding Hood in Greek literature. The brilliant analysis concludes with the dictum that, "It is the particular beauty of fairy tales that no one interpretation is the true one, no one version is correct. The ingredients of the tale can be simmered and stirred, flavoured and served up in a thousand different ways."

Running counter to the imperialist claim of children's literature as a European invention and manifestation and departing from the premise about an identifiable body of African children's literature, Sihem Arfaoui Abidi's paper, "Reading against African Children's Literature: Nationalist Didacticism in Fatima Mernissi's *Dreams of Trespass: Tales of a Harem Girlhood*" presents *Dreams of Trespass* as an African children's text that reads into national education as a means to and a backbone of childhood education.

In "A Pierced Tongue: Narration and Identity in Young Adult Novels in Verse", Amber Dinquel shows the blossoming of the young adult novel in verse as a relatively new genre through an analysis of two verse novels: Ellen Hopkins' *Impulse* and Patricia McCormick's *Sold*.

Enkelena Shockett's (Qafleshi) innovative paper, "Some Aspects of the Children's Literature in Albania" focuses on the peculiarities of the translated children's literature in Albania starting with titling in one hand and a couple of dominant motifs vested under the features of nationalism and internationalism on the other.

In his analytical paper, "(De) Centering Hierarchies: Programming Children in Hansel Ndumbe Eyoh's *Munyenge*", Kelvin N. Toh says that Eyoh's *Munyenge* (being a story written for children) is built on binaries—the ruler and the ruled, men and women—and these binaries only enforce the myth of the superior self as opposed to the inferior 'other'. Eyoh's play in this context is a tool to programme the child's mind with emphasis that this 'centre' is a perpetual state and no effort should be made to deconstruct.

Children's Literature Translation (ChLT) theory, being a 'young' strand of translation theory with origins in comparative studies, is effectively explored in Elena Xeni's paper, "Theoretical Framework of Children's Literature Translation" which provides an overview of these theories to highlight their relevance for ChLT.

The scholarly paper, "Unobtrusive Dissemination of the Didactic Teachings through the Indian Folk Lore" by Devika, Sushila Rathore and Virendra Singh Nirban discusses in detail "the richness of Indian folklore deeply infused with striking expression which has successfully made its way to the hearts of children and elders, boys and girls, learned and illiterate, firmly retaining its individual aura and diffusing its universal appeal, entirely unique and rich in its own way".

Sushmita Bhattacharya's critical paper, "Children in Victorian Fiction" presents childhood as the core theme in Victorian fiction in which the eminent writers of the age gave new inclusiveness and depth to the portrayal of the inner recesses of the child-mind.

"Violence in the Schoolboy Stories of Sukumar Ray" by Saurav Das Thakur aims at understanding this politics of foregrounding and silencing on the one hand and modes of subversion of that politics on the other as practised by the 'authority' and the 'others' in Sukumar Ray's Bangla schoolboy stories, anthologised in *Pagla Dashu.* It seeks to explore the various forms of violence it produces—in the urban schools in the age of colonialism in the adult world. It also tries to discuss how such 'violent' politics of subjugation and subversion was not something peculiar to the colonial institutions like the school alone, but also affected certain traditional indigenous institutions, like the family.

Drawing our attention towards the disappearing heritage of fairy tales that were once an oral legacy of every Indian child, Saurabh Kumar Singh in his analytical paper, "Fairy-tales and Fantasy as the Upholder of Values in Children's Literature: A Visit to *The Winged Horse: Fairytales from Bengal*", has tried to "show how the elements of fairy and fantasy have the capacity to deliver some useful and valid observations on elementary values, morals, and principles". Written not merely to amuse and entertain children, these stories serve a greater purpose of disseminating "commonsense, humility, decency, bravery, discipline, loyalty, and many other positive values for our own small children which are essential for the betterment of any civilized society".

In her article, "The Place of Books for Children and Adolescents in the Literary System", Vandana Singh remarks, "The trend and place of books in literary system changed as per the genre prevalent in different centuries.... Obviously the books reflecting the socio-economic and cultural situation in 1950s might not be of much relevance in the 21st century but the fact remains that books have the universality which cannot be denied and have always been an important and significant catalyst in development of society."

Saloni Kumar's innovative paper "Roald Dahl—The Hyberbolic Fantasist" says that Roald Dahl's view of society, his contempt for corrupt authority figures, and his distrust of the system have made his works popular with the children. Dahl has successfully tried to capture the wonder of a child's imagination by mixing in his stories the element of the bizarre and has managed to create stories that children adore.

Reena Mitra's scholarly paper "Salman Rushdie's *Haroun and the Sea of Stories*: A Postmodernist Fairy Tale" presents Rushdie's work as a "typical example of a novel which enchants and fascinates children but is also relevant in the adult world of today and carries within itself a cryptic message demanding uninhibited and unsmothered liberty to express oneself".

Ramendra Kumar's paper, "Panchtantra, Ramayana and Kamishbai—The Adaptation and Translation of Tales", is a brilliant effort "to elaborate on how tales for children can be adapted to transcend boundaries of time, space, culture and genre and help create a body of literature which is endearing and enduring".

"Vijay Tendulkar's Children's Plays: A Synthesis of Children's Fantasy and Social Commitment" by Beena Agarwal establishes that despite the abundance of fantasy, children's books are instrumental in deciding the direction of their consciousness in the totality of human experiences. "Such books", says Dr. Agarwal, "are culturally formative and of massive importance educationally, intellectually and socially. Perhaps more than any other text, they reflect society as it wishes to be, as it wishes to be seen, as it unconsciously reveals itself to be."

Anirban Gupta in his comprehensive paper, "In Love with Fantasy: The Fleeting and Seductive World of Lewis Carroll's Fiction for Children", focuses on Carroll's merits as a children's writer. According to him, "Carroll's treatment of fantasy, of allegory and mimesis of the mundane (everyday) human reality in the generic domain of fantasy is unique in the annals of literature.... Alice's imaginative visit to the land and its people, her curious involvement in their customs and rituals and the eventual flight back to her own world—gives rise to new versions of realism, or a blend of proto- and neo-realism, based upon more authentic standards of interviewing reality."

In her paper, "Portrayal of Children Characters in the Short Stories of Ruskin Bond", Norah Nivedita Shaw studies in detail the varied child characters in Bond's fiction.

Bhaskar Roy Barman's paper "Folklore as a Genre" offers a scholarly exploration of the world of folklore, mythology and telltales, and shows how these three different genres are related to one another.

Shampa Ghosh's paper "'In Essence Divided'—The Border as Metaphor" asserts rather poignantly, "What Rowling is essentially out to prove is that there are no rigid borders between opposing forces. Just as Harry is joined to Voldemort through his cursed scar so evil is linked to goodness, cruelty linked to magnanimity and morality to immorality but as Dumbledore points out in *The Order of the Phoenix*, 'in essence divided'".

Representing the combined efforts of scholars, the book is multifocal and inclusive, which would not have come to fruition without the help of many people. Needless to say, *Canons of English Literature* would not have existed but for the efforts of the contributors who conscientiously and patiently wrote and sometimes rewrote their articles at my request. Hence, I wish to thank all the contributors from India as well as from abroad for being an indispensable part of this venture and lending it a cosmopolitan outlook and a global approach.

I also wish to thank Dr. K.R. Gupta, Honorary Advisor, Atlantic Publishers and Distributors for the confidence evinced in me and for seeing the book through the press.

I sincerely hope that book will find the favour of students and teachers of English literature, particularly children's literature, and researchers in those fields.

Sunita Sinha

Acknowledgements

I am grateful to many people for their worthful support in preparing this book. I am especially obligated to my family, friends, colleagues and contributors for continually inspiring me to conjure art and scholarship that endeavour to confer valuably to the academic canon. *Canons of Children's Literature* aspires to stir the minds and hearts of the readers with a vision and wonder of the children's world in ways which reveal something already familiar, in new and enlightening dimensions. For the inspiration to visualise this book, I looked up to the realm of children, for the fact remains that "we need metaphors of magic and monsters in order to understand the human condition". Last but not least, I am indebted to Dr. K.R. Gupta, Honorary Advisor, Atlantic Publishers & Distributors (P) Ltd., for publishing this book.

Sunita Sinha

Contents

1

Truth and Power in the Magical World of Children's Literature

Joyashri Choudhury

Can you separate the child in you? It is well nigh impossible and neither should one encourage any such urge. The child in us is very special. A child wishes for things to happen whereas an adult has lost the faith of wish-fulfillment. Because a child wishes for fairies to inhabit his world, a child quickly can escape into a world full of fantasy and make-believe, where only good happens and everything ends on the note of, "...and they lived happily ever after". As Sarah Smedman says, "Hope is a vital dimension of a children's book." U.C. Knoepflmacher explains that the double perspective of child and adult that Ruskin Bond had implanted in his 1841 text (*The King of the Golden River*) would be perfected in their more complicated fantasies for young readers of both sexes by writers like Thackeray, George MacDonald, Lewis Carroll, Jean Ingelow, Christina Rossetti and Mrs. Ewing. *Goblin Market* (1862) by Rossetti confronted this psychological dilemma and proved to be appealing to both adults and children.

F. Gordon Roe says that adult books like *Redgauntlet* and *Oliver Twist* were appropriated by children and books written for children were equally devoured by adults. How many of us can really forget those Red Riding Hood and Brer Rabbit days? Heidi, Cinderella, Jack and the Bean Stalk have all stayed with us. Thackeray explains this phenomenon thus: 'The boy—critic loves the story. Grown up, he loves the author who wrote the story. Hence, the kindly tie is established between writer and reader, and lasts pretty nearly for life.' Thackeray had in mind Sir Walter Scott here, but he also refers to "Frank" in Maria Edgeworth's *Moral Tales for Young Children,* 1801.

Books read in childhood affect the adults we become at many levels, and so studying children's literature in some ways involves renegotiating the children we were as readers, emphasises Kimberley Reynolds, in her introduction to the book, *Modern Children's Literature. The Child that Books Built* (2002) by Francis Spufford explores this very interesting angle. 'Once upon a time last forever.' 'We don't' need lists of rights and wrongs, tables of do's and don'ts, we need books, time and silence. 'Thou shalt not' is soon forgotten but 'Once upon a time lasts forever', says Philip Pullman. Roger Boyes writing in *The Times*, London, reminded the world once again of the joy, euphoria and the return of the rats from an immortal legend in the sleepy town of Hamelin, Berlin in the promotion of the 725th anniversary of the Pied Piper. "Rats!" wrote Robert Browning in his famous poem, "They fought the dogs and killed the cats, and bit the babies in the cradles, and the cheeses out of the vats, and licked the soup from the cook's own ladles!" This was supposedly in 1376 (the Brother's Grimm set the date as 1284 in their version) when a man in strange attire playing a pipe lured the rodents out of the houses and met their doom in the Weser river. When the ungrateful town council did not pay up, the piper led away the town's children and they were never seen again, writes Boyes [Hamelin (Hameln in German) Browning added an extra vowel to help with the scansion of the poem].

The Beginning

Unearthing the roots of children's literature can be tricky. The Hornbooks of the later medieval period as well as the Chapbooks, precursors of the Penny Dreadfuls can lay a claim for such beginnings. Some stories popular among children were written in the 15th century. Thomas Malory's *Morte d' Arthur* (1486) and the *Tales of Robinhood* (1450) were not written with children in mind, but children have been fasicinated by these stories. In 1658, Jan Amos Komensky, published the illustrated informational book, *Orbis Pictus* in Bohemia. During this time, Charles Perrault laid the foundation of the fairy tale in France. His stories include *Little Red Riding Hood, Sleeping Beauty, Puss in Boots and Cinderalla.* In 1744, John Newbery published *A Little Pretty Pocket—Book in England*. Some would like to believe that the old romance, *Sir Beavis of Hampton* has a better claim. A version of this romance, was published in 1846, Richard Jefferies young hero in the children classic, *Wood Magic* (1881) and its sequel *Bevis: The Study of a Boy* (1882), James Janeways *A Token for Children* and Henry Jessey and Abraham Chear's *A Looking Glass for Children* of the 17th century may as well stake a claim. Some scholars prefer Bunyan's *Pilgrim's Progress* (1678), the preface to Part 11 (1684) as the beginning of children's literature. Others prefer Tommy Thumb's *Song Book* in 1744, and the appearance of the nursery rhyme tradition in Britain as a better starting point.

The appearance of fantasy and Lewis Carroll's Alice who shouted in her nurse's ear, "Nurse! Do let's pretend that I'm a hungry hyaena, and you're a bone", ultimately did succeed, to some extent, at least to lay to rest the Victorian moralistic tone of religious tracts, depicting exemplary children. According to Sylvia Kasey Marks, in 1839, this type of writing came full circle "with the publication of Catherine Sinclair's *Holiday House*". Childhood was seen now as a "central vehicle for expressing ideas about the self and its history".

Jack Zipes in the *Norton Anthology of Children's Literature* trace the history of juvenile literature from what is probably the first children's book, *Orbis Sensualium Pictus*, an illustrated Latin grammer by Johann Amos Comenius published in 1658. He writes that the attitude towards children began to change in the mid-18th century. Most early children's books were didactic and had a religious flavour. In 1762, Rousseau in his, *Emile, or On Education*, wrote that children are intrinsically innocent and should be educated apart from corrupt society, a view later taken up by the Romantics. In the mid to late 19th century, with the rise of the 'isms', Darwinism, Freudianism, Communism, Shavian socialism—

children were recognised as people and their literature became less heavily didactic.

Construction of the Child

"Children are made readers on the laps of their parents", writes Emilie Buchwald. In the opinion of the novelist Orson Scott Card, "one can make a good case for the idea that children are often the guardians of the truly great literature of the world, for in their love of story and unconcern for stylistic fads and literary tricks, children unerringly gravitate towards truth and power."

Toddlers to teenagers standing on the brink of adulthood are avid listeners and readers of children's literature. In *Milly-Molly-Mandy* by Joyce Lankestar's Brisley and *Little House in the Big Woods*, by Laura Ingall's Wilder, the text shows how parents treat the job of parenting as important. Kimberlay Reynolds in her article on "Sociology, Politics and the Family: Children and Families in Anglo-American Children's Fiction 1920-60", writes that in many ways the construction of the family as a self-sufficient loving and successful unit in a stress free, often rural or semi-rural environment, pervaded English-language children's literature for most of the 20th century. Parents are wary of fairytales, nursery rhymes and voyages of discovery such as Snow White, Hansel and Gretel, Bambi and *A Series of Unfortunate Events.* These stories succeed in removing the adult influence, letting the central character learn to cope on his or her own. Parents feel that such stories would make a child least prepared for the unhappy aspects of life to be encountered in adulthood. But this sort of adult characters, isolated from adult support, makes a child to make the transition to childhood, a less painful job. The school story became a common device for this beginning with Tom Brown's *School Days* (1857) by Thomas Hughes and F.W. Farrar's *Eric, or Little by Little*, although the framework had been explored as early as 1749 by Sarah Fielding in *The Governess, or The Little Female Academy*. Life begins for Tom Sawyer and Huckleberry in the Mark Twain stories once Aunt Polly's ineffectual tutelage is shaken off Aunt Polly's 'colonisation' is over. Critics like Peter Hunt, Perry Nodelman, John Stephens and Roderick McGillis argue that children are often 'colonized' by adults. Instead of making children speak for themselves, adults often speak on behalf of them. In the classic British novels, *Tom's Midnight Garden* (Phillipa Pearce) and *Jessamy* (Barbara Sleigh) the responsibility is enhanced by isolating the child not just spatially but in time through the use of *timeslip*. Ransom used this device of children acting for themselves, extensively in his *Swallows and Amazon Series* and included poignant discussions of it.

Gender, ethnicity, religious background act as factors in the construction of the child. Children are not one group. Feminist children's literature writer Lissa Paul shows how boys and girls read differently. Publishers were shrewd observers of this. When John Newberry published *A Little Pretty Pocket-Book* in 1744, he included toys with the books—balls for boys, pincushions for girls.

Jacqueline Rose and Karin Lesnik-Oberstein argue that identities are created and inherent, and that in the case of an identity such as 'childhood' it is created by 'adults' in the light of their own perception of themselves. That is 'adulthood' defines 'childhood' in relation to differences and similarities it perceives to itself. This is a post-structuralist approach. It is very akin to thoughts expressed in gender studies by Judith Butler and is accepted in sociological and anthropological studies of childhood.

The Hidden Messages in Children's Literature

Freud saw similarities between creative writing and day-dreaming. Children are fantastic daydreamers. Their daydreams get realized in these children's tales. And fantasy gets transformed into reality for a child.

In addition to a child's interpretation of a text, there is in it a hidden meaning, which a child would be able to unearth only from help from an adult. Susan Hancock in "Fantasy, Psychology, and Feminism: Jungian Readings of Classic British Fantasy Fiction", says that displacement and condensation are space where repressed fears are disguised, often by combining them with elements from daily life and making a single, condensed image or dreamscape, which fools the conscious into allowing repressed material to be expressed. Because they are disguised and condensed, such images work like symbols and metaphors in literature—they require interpretations—underlying the similarities between the analytical and critical processes.

Most early children's books were didactic and had a religious flavour, intended to civilise any potential sinners. It is striking in the Norton Anthology of children's literature, to see the way certain forms cross cultures. Lullabies have universal forms with elongated vowels, long pause and common themes of separation, hunger, bogeman, death—as if singing of these terrors could banish them from a child's dream world. *The Lullaby of a Female Convict to Her Child, the Night Previous to Her Execution* of 1807 is stunning. The book traces the evolution of such works as Hush-a-bye, baby, on the tree top from its origins as an African-American slave song, "All the Pretty Little Horses." That version ends with the horrifying image—"Way down yonder in the meadow lays a poor little lambia/The bees and the butterflies pickin out his eyes/The poor little thing cries, 'Mammy', London Bridge is falling down", says Jack Zipes, contain coded references to the medieval custom of burying people alive in the foundations of bridges. Fairytales have always been the hiding places for the subversives. *The Griffin and the Minor Canon* by Frank Stockton is a condemnation of cowardice and social hypocrisy, *The Happy Prince*, by Oscar Wilde, a critique of the aristocracy.

Hans-Heino Ewers, the director of the Institut fur Jugendbuchforschung (Institute for Children's Literature Research) at the Johann—Wolfgang Goethe Universitat in Frankfurt and an influential scholar of children's literature, is the author of *Fundamentals Concepts of Children's Literature Research: Literary and Sociological Approaches*. This work is a translation and revision of his, Literatur fur kinder and Jugendliche: eine Einfuhsung in grundlegende Aspekte des Hanlungsund Symbol-Systems kinder-undJugendliteratur (Munchen: Fink, 2000). Ewers employs structuralist ideas such as Gennette's concepts of the epitext, paratext, and the peritext to explore the "twofold communication" that he regards as normative for literature aimed at a young reading audience. He seeks to limit "intended children's reading" (as opposed to actual children's reading) thus: "School reading material should also be excluded from the second corpus (actual children's reading) which would then include all the texts or works that are actually read by children outside of school instruction and unconnected with it. "The historical consciousness that permeates Ewers approach is acutely aware and conditioned by the evolution of pedagogy and didactic literature in Germany. Ewers presents a theoretical discussion of the encoding of messages in children's literature, employing the ideas of Umberto Eco and other semioticians to analyse historical form of children's literature as didactic literature, as art, as revival of folk literature, as well as children's literary concepts and literary discourse.

Books read in childhood affect the adults we become at many levels, and so studying children's literature in some ways involves renegotiating the children we were as readers, emphasises Kimberley Reynolds, in her introduction to the book, *Modern Children's Literature. The Child That Books Built* (2002) by Francis Spufford, explores this very interesting angle.

Marketing

Children's books venture into new formats, new media and innovative design well ahead of adult publishing. Kimberley Reynolds says that in order to combine excitement and affordability, publishers, writers and illustrators for the young have always pushed back the boundaries of technology and design. John Sutherland remarks that it was not until the 1850s that a stable commercial infrastructure for children's fiction was established. Children's fiction as an enterprise began with the setting up of magazines such as 'Sunday at home', and the emergence of novelists such as George E. Saggent whose *Roland Leigh: The Story of a City Arab* (1857) pioneered a string of similar chronicles of virtuous heroes. From 1857 to 1885, the average number of new adult fiction titles appearing each year was 429, while the figure for 'juvenile works' was 470. An interesting point to note is that in 1894, the 'Publishers Circulum', made an announcement that it would stop counting the juvenile titles separately because so-called juvenile works are nowadays so well written that often they suit older readers quite as well as those for whom they are primarily intended.

Hans-Heino Ewers in the *Fundamental Concepts of Children's Literature Research: Literary and Sociological Approaches* reflects on the systematising and professionalizing of the distribution, evaluation, teaching and public discussion and consumption networks of children's literature in Germany. "From its extremely favourable position in the late 18th century, children's literature sank in the eyes of the educational and literary elite to being a purely commercial element of the book market with little literary or educational value". Consequently the field came to be dominated for a time by "religious denominational evaluation authority". "The secular school system that was being established in Germany at this time was based on contemporary children's books, which in the views of numerous pedagogic authorities should not even form part of children and young people's leisure reading". J.D. Stahl in the review of this book, which has been translated from the German by William J. McCann, further remarks that although children's books continued their reputation as "tendentious writing" this further diminished their value in the eyes of the elite. J.D. Stahl continues: It was only through the efforts of "Jugendschriftenkritik" (youth writing criticism) that the value of children's literature and literary criticism of that literature reestablished "cultural respect" for children's books. Through the establishment of a public library system in Germany at the end of the 19th century and the beginning of the 20th century, the supply of books for and to the child came to be dominated by an evaluation system oriented towards examining children's literature "for its educational quality, for whether it could be used in libraries and for whether it could be made use of in schools."

In "Children's Literary Polysystems and their Providence", Ewers seeks to create, as J.D. Stahl in his review tells us, a meta-description of the production, consumption, distribution and evaluation system of children's literature, which he regards as a 'chain of spheres of action'. He appears to lament that there is no conformity or dominance within these various spheres of action, as there once was in the movement spurred by Heinrich Wolgast's "Das Elend unserer Jugendliteratur", which celebrated children's literature as art (as opposed to didacticism) and which was some time the only secular evaluation authority of more than regional importance confronting the commercial book market and the denominational suppliers of literature.

I would like to conclude with the thoughts of Philippa Pearce reflected in her paper on *The Making of Stories for Children*, "The handing on of stories to children is part of a great oral tradition. We always know that fiction was lying. Now I hope to show that it is also based on a kind of calculated inaccuracy; above all in carelessness in its literal sense. Stories for children, their literature, which is a part of all literature, is carefree; and so it should be."

WORKS CITED

Carpenter, Humphrey and Mari Prichard. *The Oxford Companion to Children's Literature.* New York: Oxford University Press, 1999.

Nodelman, Perry. *The Pleasures of Children's Literature.* New York: Longman, 1996.

Reynold's, Kimberley. *Modern Children's Literature: An Introduction.* New York: Palgrave Macmillan, 2005.

Zipes, Jack et al. *The Norton Anthology of Children's Literature: The Traditions in English.* New York, London: W.W. Norton and Company. Internet sources.

2

Classical Fairy Tales and Greek Children's Literature

George Papantonakis

INTRODUCTION

The Impact of Fairy Tales on Children's Literature

This article focuses on how the folktales by Andersen, Perrault and the brothers Grimm were received by Greek publishers and Greek authors of fiction for young people. Investigating their treatment revealed different paths in transcribing and transforming fairy tales known worldwide into literary texts. First, as an expression of a people's soul, folk tales influenced authors personally, and many of their heroes inspired and fostered children's literature creatively. The examples we have studied show us the different directions in which the authors of children's books can transform a fairy tale or even the folk tradition itself. The fact that fairy tales are sometimes used to depict social reality demonstrates their *flexibility* as well as their *collective* or *social nature* that co-exists with personal inspiration, and 'records' cultural reality, either positively or negatively. The use of fairy tales to represent a specific historical reality also proves that they contain a certain *historicity*, which can be correlated with specific historical facts, and incorporated into children's and young adult's fiction. These functions can be found easily in Greek children's and young adults' fiction. For the needs of this paper, I have investigated generally how fairy tales are received in other countries as both folk tradition and fiction for children and young adults. This research showed that all nations have accepted the fairy tales of Andersen, Perrault and the brothers Grimm in their own way. Therefore, we are dealing with a universal phenomenon. Gail de Vos and Anna E. Altmann in their book *New Tales for Old: Folktales as Literary Fictions for Young Adults* (1999: v) maintain that "well-known folk and fairy tales are being retold in ever increasing" numbers worldwide. In addition to novel-length reworkings, such folktales are creatively revisited in short stories, poetry, film, and other forms of art throughout the folk culture and in young adults' literature. De Vos and Altmann also note that in the past ten years or so, folktales like "Cinderella", "Hansel and Gretel" and "Little Red Riding Hood" have been retold as novels; they have compiled an annotated bibliography that makes identifying these literary explorations much easier (1999). They also emphasize the importance of variants and stress that "no single meaning can be the only true one, and that any meaning is shaped by the context in which a story is written and read or told and heard" (1999: 16). Another interesting book is *Folktales from Northern India* (2002) by William Crook, a prominent British folklorist in India, and the transcripts of the translator Pandit Ram Gharib Chaube, which are considered an essential contribution to anthropology, literary history, the history of folklore and cultural studies. Vanessa Joosen also studied the retellings of "Snow White" in her paper "Disenchanting the Fairy Tale: Retellings of 'Snow White' between Magic and Realism" (2007). She examined fairy-tale retellings and believes that the concept of intertextuality is often introduced to explain the relationship between a retelling and the traditional fairy tale(s) to which it refers in another of her studies published in *Marvels and Tales* (2010). Extending the fairy tale in a different direction, postmodern literary texts from the late 1960s to the first decade of 2000, hold a mirror up to the foundational narratives of Western literature and culture, those fictions that, like the fairy tale, have framed and naturalized the social arrangements of the contemporary Western world (http://www.answers.com/topic/north-american-and-canadian-fairy-tales).

Comparisons between stories in Greek books and the originally translated French and German fairy tales show different results as regards both their adaptation and transformation, according to Maria Kalimbrou (2007: 54). She also maintains that there is no single way to transform European fairy tales into the format they take on in Greek popular booklets. It can likewise be said that a close and detailed analysis of folk tales demonstrates that the adaptation of the original translated texts ranges from the free, creative and innovative handling of the originals to a word-for-word translation.

HOW FAIRY TALES ARE ADAPTED BY CONTEMPORARY GREEK AUTHORS OF CHILDREN'S FICTION

Fairy tales are retold in Greek children's and young adults' literature in the following categories:

Intratext Fairy Tales of a Symbolic or Allegorical Nature

The author focuses on the point in the fairy tale that serves his plot and incorporates the text into his fiction. It can be limited to a simple reference to the title of the fairy tale with its symbolic or allegorical meaning (*Tina's Web* by Zei). Handling the original tale in this way enriches the story and aims to explain, deepen, justify or comment on reality by incorporating it at a particular point into the story, as the reality is structured by the historical framework and makes the historical reality of the novel more understandable for both the hero and the reader.

Fairy Tales as Meta-texts

Handling fairy tales as meta-texts leads to their adaptation and utilisation in an integrated and autonomous piece of fiction. John Stephens uses the term 'metanarrative' in an attempt to show that any adaptation is a secondary text created at a very specific time and place and reflects a particular ideology. We have found four such retellings of fairy tales: *The Wolves and Little Red Riding Hood* by Maria Pyliotou (1976), *In the Concrete Forest* by Loty Petrovits-Androutsopoulou (1981), *The Rebellion of the Fairy Tales* (1982; reprinted in 2004 as: *Rebellion of Dreams*) by Zoe

Valasi, and *Even Bad People Have a Soul*, by Sophia Paraschou. The first two novels are adaptations of Little Red Riding Hood, giving it a socio-political character. The other two also transfer heroes from other fairy tales to the contemporary world.

Fairy Tales as Peri-text

It is very useful for a scholar to observe carefully the peri-text in books for children and young adults that are adaptations of classical folk tales. In such cases, the title, abstract and comments on the back page of the book jacket comment on and reveal the author's tone and mood as well as the use of the metatextualized fairy tale in question. In any event, the adaptation always takes into account the Greek reader and cultural reality at the time of writing. For example, in the novel *In the Concrete Forest* by Petrovits-Androutsopoulou, perhaps only the word 'forest' suggests *Little Red Riding Hood*, of which this book is a meta-text. The title represents Athens, whose residential environment has been reshaped over the years to meet the needs of a rapidly expanding population. The city has become a forest of concrete apartment blocks that provide the background to the story of *Little Red Riding Hood.* The novel describes the dangers lurking in the big city drawing an unsuspecting person into drug use. In contrast, the title of the novel *The Wolves and Little Red Riding Hood* by Maria Pyliotou is a direct reference to the known fairy tale, and the first edition of Valasi's novel *Rebellion of the Fairy Tales* refers to many fairy tales.

HOW LITTLE RED RIDING HOOD WAS RECEIVED IN GREEK CHILDREN'S LITERATURE

Treatment of the Fairy Tale in Children's Literature World-wide

No fairy tale has been retold over the centuries as frequently as Little Red Riding Hood. It is part of the literature of 'inexhaustible possibilities', causing one to marvel at the countless and innovative ways in which the tale has been recycled in recent decades. The story could perhaps be regarded as hypertext, because most authors have included it in their books as either meta-text or intra-text. This suggests that age-old folk tales have the amazing ability to adapt to new social and cultural contexts (cf. Becket 2002: xvi).

This particular fairy tale has been adapted in many other countries as well. The study entitled *The Trials and Tribulations of Little Red Riding Hood* by Jack Zipes (1993: 48-49) gives us a lot of information about how the story has been treated all over the world (France, Germany, England, Ireland, U.S.A. and in many other countries). After World War II, *Little Red Riding Hood* kept being changed in Europe and the U.S.A. Contrary to the adaptations of the *Little Red Riding Hood* tradition in the 1920s, '30s and '40s, the new versions of the tale were addressed to both children and adults (Zipes, 1993: 58). This study and my internet research proved that the adaptation of the fairy tale[1] has also attracted the interest of scholars.[2] In world literature for children and young adults, the tale has been adapted in various ways. Sometimes it retains the heroine's name and the basic structures of the tale, and is easily recognized by the young reader. At others, the name is changed and the basic structures are modified and adapted to fiction for children or adults. Many structures may be retained, but they can always be changed.

The Fate of Little Red Riding Hood in Greek Children's Literature

Original production: The tale itself

In Greece, *Little Red Riding Hood* has generally followed the course of adaptation. Although in Germany this tale came second to the Bible in children's preferences, in Greece it was first (Anagnostopoulos, 2002: 123). The fairy tale has been received in Greece on the basis of two interesting reception mechanisms. The first comprises *faithful adaptations* and shows that the majority of translated texts remain faithful to the original tale. The second mechanism indicates that the patterns by which folk tales and fairy tales are transformed into fiction are the *creative transformations of the originals*, as Kaliambou argues (2007: 54). All the transformations we found in Greece belong to the latter category.

The main Greek version of the tale is found on the Aegean islands (Evvia, Sporades), on Mykonos in the Cyclades and on the island of Skiathos as *Chalkoskoufitsa* (chalkos = bronze—coloured in comparison with the original name which is in Greek *Kokkinoskoufitsa, kokkino* = red). The tale retains its basic structural features (she leaves home to see her grandmother, meets the wolf who extracts information from her and then devours her grandmother and herself). There is no hunter or woodcutter to save her. She is rescued by her parents. Her mother, worried by her long absence, goes to the grandmother's house, sees the wolf resting and informs her husband, who kills the wolf and plucks both the grandmother and her granddaughter alive from its belly (Angelopoulou and Brouskou, 1999: 465). The original fairy tale (ATU, 333) notes the presence of the father, who intervenes, albeit at the last moment, whereas in the versions of Perrault and the Grimm brothers, the father is absent.

In the Cyclades (Mykonos), the wolf is replaced by a dragon and Red Riding Hood by a little boy, who on his way to see his grandmother, meets the dragon, gives it the information it wants, and then the dragon devours the boy's grandmother. His mother, worried, goes to her mother in search of her son, places her iron shoes on the well and sighs, at which point the ground opens up and swallows her (Angelopoulou and Brouskou, 1999: 467). In this version, all family members are eaten by the dragon.

In Central Greece, the tale is found under the title "The Ogre". Here the ogre is the wolf, who eats the girl's mother, pretends to be the mother and then eats the girl as well. Neither of them is rescued, as is the case in the Mykonos version.

In Epirus, the story is told under the titles "The Evil Mother-in-law", "The Bear" and "The Terrible Mother-in-law". In all three versions, the mother-in-law asks her daughter-in-law to exchange hair colours from black to white and vice versa. The daughter-in-law asks God to change her into a bear so she can eat her mother-in-law. She is changed into a bear and eats both her mother-in-law and her son, i.e.

her own husband. But she does not eat her daughter. The mother makes her husband's sister eat her brother and drink his blood. The sister, however, deceives her and escapes into the forest where she is saved with the help of some deer. And then she marries a prince. In these variations we can see elements of the cruelest versions that are contained in the Zipes book.

LITTLE RED RIDING HOOD IN GREEK CHILDREN'S LITERATURE

Illustrated Adaptations of the Fairy Tale

Quite a few illustrated adaptations of this fairy tale have been published for small children in Greece. We shall confine ourselves here to those that present special interest. Christos Boulotis begins his story from the end of the known fairy tale, when the world-famous heroine marries the son of the hunter who killed the wolf. Of this union, twelve little girls were born who do everything they can to live an adventure similar to that of their famous mother. However, the forest was destroyed many years earlier, and the wolves had gone away to distant mountains. So the twelve little girls ordered a wind-up wolf from China that was like a real one.

Another post-textual utilisation of the fairy tale is one in which the heroine has a different name, as declared by the title of the novel by Antonis Papatheodoulou (2000), *Little Red Broom* (Kokkinoskoupitsa). The story is about a witch's broom that teaches a child to fly. The witch is evil and dangerous, but the child transforms her into a peasant girl. This is an odd version of Little Red Riding Hood that includes a sexual allusion: the big bad wolf is an evil witch-mother who is keeping her daughter, Little Red Broom, prisoner so she cannot fall in love and leave; a plan which fails in the end. Finally, in the illustrated history by Lefki Molfesi *Angelykos and the Two Sisters* (2002), the big bad wolf is represented as a housewife who darns socks.

Little Red Riding Hood as an Intra-text Fairy Tale

In children's literature, authors have received and utilized the fairy tale in miscellaneous ways. Thus, Red Riding Hood becomes a rag doll in Manos Kondoleon's novel *The 33* (2000:

65-66). In her book *The Hegia*, Sari notes that during the carnival (Hegia is the name of the feast held on the last Sunday before Lent) when people dress up, they often wear Red Riding Hood costumes. In many cases, authors change the name of the heroine (Psarafti, 2001: 81-83), a tactic that can also be observed all over the world (Zipes, 1993).

Its intra-text use reveals significant functions, apart from its contributions to promoting the story. In the novel by Sofia Zarabouka, *Friends, Close Friends* (1998: 16) the fairy tale is used to ridicule a situation by alluding to Red Riding Hood with a basket of figs for the heroine's mother. Giannis Bartzis in his science fiction novel *UFO in Digeliotika* (1990: 16) depicts his heroes admitting that children in our era are no longer fond of fairy tales like Red Riding Hood, which is why the little hero's grandfather tells him a modern fairy tale.

The intra-text folk tale once had a political dimension. In Alki Zei's novel *Wildcat Under Glass*, the two sisters Melia and Myrto had a basket that their Aunt Stamatina would fill for them to take to their cousin Nikos who was in hiding because of his left-wing ideology (1987: 87-88). Thus Nikos played the role of the grandmother, Stamatina was the mother giving orders, the two sisters were Red Riding Hood and all the people who shared the views of the dictators and persecutors of Nikos were the wolf. In the novel by the same author, *Tina's Web* (2002: 27). Tina's grandmother argues that the wolf ate Red Riding Hood because it was a fascist. In this way, the author passes down the message indirectly that communists are persecuted because of their ideology, and obliged to hide. In the novel by Litsa Parafti, *Breaths and Whispers of the Forest* (2000: 122) dangers are lurking that can hide in any unfamiliar place. A boy is willing to accompany a girl into a ravine to gather blackberries "so that the wolf does not show up and eat Red Riding Hood". Again, the fairy tale is used as the second term in a comparison, as it provides an opportunity to draw various parallels, and sometimes sexual symbolism is hinted. In Parafti's novel *Dreams of Silk* (2002: 69), a handsome Italian deceives his married lover (who leaves her husband for him) and is likened to a wolf.

RED RIDING HOOD AS META-TEXT

We encounter the tale of Little Red Riding Hood as meta-text in four works of fiction, two of which lend it historical or social content whereas in the other two, it constitutes part of a story in which many other known fairy tales are utilized. In these texts, Red Riding Hood plays an important role in the story.

Red Riding Hood as Historical Signifier

The tale of Little Red Riding Hood proved to constitute a good wrapping in which to present the story of Cyprus after 1974, starting out with the assault on Makarios and ending with the post-invasion refugee problems.[3] Maria Pyliotou in her novel *The Wolves and Little Red Riding Hood* focuses on the President of the Cypriot Republic, Archbishop Makarios. The symbolic character lent to the text by the tale of Little Red Riding Hood and its influence as fairy tale on a child renders historical reality in a particularly inventive way, proving the multiple meanings of fairy tales and the political repercussions they can have. In the case of Cyprus, the traps were set by the Greek junta as the big bad wolf who devours the grandmother (Cyprus), and Red Riding Hood (her children). From this contemporary folk tale the hunter-rescuer is absent. But he can be found in a text by Dinos Dimopoulos as the United Nations, with its collective nature, but totally formal and passive role in Cyprus. Thus, the fairy tale of Red Riding Hood can be recognised in its historical, political and national dimensions in contemporary children's literature for Greeks the world over, with the heroes devoured, the people refugees, the wolf with a full stomach, and the hunter a mere spectator whose presence is characterised by pious words; the end is a divided Cyprus.

Historical events are thus represented in a work of fiction that does not appear to be far removed from historical reality. Respect for people and human rights is commended, while the inability of certain institutions to function, such as the UN (woodcutter, hunter or father of Red Riding Hood), is touched upon. The clash of the weak, innocent people of Cyprus (Red Riding Hood) with the powerful political, military and financial establishment (wolf) that regulates the fates of nations did not change the status quo.

The Fairy Tale as Meta-text and the Theory of Literature

In the novel by Sophia Paraschou *Even Bad People Have a Soul*, the big bad wolf organizes a conference to exonerate the 'bad guys' in fairy tales from the charge of being evil. So the wolf sent letters to all these evil characters to invite them to submit the topic of their speech as well as to authors including Oscar Wilde, the Grimm brothers, and Greek children's writer Eugenios Trivisas. He did not invite Perrault or Andersen, who attended the conference uninvited. The wolf considers the authors responsible for quite arbitrarily assigning the role of 'bad guy' to wolves, sorcerers, dwarfs, stepmothers or evil sisters who terrify millions of children. Interest is focused on the stereotype of the big bad wolf and numerous cases are cited in which he appears in folk tales, with emphasis on Red Riding Hood.

On the pretext of the fairy tales, including Red Riding Hood, Paraschou's novel raises issues related to the theory of literature, regarding the power of the author, the reader and the fictional hero, and argues for the view that the strongest is the fictional hero, because he continues to exist even after the author and reader die. One of the Grimm brothers disagreed with these views, put forward the idea that the reader has the last word (*reading response theory*) and emphasized his role in the reception and assessment of a literary text. Perrault argued that when he wrote his fairy tales, he did not know that they would be read by children, because he wrote them for the high society ladies and cites Little Red Riding Hood as an example (cf. Zipes, 1993: 7). The shift from the adult to the child reader was made by the Grimm brothers, who argued that their mission was to keep tradition alive. They defended themselves against the charge of preserving the 'bad guys', with the argument that such tales help children develop their imagination and give form to their fears. These views raised concerns about the right of the author to re-narrate a fairy tale as he or she chooses, notwithstanding the views of M. Tatar (1992: 20), "Fairy tales are not written in granite. My own experience has shown that we continue to rewrite the tales as we reread them, even though the words on the page remain the same. But it is important to remember that what we produce in our retellings and rereading discloses more about an adult agenda for children than about what children want to hear. Thus, fairy tales may not offer much insight into the minds of children, but they often document our shifting attitudes toward the child and chart our notions about childrearing in remarkable ways."

The views of the conference participants, i.e. the 'bad guys' in fairy tales, including the wolf, imposed censorship and insisted that texts be re-written for reasons related to their public image, marking a new form of censorship of an intra-textual nature, independent of previous forms of censorship. It was due to the reaction of some fictional heroes (among whom was Red Riding Hood) who demanded that authors re-examine their position and change the unethical traits that a particular culture had attributed to them. This was a strict censorship imposed by fictional characters and an effort to manipulate their authors. The situation is saved by the contribution of the children, who prefer their fairy tales unaltered. Thus, the archetypal patterns of the human figures and situations remain unchanged and any effort to change and reverse them harbours threats of other forms of exaggeration. This is why the children at the wolf's conference demanded that archetypes familiar to them be retained, rejecting the pedagogical censorship proposed by the wolf with his argument: "But we didn't spoil them, my dear, we actually made them better. There won't be any bad people any more to scare you. You will be able to read Red Riding Hood without being afraid of the Big Bad Wolf" (Paraschou, 2004: 127). The insistence on tried and true forms of fairy tales with their archetypal patterns is due to the fact that the presence of the 'bad guy' throws the character of the 'good guy' into relief, which is why, as the little girl argued, "without the wolf, Little Red Riding Hood would have been just a silly girl who didn't listen to her mom" (Paraschou, 2004: 127). This of course happens only when children have read the traditional versions. The conference ended and, as the wolf leaves, he reverts to his old self, and cries "Blessed is the hand of the author who made me eat granny!" In this way, tradition overthrows the effort of modernity to take over by proposing the re-narration of the texts of traditional children's literature and making the 'bad guys' into 'good guys'.

Little Red Riding Hood as a Depiction of Social Pathogeny

In the novel by Petrovits-Androutsopoulou, *The Concrete Forest*, the same structure is followed as that of the fairy tale, and the author changes only the names or occupations of the characters. Here, Red Riding Hood (*Kokkinoskoufitsa*) becomes Connie Skoufitsi, who is sent by her mother from Boston to Athens to help look after her sick grandmother. In Athens, she meets Lykidis (*lykos* = wolf), a kind, middle-aged man who is also a drug-dealer. Connie tells him the reason for her visit (she misconstrues her parents' instructions thus creating the conditions for her to be 'devoured') and causes her grandmother to be become addicted to narcotics. Lykidis tries to lure Connie into the same trap (to 'devour' both the grandmother and Connie). Rescue arrives in the person of Sotiris Kynegos (sotiris = saviour, kynegos = hunter). Petrovits-Androutsopoulou manages the tale by relying on the social ideology of the period in which it was written, as it depicts the threat of narcotics in a concrete megalopolis like Athens. The concerns raised by the fairy tale regarding the parents' ignorance of the dangers in the forest, the role of the forest, the fact that the parents are not worried about Red Riding Hood's long absence, the appearance of the hunter or woodcutter and her rescue remain essentially the same, but are interpreted on the basis of the historical and social context of the period in which the story was written. The walk through the forest in the fairy tale becomes, in Petrovits-Androutsopoulou's novel, a trip through a concrete forest of apartment blocks in Athens and an ordeal for the young heroine. The concrete forest, like the forest in the folk tale, represents the dangers that threaten a young girl like Connie, who is guided by parental models and maternal instructions, and seems to have everything necessary to make a safe journey in a large city (dangerous forest). As the wolf in the fairy tale takes advantage of the unsuspecting innocent child, so Lykidis in *The Concrete Forest* tries to exploit the youthful Connie and lure her into drug addiction.

Lykidis is forceful and clever enough to resort to deceptive methods, like the wolf in the fairy tale. Because of her innocence and youth, Connie cannot see his ulterior motives, gives him the information he wants and is led astray. The novel, like the fairy tale, is structured around the contrasting states of disobedience/deprivation and appropriation. Connie harms her grandmother unwittingly, as she hands her over to Lykidis to exploit financially, just as in the fairy tale Red Riding Hood puts her own and her grandmother's life into the hands of the wolf. Lykidis grabs the grandmother's money and endangers her life as well as that of her granddaughter. Rescue will come from a young man named Kynegos (hunter), an unexpected support whose intervention saves the heroine.

Rebellion of Dreams

In the novel by Zoe Valasi, *Rebellion of Dreams*, Little Red Riding Hood, with many other fairytale characters, leave fairyland and enter the 'real' world of fiction, to which they have trouble adjusting. In this effort, Red Riding Hood takes initiatives to protect the financial and commercial activities in which Puss-in-Boots involves the fairytale heroes. She is depicted as a person who follows the era in which she lives in the real world of fiction. She supports Puss-in-Boots's commercial activities and does not hesitate to take the magic mirror away from Snow White to sell it. She is generally depicted as someone who moves comfortably, is always foresighted and ready to help the other heroes. This is a representation of the fairytale heroine who is in full harmony with the demands of an era that wants women to be dynamic and to take an active part in the social, financial and civic life of the society.

Conclusions

Our study has proved that "It is the particular beauty of fairy tales that no one interpretation is the true one, no one version is correct. The ingredients of the tale can be simmered and stirred, flavoured and served up in a thousand different ways", as Gail de Vos and Anna E. Altmann (1999: v) state.

It is typical that, despite the scanty presence of the fairy tale in Greece, the Greek people did not adopt the cannibalistic model in which Red Riding Hood boils and then eats her grandmother's entrails, without of course knowing what she was cooking, under the watchful eye of the wolf. But even in the few local variations, Red Riding Hood is sometimes replaced by a boy (or the daughter by the son/grandson) and the wolf by a dragon or ogre; whereas the hunter is absent (Zipes, 1993: 63). However, the radical variations that transform Red Riding Hood into a fearless, independent girl (Valasi, Petrovits-Androtsopoulou), like the versions that replace the wolf, undermine the appropriation of the traditional cultural model. Molfesi's *Angelykos* (=Angel-wolf) shows that the first obvious explanation for this is that wolves no longer represent a serious threat to human beings, if they ever did, which Zipes discovers, based on the different versions of Red Riding Hood worldwide. Moreover, the wolf as a representative of sexuality in general is less of a threat today, because the fear of sex has diminished, owing to a higher degree of scientific control over the body. We can confirm this by the fact that in Greek children's literature, there are very few cases in which the wolf represents a sexual threat (Zipes, 1993: 65). In the Greek children's books that we have been studying, an effort has been noted on the part of authors to counterbalance male dominance by promoting images of girls and women with various abilities and roles. In any event, the confrontation between re-writing or re-telling old fairy tales and retaining them as they are reveals how people deal with fairytale heroes as archetypal patterns of human nature that are found in reference to social and historical contexts.

Furthermore, fairy tales as meta-text became known as the fictional battlefield on which theories of literature clash. This is precisely what one derives from them. The wolf's conference and the effort to rehabilitate the 'bad guys' in fairy tales socially and morally was merely an excuse to present mutually conflicting theories of literature and the struggle between tradition and modernity. This is a game between 'being' and 'seeming'. The former raises more substantial issues, themes of writing and reading, responsibility to fictional heroes, while the latter alludes to the reason for their appearance.

The main discovery is that this particular fairy tale, as fairy tale, has not been adapted broadly in Greece, in which there are very few variations, as we have confirmed. In several of these, however, the wolf and Red Riding Hood have been replaced by an ogre, grandson or daughter respectively. The only constants remaining are the questions and answers, as noted by Tatar (1987: 40-43), and the forest, which are present in all variations, irrespective of the gender, age and form of the protagonists.

NOTES

1. Donald Haase in his collective study *Fairy Tales and Feminism: New Approaches* (2004) monitors the evolution and adaptation of fairy tales from a feminist viewpoint in many countries (Iberia and Latin America, Argentina, India). In his study "Response and Responsibility in Reading Grimm's Fairy Tales" (2003: 230-49), he monitors the responsibility with which later writers, especially critics, respond to the fairy tales. Altmann and Gail (2001) study the tale of Beauty and the Beast, and its re-writings in young people's literature, prose and poetry, on film and television.
2. For example, Ross King in his work *Traditional Korean Fairy Tales and Contemporary Korean Fiction: A Case Study of 'The Woodcutter and the Nymph'*. (http://www.asia.ubc.ca/fileadmin/user_upload/asian_studies/faculty/elena_yugai/Publications/RKing_2005_Traditional_Korean_fairy_tales_and_contemporary_Korean_fiction.pdf), discusses the problem of traditional culture in a "modern" world, and studies the case of "The woodcutter and the nymph" and its various versions and retellings for adults in Korean children's and young adults' literature.

3. The historical dimension of the fairy tale is already known, from the time French troops occupied the Rhine region and loaded the tale down with anti-French and anti-English references. Thus, the wolf embodies a dual identity, the French revolutionaries who came to liberate German youth and/or the French conquerors who came to destroy the virtues of Germany. Red Riding Hood symbolized innocent German young people who were initially carried away by the revolutionary fervour of the French but were then oppressed by the cruelty and barbarism of the revolutionaries.

BIBLIOGRAPHY

Primary Sources

Bartzis, Yannis. *UFO in The Village Digeliotika.* Athens: Kastaniotis, 1990.

Carmen Gaite Martin. *Caperucita en Manhattan/Little Red Riding Hood in Manhattan* (Escolar De Literatura/School Literature). Madrid: Siruela, 2006.

Fakinou, Eugenia. *A Summer Story.* Athens: Kedros, 1986, 16.

Kondoleon, Manos. *The 33.* Athens. Patakis, 2000, 65-66.

Papatheodoulou, Antonis. *Little Red Broom.* Illustr. Stavros Palanzas. Athens: Minoas, 2000.

Paraschou, Sophia. *Even Bad People Have a Soul.* Athens: Psychogios, 2004.

Petrovits-Androutsopoulou, Loty. *In The Concrete Forest.* Athens: Patakis, 1981.

Psarafti, Litsa. *Angels of the Sky.* Athens: Patakis, 2001.

——. *Breaths and Whispers of the Forest.* Athens: Kedros, 1993.

——. *Dreams of Silk.* Athens: Patakis, 2002, 69.

Pyliotou, Maria. *The Wolves and Red Riding Hood.* Nicosia, 1976.

Sari, Georges. *The Hegia.* Athens: Patakis, 1998, 21.

Valasi, Zoe. *Rebellion of Dreams.* Athens: Patakis, 2004 (1st edition: *Rebellion of Fairy Tales*, 1982).

Varella, Angeliki. *The Match Begins.* Athens: Patakis, 2001.

Zarabouka, Sofia. *Friends, Close Friends.* Athens: Patakis, 1998, 16.

Zei, Alki. *Tina's Web.* Athens: Kedros, 2002.

——. *Wildcat Under Glass.* Athens: Kedros, 1987, 84.

Illustrated Books

Boulotis, Christos. *12 Red Riding Hoods and The Wind-Up Wolf.* Illustr. Fotini Stefanidi. Athens: Papadopoulos, 2007.

Mania, Christine. *Cinderellas Around the World.* Illustr. George Sgouros. Athens: Intro Books, 2007.

Molfesi, Lefki. *Angelykos and His Two Sisters.* Athens: Periplous, 2002.

Rossi-Zairi, Rena. *7 Snow Whites and the Dwarf.* Illustr. Natalia Kapatsoula. Athens: Minoas, 2003.

Essays

Altmann, Anna, and de Vos Gail. *Tales Then and Now: More Folktales as Literary Fictions for Young Adults.* New York: Greenwood Publishing Inc., 2001.

Anagnostopoulos, V.D. *Art and the Technique of the Fairy Tale.* Athens: Kastaniotis, 2002.

Angelopoulou, Anna and Brouskou, Aegli. *Processing of Fairytale Types and Variations AT 300-499.* Athens: N.H.R.F., 1999, 465-68.

Beckett, Sandra. *Recycling Red Riding Hood.* New York and London: Rutledge, 2002.

Beckett, Sandra. *Red Riding Hood for All Ages: A Fairy-Tale Icon in Cross-Cultural Contexts.* Detroit and Michigan: Wayne State University Press, 2008.

Crook, William and Chaube, Pandit Ram Gharib. *Folktales from Northern India.* Edited and with an introduction by Sashana Naithani. ABC-CLIO Classic Folk and Fairy Tales. Santa Barbara: ABC-CLIO, 2002.

De Vos, Gail and Altmann, Anna. *New Tales for Old: Folktales as Literary Fictions for Young Adults.* Englewood, CO: Libraries Unlimited, 1999.

Haase, Donald. "Response and Responsibility in Reading Grimms' Fairy Tales." *The Reception of Grimms' Fairy Tales: Responses, Reaction, Revisions.* Ed. Donald Haase. Detroit and Michigan: Wayne State University Press, 2003, 230-49.

——. *Fairy Tales and Feminism: New Approaches.* Detroit and Michigan: Wayne State University Press, 2004.

Joosen, Vanessa. "Disenchanting the Fairy Tale: Retellings of 'Snow White' between Magic and Realism". *Marvels and Tales,* 21.2, (2007), 228-39.

Kaliambou, Maria. "The Transformation of Folktales and Fairy Tales into Popular Booklets". *Marvels & Tales,* 21.1 (2007), 50-64.

King, Ross. "Traditional Korean Fairy Rales and Contemporary Korean Fiction". 24 April 2011 <http://www.asia.ubc.ca/fileadmin/user_upload/asian_studies/faculty/elena_yugai/Publications/RKing_2005_Traditional_Korean_fairy_tales_and_contemporary_Korean_fiction.pdf.>

Stephens, John and McCallum, *Robyn. Retelling Stories, Framing Culture. Traditional Story and Metanarratives in Children's Literature.* New York and London: Garland Publishing, Inc, 1998.

Tatar, Maria. *The Hard Facts of the Grimm's' Fairy Tales.* Princeton and Oxford: Princeton University Press, 1987, 40-43.

——. *Off With Their Heads: Fairy Tales And the Culture of Childhood.* New Jersey: Princeton University Press, 1992, 3, 10, 35-39, 49, 209-10.

Zipes, Jack. *The Trials and Tribulations of Little Red Riding Hood.* New York and London: Routledge, 1993.

3

Reading against African Children's Literature: Nationalist Didacticism in Fatima Mernissi's *Dreams of Trespass: Tales of a Harem Girlhood*[1]

Sihem Arfaoui Abidi

> To assert that only our conception of childhood can result in children's literature, a literature that only we are able to judge as literature in terms of its literary value (which for some reason must include 'entertainment'), is the kind of cultural imperialism and ideological colonialism that modern critics—often seek to avoid. (sic. qtd. in Nodelman and Reimer 83) [2]
>
> I was very proud to have a role to play, even though it was a silent and marginal one [...] it did not matter what role you played, as long as you were useful. The essential thing was to have a role, to contribute to a common goal. (Mernissi 126)

Ideological Interpellation

To the extent that the conception that Children's Literature is a European invention in origin and should remain so is a common view, the category African Children's Literature could sound a bit awkward and surprising for some readers and cultures.[3] This way, from the perspective that Children's Literature has always been associated with such canonical texts as *Alice in the Wonderland*, the venture of this article to go beyond this elitist configuration, by exploring the area of African Children's Literature, may be as challenging as the assumption of the latter as an identifiable body. In this respect, what motivates the interest of this paper in African children's texts is the fact that critic Philomena Osazee Fayose goes a step further as to distinguish "three distinct periods in the publishing of children's books in Africa: 1960-c.1974, 1975-85, and 1985 to the present" (929).

As an English text published in 1994 yet written by the Moroccan woman writer Fatima Mernissi, *Dreams of Trespass: Tales of a Harem Girlhood* can be considered as an African children's book which technically falls in what Fayose speaks of as the third phase in the history of this literary corpus. Most essential of all is the argument advanced in this paper about *Dreams of Trespass* as a memoir wherein the discourse of childhood both informs and is informed by ideas of nationalism. By moving within the broader orbit of the strong connection between text and context, the present article shall benefit from the conception that "cultural and historical antecedents, social, political, economic issues give rise to regional, national or ethnic differences" (Fayose 927). It also shares the postcolonial perspective that "literature interpellated and continues to interpellate its readers into social and political thinking; in other words, literature deals in ideological matters" (McGills 893). By definition, literature is politicized.

More particularly, let us remind ourselves that "[w]e are implicated in and complicit with ideological and political positions and hailings" and "that ideology is at work even in that literature that seeks to 'echo or awaken...thoughts or feelings of human communality'"[4] (McGills 898). In this same context, E. Oluwasanmi et al. equally insist that the relevance of children's books "to their own environment in textual content and illustration" is a quintessential edifice in both the emergence and growth of this corpus (qtd. in Fayose 929). Such concurrent readings represent sufficiently strong enhancements to reconsider Children's Literature in Africa, through the suggested example of Mernissi's *Dreams of*

Trespass, with a special eye to its correlation with nationalism. They help shape nationalism, both in the sense of a "mnemonic space of popular resistance" and as a category encompassing the coalition of the masses, as concerns of a certain depth in Mernissi's children's text (Mowitt 169).

At this point and from the point of view of a reader with no particular knowledge of the considered text or the geo-political circumstances it describes, an introduction of Fatima Mernissi and the publication history of *Dreams of Trespass* and structure arise to the status of a necessary prerequisite. On the basis of Anne Donadey's *Recasting Postcolonialism: Women Writing Between Worlds* (2001), Fatima Mernissi, a Moroccan woman writer and sociologist holding an American Ph.D., publishes in English, such as *Beyond the Veil* (1975), as well as in French (148). In a pointer to the international significance of Mernissi's *Dreams of Trespass*, critic Donadey equally adds that "although Mernissi lives and works in Morocco, her memoir's target audience is international due to her choice of writing in English" (148). In her view, Mernissi's "knowledge of English allows her to bypass the dangers of writing about the self in the language of the former colonizer", especially that "English is a more neutral language, one that may allow writers to distance themselves from the text and possibly reveal certain things that may be difficult to say, and even more to write, in Arabic, the language of the sacred text" (148). In the meantime, the same critic stresses that the writer's choice of writing this memoir in a language unfamiliar to the majority of Moroccan people puts certain constraints on Mernissi's memoir such as the obligation to provide detailed explanations (148).

In addition to this, Mernissi's *Dreams of Trespass* falls under the genre of African children's literature, precisely because it only covers the childhood years of a North African Moroccan girl between the ages of four and nine (Donadey 148). In this respect, Melissa Matthes describes the involved book as "Fatima Mernissi's account of her early girlhood in a Moroccan harem in the city of Fez" in the sense that it "recounts life in her childhood harem from her earliest recollections" (73) until she is declared by an older cousin to be 'officially mature', that is, when she is approximately tiptoeing into her ninth year (Mernissi 219). As to the structure the considered memoir, we should mention that the latter "is organized according to the structure of *The Arabian Nights*", including the latter's framing device and some of its stories (Donadey 150).

With this biographical and critical background in view, it should be indicated that the purpose of this paper is to examine the inherently solid connection that this narrative generates between childhood and national education, hence, the commitment announced in the title to read against African Children's Literature, with a special focus on nationalist didacticism. In this respect, speaking of 'reading against' *Dreams of Trespass*, this paper intends to see through the ways in which Mernissi's text attempts to "manipulate one's emotions and influence one's understanding and moral judgments" (Nodelman and Reimer 26). It suggests indicating the political and social assumptions of Mernissi's text and bringing them to the reader's consciousness (Nodelman and Reimer 152). On the basis that Mernissi's text mirrors a personal narrative which is situated during the expansion of the European empire in the twentieth century, meaning the colonization of Morocco by Spain and France in 1912, this article will focus on the informative impact of the national scene in Morocco on *Dreams of Trespass*.[5] It reads into Mernissi's childhood narrative as an ideological vehicle for representing the Moroccan national experience during and after Western encroachment. One of its main assumptions is that the considered text mirrors a nationalist activism that makes of the notion of Morocco as an independent nation inseparable from the modernization and emancipation of Moroccan women.

European versus Third World Nationalism

Given that the present paper aligns itself with the general umbrella theme of "Nations of Childhood", as a paramount guideline, to proceed with a brief literature review of the concepts nation and nationalism, both of which amount to key contextual axes along which the argument of the whole paper is developing, seems a required step. Most often understood as a large group of people inhabiting the same country and governed by one civil law, the term nation and its existence rely on such prerequisites as "a great multitude of men" who "must obey the same laws and the same country" and "inhabit [...] a defined country" which "must be circumscribed by frontiers" (qtd. in Foucault 142).[6] Within a Foucaultian framework, it is also possible to reject the limited consideration of a nation as "something that is defined by its territorial unity, a definite political morphology, or its systematic subordination to some imperium" (Foucault 134). Instead, a "nation can exist as a nation, and can enter history and survive through history, only if it is capable of commerce, agriculture, and handicrafts; only if it has individuals who are capable of forming an army, a magistrate, a church, and an administration" (Foucault 220). Foucault equally reminds us:

> The essential function and the historical role of the nation is not defined by its ability to exercise a relationship of domination over other nations. It is something else: its ability to administer itself, to manage, govern, and guarantee the constitution and workings of the figure of the State and of State power. Not domination, but State control. The nation is therefore no longer a partner in barbarous and warlike relations of domination. The nation is the active, constituent core of the State. (sic. 223)

Thus, the extent to which the existence of a nation "is linked to the rise of a merchant class and capitalist economic system, a centralized, bureaucratic state, a common language, and an educated public", rather than the ideals of expansion in other countries, is one of the fundamentals that gives the term nation its historical meaning (Baker 13).[7]

In parallel with this latter framework which describes a European model of nationalism, we should not overlook the Third World perspectives of national consciousness during colonization. As a matter of fact, nationalism in colonized nations is credited ambivalent implications of resistance which engulfs at least two main traits or domains, that is, in terms not only of political/cultural activism, but additionally of armed struggle against the colonizer. However, because history abounds with instances where "the colonized intellectual has thrown himself headlong into Western culture", there is an emphasis of the fact that political activism by itself is not sufficient in the national-building (Fanon 156). As Fanon puts it, "[w]e should not therefore be content to delve into the people's past to find concrete examples to counter colonialism's endeavours to distort and depreciate. We must work and struggle in step with the people so as to shape the future and prepare the ground where vigorous shoots are already sprouting" (168). As such, the political, the cultural and the military should go hand in hand in the context of national activism and resistance.

With respect to military resistance, Fanon openly states that "when it comes to talking about that one thing in a man's life that involves opening up new horizons, enlightening your country and standing tall alongside your own people, then muscle power is required" (167). Homi K. Bhabha equally considers the repossession of land and territoriality "in order to ensure the security of national polity and global unity" the primary purpose of decolonization (xi). He furthers that, "the colonized emerges as a guerrilla in camouflage waiting for the colonist to let down his guard so that he might jump; each obstacle encountered is a stimulant to action and a shield to hide the insurgent's intention to take the colonist's place" (xxxviii). In a similar context, Jean-Paul Sartre deems the rural masses "the true reservoir for the national and revolutionary army" (XIV). Although suggestive of different standpoints, such readings converge on assuming the mobilization of a collective action a pre-condition in national liberation.

With these framing remarks, what is of interest to this paper is the historical embeddedness of *Dreams of Trespass* through its allegiance to nationalism. It is the use of this children book as a vehicle to express the national concerns of colonized Morocco and formulate the latter's national consciousness and experience. What contributes in bringing further notice to this issue of ideological interpellation is the fact that Mernissi's work emphasizes such ideologically-embedded topics as armed resistance and the education of women as part of the Moroccan nationalists' political platform (Donadey 151).

Armed Resistance and Anti-colonialist Heroines

Dreams of Trespass seems to impart that what puts the nation on the stage of history is the national liberation based on armed struggle (Fanon 180). To this extent, it intentionally mentions several names of nationalist heroes and heroines in Morocco such as Al-Hiba in the South at the edge of the Sahara who resisted until 1934 (Mernissi 36). In a significant way, Mernissi expresses her pride as a child, who is born in the Atlas region, because the latter, she clarifies, is the birthplace of a nationalist hero called Hamou Zayani "who kept the French at bay until 1920" (Mernissi 36). In addition to this, the memoirist refers to nationalist symbols in the North such as Abdel Krim, entitled the prince of fighters, who was defeated only in 1926 (Mernissi 36). Of similar appeal to Mernissi as a child are the nationalist heroines. In this vein, critic Alison Baker explains that, in the center of Morocco, in the Middle Atlas mountains, "according to oral tradition, women followed the male fighters into battle, loaded their guns, and even carried guns themselves to take their turn fighting when the battle got really intense" (19). The same critic informs us:

> Women participated in active, even armed, resistance against the colonizers from the very beginning of the protectorate, especially Berber women in the Rif Mountains, the Muddle Atlas, and the Anti-Atlas and Sahara in the south. In 1913, one year after the establishment of the protectorate, the women in the Khemisset organized the first known demonstration against the French. It was so large and effective that the French had to resort to the military to bring things back under control. (18)

At this level, the colonizer had to fight the colonized at least at two camps. In reinforcement of the notion of anti-colonialist female nationalists, Mernissi shows further zeal when she relates the heroic journey of Tamou, a relative to the Mernissi family, and a symbol of the Berbers' nationalist struggle in the South. Tamou appears in 1926, "after the defeat of Abdel Krim by the combined Spanish and French armies. She appeared early one morning over the horizon of the flat Gharb Plain, riding a Spanish saddled horse, and dressed in a man's white cape and a woman's headdress so that the soldiers would not shoot at her" (Mernissi 50). Out of admiration for this relative heroine, Mernissi recounts all the details of her adventures and background, indicating that "Tamou was a Riffan and a war heroine. Morocco was full of admiration for the Rif people, the only ones who had kept on fighting the foreigners long after the rest of the country had given up, and here was this woman, clad as a warrior, crossing the Arbaoua frontier into the French Zone all by herself to look for help" (Mernissi 51). Further on, she comments "Tamou became a legend the moment she appeared. She made people aware of their inner force and their capacities to resist all kinds of fates" (Mernissi 53). In this sense, *Dreams of Trespass* does function as a tribute to the Rif's heroines and fighters, as iconic models of national struggle.

Mernissi's *Dreams of Trespass* indicates that women are a central part in the nationalist struggle of Morocco for independence, given that they have provided an essential component in the political agenda of Moroccan nationalism, in addition to their participation in the war of resistance to colonization. Critic Baker states:

> Following the defeat of Abdelkrim in the Rif War in 1926, there was a shift from armed resistance based in rural areas to political resistance based in the cities. The Moroccan nationalist movement was initially out of a concern among a few individuals in the cultural and intellectual elite that the values of Moroccan Islamic culture and society were being subverted by France [...] It was in this context that the young Moroccan nationalists turned their attention to the status of women. (20)

It is also in this context that the considered memoirs unravel the fact that Mernissi is born and educated in a family of nationalists (Mernissi 36). Though her grandfather was a slave-holder and tradesman, later one he adopts the principal nationalist slogans such as the abolition of slavery and monogamy (Mernissi 36).

Political Activism and the 'New Woman'

The following section brings to the foreground the ways in which Mernissi's memoir emphasizes the overarching part devoted to the education of Moroccan women in the political agenda of the Moroccan nationalists of the 1940s. It stresses the interactive relationship between the emergence of Moroccan nationalism during the French Spanish colonization of Morocco and the education of local women as an edifying infrastructure for the progress of a Moroccan nation. In this respect, Baker considers the emancipation of Moroccan women a prerequisite in the nationalist movement in Morocco, particularly, upon suggesting that the education of women "as one of the most effective means of fighting ignorance in the family" (22). In fact, from the perspective that "[w]omen were the guardians of Moroccan tradition, and the family was the basic cell of Moroccan Muslim society", also "the mother of all social institutions" (Baker 28), the nationalist leaders in Morocco "took up the cause of girls' education" and "created their own free schools where instruction for girls (and boys) would focus on the Arabic language, the Koran, and nationalism" (Baker 22). This is in addition to the notion that "[t]he status of Moroccan women—their seclusion and lack of education—had become an embarrassment to French-educated Moroccan men who wanted to show that they were civilized and modern by getting rid of everything that was backwards in the old society. Thus, they imagined a 'new woman' who was presentable in colonial society, yet whose primary role was still in the home" (Baker 21).

Moving along a similar orbit, Mernissi's *Dreams of Trespass*, in turn, represents the modernization of women in Morocco as a paramount step to the achievement of independence. This is the reason why most of the Mernissi children go to the nationalist schools while the brightest few attend the college (Mernissi 86).

> [t]he nationalists, who were fighting the French, had promised to create a New Morocco, with equality for all. Every woman was to have the same right to education as many as well as the right to enjoy monogamy—a privileged, exclusive relationship with her husband. In fact, many of the nationalist leaders and their followers in Fez already had only one wife, and looked down on those who had many. Father and Uncle, who espoused the nationalist views, each had only one wife. (Mernissi 24)

Towards the end of Mernissi's tales, the national consensus on a modern education of women is embodied as a turning-point in the history of nationalism in Morocco, especially, when we consider the following reference:

> The entire town was turned upside down when the religious authorities of the Qaraouiyine Mosque, including Fquih Mohammed al-Fassi and Fquih Moulay Belarbi Alaoui, supported women's rights to go to school, and with the backing of King Mohammed V, encouraged the nationalists to open up institutions of learning for girls. Upon hearing the news, Mother immediately petitioned Father that I be transferred from Lalla Tam's Koran school to a "real one," and he responded by calling for an official family council meeting. (Mernissi 196)

According to this passage, Fatima herself gains the benefits of the expansion of nationalism in Morocco. As she puts it, "[t]he change was incredible, and I was elated" (Mernissi 197). Fatima's elation mirrors itself in her recent attendance of a modern school where she "learned by heart many of the nationalist songs that we sang in school, and Father was so proud that he would ask me to recite them in front of Grandmother Lalla Mani at least once a week" (Mernissi 199). In this sense, a modern school is assumed not only to improve women's status but also to enhance the transition of this nationalist consciousness to the younger generation.

At this level, *Dreams of Trespass* best depicts women's roles in passing on the modernizing spirit of the nationalist agenda in Morocco to their children. For one thing, even if Fatima dresses in the traditional Moroccan garment, the caftan, especially on religious festival days, her mother insists on dressing her "in the latest Western fashions—short, fluffy lace dresses with colored ribbons and shiny black shoes", Fatima also (Mernissi 85). In the mother's perspective, "'[d]ress says so much about a woman's designs,' she said. 'If you plan to be modern, express it through what you wear, otherwise they will shove you behind the gates. Caftans may be of unparalleled beauty, but Western dress is about salaried work'" (Mernissi 85). Likewise, even Fatima's grandmother hints to "the creation of the beautiful, new Morocco, the Morocco that I, her little granddaughter, was going to step into. 'Morocco has changed quickly, little girl,' she often told me, 'and it will keep on doing so'. That prediction made me feel very happy. I was going to grow up in a wonderful kingdom where women had rights, including the freedom to smuggle up with their own husbands every night" (Mernissi 36-37). Suffice it to mention that, in New Morocco, "we will have one man, one wife" (Mernissi 37). Even this note of humour does not undercut its indication of the great enthusiasm for a monogamous Modern Morocco.

So far, it could be noticed that, in the background of Fatima's elation, so to speak, her mother's recommendations and her grandmother's expectations lies the nationalist penchant for taking France itself as a model of nation formation (Baker 20). In the early 1930s, critic Baker indicates, young Moroccan men educated in France, who took Europe as their point of reference, dominated the debate on women's emancipation (20). Fatima herself is a representation of this project, since her grandmother keeps reminding her, "[y]ou will be a modern, educated lady. You will realize the nationalists' dream. You will learn foreign languages, have a passport, devour books, and speak like a religious authority" (Mernissi 64). Everybody around Fatima enhances her status as a potential representation of New Morocco.

Union against Conquer and Divide

Considering all these complementary perspectives on the struggle against anti-colonialism, Mernissi's *Dreams of Trespass* reveals that all components of the Moroccan nation, ranging from the monarchy to women and children, spared no effort in their resistance to the French-Spanish rule. In fact, in January 1944, when the child-narrator was barely four, the Moroccan King Mohammed V, "backed by nationalists all over Morocco, went to the top-ranking French colonial administrator, the Résident Général, to make a formal demand for independence" (Mernissi 23-24). In her childhood narrative, Mernissi also shows that what brings Moroccans together is the idea that Morocco "had existed undivided for centuries, even before Islam came along fourteen hundred years ago. No one ever had heard of a frontier splitting the land in two before" (Mernissi 1). As a result, "the moment when the Spanish and the French crossed the Moroccan frontier, making the North Spanish and the South French, signals a turning-point in the historiography of Morocco" (Mernissi 2).

In the spirit of a nationalist unity against the imperialist dictum of Conquer and Divide, *Dreams of Trespass* emphasizes that this resistance not only takes precedence over any other issue but also dictates solidarity even among family members. As far as women are concerned, the common goal of regaining the notion of Morocco as a wholesale nation is the reason why the claim of Fatima's mother for an independent nuclear family almost goes without notice in the Mernissi family. "Mother, who hated communal harem life and dreamt of an eternal tete-à-tete with Father, only accepted what she called the '*azma*' (crisis) arrangement on the condition that no distinction be made between the wives" (Mernissi 6). Apart from the great reserve that surrounds every demand of modernizing the family structure, even the fact of skipping a meal on the communal dinner table in the Mernissi family, Fatima tells us, "was considered terribly rude and too openly individualistic" (Mernissi 76).

> Eating at fixed hours was what Mother hated most about communal life. She would nag father constantly

> about the possibility of breaking loose and taking our immediate family to live apart. The nationalists advocated the end of seclusion and the veil, but they did not say a word about a couple's right to split off from their larger family. In fact, most of the leaders still lived with their parents. The male nationalist movement supported the liberation of women, but had not come to grips with the idea of the elderly living by themselves, nor with couples splitting off into separate households. Neither idea seemed right, or elegant. (Mernissi 75-76)

The rationale seems to be that the preservation of the extended family structure embodies a solid ground on which to build an agenda of resistance to colonization. As future citizens of a New Independent Morocco, even the Mernissi children share a sense of responsibility for holding the Moroccan family strongly together. In their eyes, one way of achieving this cohesion is by never uttering the word 'harem' in public, since that word causes along serious disputes between the harem women (Mernissi 40).[8] All that the children could do is try to figure out the concept and its embedded meanings in total discretion.

Salafiya Islamic Reforms

In essence, it is what is termed the neo-salafiya thought which passes on the equal responsibility of the Mernissi adults and children, men and women, for protecting the maximum level of cohesion. In this same context, Baker reminds us of the salience of "the conception of the family that was at the core of" this Islamic nationalist movement, explaining that,

> [t]he Islamic reformers didn't promote the education of women or defend the rights of women under Islamic law primarily in order to let women develop as human beings, but rather to buttress the Muslim family, and through the family, to reinforce social cohesion, and women were important because of their traditional roles at the heart of the family. Thus the reforms sought to strengthen the basic structures of the old society, especially the bourgeois family, not to change them. (22)

This particular passage puts in evidence the significance of the communal family as a backbone of the nationalist reforms. It downplays a strong sense about the primacy of family solidarity, as an embryo of national consciousness, inasmuch as it manifests the degree to which Moroccan nationalists bet on family ties as a microcosm of national union.

In consequence, it should be noted that the emphasis of *Dreams of Trespass* on the valorisation of each Western aspect about women's status is not tantamount to mirroring an utter rejection of the traditions that keep Moroccans as a united nation. On the contrary, Mernissi depicts the latter stance at the very extreme of the father's attitude which evinces a rejection of the complete westernization of the younger generation. In the context of clothes, for instance, the memoirist's father notices in a critical tone:

> "But what good does our wearing traditional dress do," father joked one day to my young cousins sitting around him, "when all you young people dress like Rudolf Valentino?" Without exception, they all wore Western attire, and with their short hair uncovered and cut above the ears, they looked very much like the French soldiers standing at the end of the street. "One day, we will probably manage to throw the French out, only to wake up and find out that we all look like them," added uncle. (Mernissi 85)

In so saying, the Mernissi advocates of Moroccan nationalism show their pre-occupation with the questionable adherence to Europe as a model for rebuilding a modern Moroccan identity. They are closer rather to a form of nationalist leadership which "based its ideology of social reform, and especially its ideas about women, not on European models but rather on the Salafiya Islamic reform movement," coming through Syria and Egypt (Baker 21). According to the Salafiya movement, "Islam and the Koran provide guidance for all times and places. If the Muslim world is stagnant, it is because Muslim populations have either neglected or misinterpreted Islam. What is needed is *ijtihad*, an established method of going back to sources in order to interpret the general principles of Islam in the light of the current situation" (Baker 21). Part and parcel of this standpoint is that independence requires modernization without effacement.

As a noticeable development in the nationalist movement in Morocco, the latter perspective reflects itself in *Dreams of Trespass* in powerful ways. In fact, the tales make reference to the encouragement of "the youth to read the classic treatises of Avicenna and Al-Khwarizmi, 'just to have an idea about the way their minds functioned. It always helps to know that our ancestors were fast and precise'" (Mernissi 87). This brings to mind Zin, Fatima's cousin whose appeal lies in his French education besides his religious knowledge. Indeed, he "worked very hard at becoming the ideal modern nationalist, that is, one who possessed a vast knowledge of Arab history, legends, and poetry as well as fluency in French, the language of our enemy, in order to decode the Christian press and uncover their plans" (Mernissi 87). Even the Mernissi family respect him "as one of the new generation of Moroccans who was going to save the country. He led the procession to the Qaraouiyine Mosque on Fridays, when all the men of Fez, young and old, turned up in the traditional white *djellaba* and fine yellow leather slippers to go to public prayer" (Mernissi 88). The notion that Zin takes up leadership in the mosque makes him loom larger for Fatima, given that it is during the Friday gatherings in this place of worshipping "that many important political decisions of the *Maglis Al-Baladi*, or City Council, were in fact settled" (Mernissi 88). At this level, *Dreams of Trespass* hinges back to Fanon's statement that "[i]n the colonial context, culture, when deprived of the twin supports of the nation and the state, perishes and dies. National liberation and the resurrection of the state are the preconditions for the very existence of a culture" (177).

Childhood and Adulthood a False Split

Although Mernissi sets the first pages of her memoirs in the 1940s, that is, "in the midst of chaos," meaning the apex of national resistance against the French-Spanish colonization of Morocco, yet the remainder of her life-writing narrates the different convulsions before the birth of an independent nation

(Mernissi 1-2). In one respect, her personal tales feature the conception that she "has indissolubly linked feminism and anti-colonialist nationalism in the Arab world" (Donadey 151). Consequently, they represent an attempt "to heal a false split [not only] between political and private life" but also between the child and the adult worlds (Matthes 84). This way, *Dreams of Trespass* is in no way the autobiographical story of Mernissi's own singular childhood. It even amounts to a national allegory "where the telling of the individual story and the individual experience cannot but ultimately involve the whole labourious telling of the experience of the collective itself"[9] (qtd. in Hefferman 472).

Through all this, Fatima Mernissi's *Tales of a Harem Girlhood* best exemplifies the notion of children as future citizens of a New Independent Morocco. One of the main messages that it imparts for these potential citizens is that "[t]o live in a combination of two worlds was much more appealing than living in just one. The idea of being able to swing between two cultures, two personalities, two codes, and two languages enchanted everyone! Mother wanted me to be like Princess Aisha (the teenage daughter of our King Mohammed V who made public speeches in both Arabic and French) who wore both long caftans and short French dresses" (Mernissi 180). Thus, although the Mernissi children have served as an indispensable complement to the political scenery, yet much of their receptive role is quite informative at the level of emphasizing the harmonious existence of tradition and modernity (Mernissi 91).

In another respect, *Dreams of Trespass* stands out as a chronicle of the military and political activism against the French-Spanish encroachment on the Moroccan nation, with a considerable narrative space allocated to Moroccan women's role in the national struggle for liberation. To this end, it is a recuperation of Fanon's view that "[t]he restoration of the nation must [...] give life in the most biological sense of the term to national culture" (177) and that one "cannot divorce the combat for culture from the people's struggle for liberation" (168). At the same time, its representation of nationalism during colonization reminds us that "the conscious, organized struggle undertaken by a colonized people in order to restore national sovereignty constitutes the greatest cultural manifestation that exists" (Fanon 178). In both forms of national struggle during the Spanish/French colonization of Morocco, Mernissi's text re-emphasises, rather than de-emphasizes, the active participation of Moroccan women. Although the fruition of this contribution in national resistance is harvested by the younger generation in the Moroccan society, still "each generation must discover its mission, fulfil it or betray it, in relative opacity" (Fanon 145).

NOTES

1. In the body of my analysis, I shall refer to the considered text as either *Dreams of Trespass: Tales of a Harem Girlhood,* or just either part of the title.
2. Gillian Adams, "Medieval Children's Literature: Its Possibility and Actuality," *Children's Literature,* 26 (1998): 4.
3. A case in point are Nodelman and Reimer who depart from the conviction that "[w]hat Europeans and European-influenced cultures currently see as the literature children obviously need and will like didn't even occur as a possibility to people in other places until Europeans began to influence them" (81).
4. V. Ramrag, "The Merits and Demerits of the Postcolonial Approach to Writings in English" in *Voices of the Other: Children's Literature and the Postcolonial Context,* ed. R. McGills, (New York: Garland, 1999), 253-67.
5. According to Alison Baker, 1912 is the year that "a weakened sultan was forced to sign the treaty of Fez, establishing a French protectorate over the largest part of his kingdom, with a Spanish protectorate in the Sahara and the North of the country" (14).
6. "Nation", *Encyclopédie, ou Dictionnaire raisonne des sciences, des arts et des métiers* (Lucques, 1758), Vol. 11.
7. For an analysis of the specificities of Moroccan nationalism, Alison Baker, "Nationalism". In her article, Baker points out that "[t]he roots of Moroccan nationalism—of the Moroccan nation—go back to the seventh century, when Arabs started arriving in Morocco. The Arabs not only conquered the country and took political power, but they also converted the

local Berber populations to Islam and began a process of Arabization, changing the ethnic make-up of the population, the language and the culture. Morocco's first national government was the Islamic monarchy founded in 787 AD by Idriss I2, who established from the very beginning a monarchy whose political legitimacy was based in blood descent from the Prophet Mohamed" (13).

8. Mernissi defines the harem "as the place where a man sheltered his family, his wife or wives, and children and relatives. It could be a house or a tent, and it referred both to the space and to the people who lived within it [...]. No other men could enter it without the owner's permission, and when they did, they had to obey his rules" (61).
9. Frederic Jameson, 85.

WORKS CITED

Adams, Gillian. "Medieval Children's Literature: Its Possibility and Actuality." in *Children's Literature,* 26 (1998). 1-24.

Alice in Wonderland.

Baker, Alison. *Voices of Resistance and Histories of Moroccan Women.* State University of New York Press: New York, 1998. 13-22.

Bhabha, Homi K. Foreword: Framing Fanon. Fanon, vii-xii.

David, Macey. Ed. *Mauro Bertani and Aessandro Fontana.* New York: Picador, 2003.

Donadey, Anne. *Recasting Postcolonialism: Women Writing Between Worlds: Studies in African Literature.* Portsmouth: Heinemann, 2001.

Fanon, Frantz. *The Wretched of the Earth.* Trans. Richard Philox. New York: Grove Press, 2004.

Fayose, Philomena Osazee. "African Children's Literature: An Overview" in *International Companion of Childrens Literature.* 2nd ed. Vol. 2. Ed. Peter Hunt. London: Routledge, Taylor and Francis Group, 2004. 891-900.

Foucault, Michel. *Society Must Be Defended: Lecture at the College de France, 1975-76.* Trans.

Heffereman, Teresa. "Apocalyptic Narratives: The Nation in Salman Rushdie's Midnight's Children" in *Twentieth Century Literature.* Vol. 46, No. 4, *Literature and Apocalypse* (Winter 2000). 470-91.

Jameson, Frederic. "Third-World Literature in the Era of Multinational Capitalism" in *Social Text,* 15 (1986). 65-88.

Matthes, Melissa. "Shahrazad's Sisters: Storytelling and Politics in the Memoirs of Mernissi, El. Saadawi and Ashrawi" in *Alif: Journal of Comparative Politics,* 19 (1999). 68-96.

McGills, Roderick. "Postcolonialism: Originating Differencc" in *International Companion of Childrens Literature.* 2nd ed. Vol. 2. Ed. Peter Hunt. London: Routledge, Taylor and Francis Group, 2004. 891-900.

Mernissi, Fatima. *Dreams of Trespass: Tales of a Harem Girlhood.* New York: Basic Books, 1994.

Mowitt, John. "Algerian Nation: Fanon's Fetish" in *Cultural Critique,* 22 (Autumn 1992). 165-86.

"Nation" in *Encyclopédie, ou Dictionnaire raisonne des sciences, des arts et des métiers.* Vol. 11. Lucques, 1758.

Nodelman, Perry and Mavis Reimer. 1992 and 1996. *The Pleasures of Children's Literature.* 3rd ed. Boston: Allyn and Bacon, 2003.

Oluwasanmi, E., E. McClean and H. Zell, eds. *Publishing in African in the Seventies.* Ile-Ife: University of Ife Press, 1973.

Ramrag, V. "The Merits and Demerits of the Postcolonial Approach to Writings in English" in *Voices of the Other: Children's Literature and the Postcolonial Context.* Ed. R. McGills. New York: Garland, 1999. 253-67.

Sartre, Jean-Paul. Preface. Fanon. xliii-lxii.

4

A Pierced Tongue: Narration and Identity in Young Adult Novels in Verse

Amber Dinquel

The young adult novel in verse, gaining notice in the past decade, is a relatively new genre. With the successful publication of novels such as Karen Hesse's *Out of the Dust*, scholars and readers alike have been forced to pay more attention to these unique texts. These novels have also sparked a debate over whether to actually consider them novels or poetry. Some critics argue that novels in verse are more closely related to dramatic poetry than to narrative. However, the majority of these texts still follow a linear narrative pattern. In addition, because of their sparse nature, the development of the narrative persona and/or characters becomes the most crucial element of the text. Another trope of the novels in verse is that most deal with difficult, emotional, and life-changing topics. Through the use of distinctive, intriguing narrative perspectives and the minimal language of verse novels, authors are able to approach challenging subjects in a manner that allows them to be accessible to their teen audiences. Furthermore, these points of view, often first person, help to build a bridge between the inherent difficulties of an adult writer composing texts for young adult audiences. This paper will strive to illustrate these points through an analysis of two verse novels: Ellen Hopkins' *Impulse* and Patricia McCormick's *Sold*.

Due to the recent emergence of the novel in verse genre, relatively little has been written by scholars and critics. Nevertheless, there are a few essential characteristics that the YA novel in verse embody. First, critics agree, young adult verse novels offer an alternative form of poetry to students. Ed Sullivan, in his column for the *School Library Journal*, comments, "Novels in verse can be an appealing, accessible introduction for students turned off by poetry or reluctant to read it. The verse authors write for these books is not like what most students are forced to study in class—it does not require analysis and explication" (44). While the verse novel may have roots in traditional epic poetry, works like Ellen Hopkins' *Crank* are a far cry from the metaphysical poets like John Donne and Andrew Marvell, whose formality often renders the text inaccessible to students. In turn, these texts offer an alternative entry point for the study of poetry and, if studied first, may present an opportunity to understand more traditional poets found in the high school literary canon. Additionally, the novel in verse constructs a merging of genres and techniques not found in other forms. While they sometimes retain some of the straight-forward narrative structure found in fictional prose, their form is more often related to novels written in diary entries or letters. In her article, "The Verse-Novel: A New Genre", Joy Alexander argues that this results from what Walter Ong calls "secondary orality", or a culture who has always known the ability for mass communication in print and therefore lacks an essential oral nature (270). She writes that secondary orality leads to experiments in narrative form and "that there has been a loosening of styles and a blurring of genres" (271). Besides their form, topics for the YA narrative in verse may appear similar to non-fiction, such as Patricia McCormick's *Sold* which introduces readers to the sex slave trade of Calcutta.

In concert with the alternative form, scholars note that YA verse novel provide a unique ground for exploring and understanding the teenage psyche. In her article "A Fresh Approach to YA Novels", Sherry Shanan observes that "the YA novel-in-poems—a nontraditional story form—is an apt reflection of adolescence, of a time when youth breaks away from authority and social convention" (35). Similar to the structure problems teens face with canonical poetry, they often feel that they cannot relate to the topics given. However, the young adult verse novel deals with themes familiar to teens in well-known settings: sex, depression, death, drugs, family troubles and academic difficulties. Moreover, the common use of first person narration in YA novel in poems is intimately linked to such faith altering topics. Shahan wonders, "Can the novel-in-verse do something traditional prose novels can't? Is it, in fact, peculiarly suited to the turbulent, but often secret, inner lives of teenagers?" (37). The authors' use of first person narration and topic choice reply that it can. Yet, some critics worry that the YA novel in verse will fall victim to the stereotype of teen angst writing (Alexander 272). Peter Hollidale, columnist for *Books for Keeps*, writes, "If things go really badly, though, this promising new form will fall hostage to outright bibliotherapy. Some recent American verse novels might well carry their own version of a familiar warning. 'If you have been affected by any of the issues raised in this poem, then please call Poetry Doc. Restore your emotional balance with bedtime reading!'" (12). Therefore, while the novel in verse is an emerging genre, amateur writers should strive to avoid "banal and lazy language" in hastily executed attempts to slap together a YA novel (Hollidale 13). The young adult verse novel requires a certain amount of artful writing, particularly in voice and character, in order to avoid these pitfalls.

Yet, as the critics note, the YA novel in verse proffers a starting point for exploring the mental and emotional landscape of teenagers. Aristotle believes tragic epic poetry lends itself well to intense emotions and is in fact, the highest form of poetry that can be achieved (Leitch 5). The young adult verse novel is not so different from the works Aristotle praised. While the language is certainly more colloquial and the plots are updated, the concepts of tragedy and high emotion still remain intimately linked to this genre as well as the length of the works (Ellen Hopkins' *Impulse* is upwards of

400 pages). The concise, free verse form also gives a distinct liberty to the writer and audience. These powerful emotions, whether they are rage, passion, mania or depression, should not be constrained and are not always well represented in prose. The freedom of the novel in verse form offers an outlet for the tumult of teenage emotions which often defy confinement. The instability of teen life is also manifested through the stream-of-conscious like narrative that flows throughout the verse novel. Poems come in fragments and sudden thoughts, rather than the lengthy reflection of a traditional novel; a true reflection of how we experience life. Alexander notes that "writers seem to find this genre to be a suitable medium for portraying a teenage character experiencing the angst of adolescence; for the reader, the narrator seems literally to be 'telling it like it is,' with immediacy and reality" (271). But this issue remains: how do authors mold these fragmented, passionate experiences into a readable story with a reliable, true to life narrator?

Narration can become a troublesome factor for the novel in verse. The majority of these texts utilize a first person point of view in order to create an intimate relationship between the narrator and reader. While some would argue that a speaker in third person creates a more impartial view, third person narration is not necessarily anymore objective than first person, as demonstrated by the use of unreliable narrators in a variety of genres. Cadden argues that "third person address is not necessarily obliged to present the positions, perspectives, and politics of all, or even some, of the characters in the text..." (146). The authors and readers find the desire for intimacy more important than objectivity. Moreover, it is the subjective nature that closely relates the verse novel to epistolary and diary novels. Subjective viewpoints also become more effective when considering the emotion encapsulated in these texts. In "Vetting the Verse Novel", Patty Campbell points out "...they are all intensely internal, focused on the character's feelings because emotion is what the verse novel—and poetry—is all about, characteristically, the action centers on an emotional event and the rest of the novel deals with the characters feelings before and after" (614). For example, in Hopkins' *Impulse*, each character (and narrator) has been admitted in a mental facility after suicide attempts. They all have experienced different situations but the crisis for all three is a failed suicide. The rest of the novel then spends its time revealing what experiences have led up to their depression and their development, or lack thereof, after being in the institution. The plot of *Impulse* aptly supports Campbell's metaphor that "the verse novel is often more like a wheel, with the hub a compelling emotional event, and the narrative referring to this event like the spokes" (615). For instance, Vanessa repeatedly harkens back throughout the text to the reaction of her grandmother and younger brother upon finding her in the bath tub with both wrists split:

> I heard my brother's scream
> Through the cloud
> that had veiled my brain,
> coloring everything crimson.
> It seemed to last forever,
> that scream. Poor Bryan.
> He's only eight,
> too little to understand
> that dying isn't something
> to fear. It's a comfort. (Hopkins 35)

Although this event may be crucial in the lives of her grandmother and brother, their depictions would taken on uniquely different tones and in particular lack the guilt that Vanessa's internal narration depicts. Vanessa notes her awareness and understanding of the event as opposed to what her brother's perception would be, given his age and lack of experience.

Even though first person narration is well-suited to the YA novel in verse, some critics caution against the lack of awareness on the part of the narrator. Because the narrator and character become so intertwined in a first person perspective, the distinction between the two blurs and may result in a lack of reflection on the part of the character. However, there is a difference between a character's voice and awareness of the narrative and the intrusion of the author as narrator. The best of these first person narratives strive to be intimate without being didactic. Patty Campbell notes that "the prevailing pitfall for writers of verse novels is pretentiousness, self-consciousness about the prosody of their words that can make the whole undertaking seem a little operatic" (613). In order to achieve the organic act that a first person narration offers, writers must avoid shaping the language into an overtly teachable moment. The consequences of an intrusive author will be discussed later in this paper, but the awareness I discuss here is a characters ability to reflect and question their own motives and actions. Scholar Mike Cadden agrees, saying, "Critics of young adult fiction have good reason to dwell on the nature of narrative authority in the young adult novel, especially the authority claimed through the consciousness of young characters" (146). The focus needs to remain on the self-awareness of the characters, rather than that of the author. In turn, the degree of a character's self-awareness may also be related to the reception of the novel. Richard Aczel comments "The notion of 'self-conscious narration' is...directly related to the qualitative aspect of narrative voice" (470). One technique that Hopkins utilizes is offering a loved one or family member in comparison to the narrator. For example, Tony and Vanessa of Hopkins' *Impulse* are certainly not in denial about what has led them to the point of self-destruction. For Vanessa, it is her experience with her mother's bipolar disorder, which she has inherited to some degree. She laments:

> Worst thing was, the older
> I got, the more I began to see
> How much I resembled Mama,
> Falling in and out of the blue,
> Then lifting up into the white. (Hopkins 21)

Hopkins employs this mirroring effect to heighten Vanessa's self-awareness. She is extremely conscious of her actions through the comparisons she draws between her mother and her own behaviour. Because Vanessa has seen the point to which her mother fragments, she knows the length her mental illness can carry her to. Awareness alone does not necessarily save Vanessa. She still requires medical intervention and behavioral therapy to change her awareness into action.

Another example of character awareness in *Impulse* is Tony, a fellow patient of Vanessa's who attempted suicide by overdose (Hopkins 15). His experiences with drugs and mental illness stem from a brutal rape which his mother refuses to believe:

> *Larry is a decent man,*
> She said, when I told her
> about it the first time.
> *A bit rough around the edges*
> *yes, but he'd never ever*
> *do such a thing, little liar.*
>
> Like an eight-year-old
> child could make up
> something so evil and
> perverse. She wouldn't
> even believe it when
> I pulled down my jeans.
>
> The proof was right there
> on my underwear, streaked
> pink with blood. (Hopkins 104)

Tony's awareness of this event trails him throughout the novel and shapes his interactions with others throughout the text (Hopkins 88). In fact, his rape at such a fragile age has caused him to believe he is gay, though he is actually sexually attracted to women. Again, first person narration becomes important here. While an omniscient narrator would be privy to events that only certain characters know, the degree of subjectivity would be altered. Alexander writes, "This increased awareness of the narrative voice in turn raises the potential for personalized subjective narration and for reading constructed as intimate conversation or even as eavesdropping" (270). Vanessa's experiences with her mother are a prime example. Besides the effect she may have had on her younger brother, the majority of Vanessa's guilt stems from an event that the reader does not discover until over a hundred pages into the novel. She came one day to find that her mother had overdosed. Instead of calling for help, she simply backs out of the kitchen, leaving her mother to die (Hopkins 130). This scene is significantly loaded with emotion and guilt, an aspect that a third person narrator would not be able to achieve without seeming far removed from the action or diminishing the horror of the action. With Hopkins' version, we not only see Vanessa's guilt we *feel* it as well. In turn, these emotional experiences give Vanessa and Tony the authority to act as narrators telling the story, without an authorial intrusion.

However, Hopkin's offers an interesting counter point in her third character, Connor. There is a good deal of self-denial on Connor's part throughout the text. While he has come to the same attempt of self-destruction as Vanessa and Tony, his attitude upon entering the mental facility is significantly different. Upon contemplating a possible roommate, he comments:

> whacked-out freak. I wonder
> how long it would take him
> to realize I'm right as sin—it's
> the rest of the world that's wrong. (Hopkins 24)

Although he had attempted to shoot himself in the heart, it appears as if Connor admits no responsibility for the act. It is as if the rest of the world had placed the gun in his hand and pulled the trigger. Nevertheless, Hopkins' employment of Connor's limited view also reflects the reality of a teen consciousness. Cadden says "In any case, by employing an all-too-reliable young adult's consciousness, the YA novelist often intentionally communicates to the immature reader a single and limited awareness of the world that the novelist knows to be incomplete and insufficient" (146). While Tony and Vanessa acknowledge outside influences on their depression and suicide attempts, neither of them embody an attitude like Connor's. They are not cocky or self-assured to the point of denial. His reaction to counseling sessions is by far the most negative as well. He wonders if he can seduce his doctor into letting him out of the facility (Hopkins 97). His response to her attempts to establish communication is automatically negative:

Dr. Starr will never buy
into "Connor the saint,"
but Dr. Boston might
award me that honor.

I've almost got her right
where I want her—on her
knees, my hands caught
in her silky blond hair as she

whispers, *I want you, Conner*. (Hopkins 96)

So how do Hopkins and other novelists deal with protagonist-narrators who lack an awareness of their position? Would this not undermine the artistry and authority that the rest of the narrators and the author exhibit? Hopkins turns Connor's self-denial into another mirror technique through her use of multiple narrators.

Multiple narrators are a common phenomenon for the YA verse novel, a form that lends itself well to the rapid changing of point of view. Ed Sullivan argues "the author's use of multiple perspectives to tell his stories would not work with prose. Verse gives authenticity and distinction to the individual voices" (45). Other than frame narratives or the closely related epistolary novels, the use of multiple voice narration is often absent from fictional prose. Campbell argues that this works because "the text I shaped in a succession of one- or two-page poems, usually titled, that end with a punch line. This provides temporary closure for the reader, a necessary resting point in the very concentrated narration" (614). This allows the reader to momentarily disperse with one point of view and move onto another, while knowing that this first narrator will later reemerge in the text. Additionally, the narration of a second or third character is often interwoven with the story of the first, as is the case for Tony, Vanessa and Connor.

The unreliability of Connor's narration truly comes to a head in the final hundred of Impulse. Part of the final step of being released from the mental facility is an extended camping trip through the rocky wilderness of the Black Rock Desert in Nevada. Unlike Tony and Vanessa, Connor's mental state has not improved during his stay at Aspen Springs. His internal narration and his behavior begin to diverge. On the road to Nevada Connor muses:

> I thought I was ready
>
> To graduate Aspen Springs,
> Move ahead with my life.
> I even quit taking the Prozac,
> To prove to myself that I could.
>
> I figured the Challenge would
> Provide enough stimulation
> To let me go cold turkey.
> Four days later I can't decide
>
> If that's why I feel like I'm
> Fresh out of hope, or if it's
> The big, ugly picture. (Hopkins 507)

However, Hopkin's use of multiple narratives allows the reader to view Connor through the eyes of Tony and Vanessa. Vanessa and Tony are constantly observing Connor on their trip and reflecting on his behavior. Vanessa says:

> My eyes travel to Tony,
> And I see he is watching
> Connor too. Finally he glances
> At me, and we offer a mutual shrug.
>
> > He scoots closer. *Don't worry,*
> > *Vanessa. Everything will be okay.*
> > *Connor knows what he's doing.* (Hopkins 520)

There is an obvious disconnect between the persona that Connor has outwardly portrayed throughout the text and his internal monologue. Yet, the reader fully comprehends Connor's internal conflict because of Hopkins multiple narrators. She makes up for his lack of authority and self-awareness through the perspectives of Vanessa and Tony, painting a full picture of Connor's true character. However, even despite his lack of agency, Connor remains a convincing character. Thomas Leitch writes, "But when we ascribe depth or authority to characters, when we talk about what makes them compelling or memorable, even we describe them as realistic, we are really talking about what makes them tellable..." (158). Therefore, Hopkins' presentation is convincing enough that Connor remains 'tellable', and a narrator whom the reader can still connect with.

Narration is particularly tricky for young adult novels because of the inherent ethical and moral dilemmas of writing for an adolescent audience. The intended audience for YA novels is at a malleable stage in their mental and emotional development. Wayne C. Booth, in his ground breaking work, The Company We Keep, argues that whether or not we are conscious of it, the texts we read are a constant influence. He writes, "Indeed, our imitations of narrative 'imitations of life' are so spontaneous and plentiful that we cannot draw a clear line between what we are, in some conception of a 'natural', unstoried self, and what we have become as we have first enjoyed, then imitated, and then, perhaps, criticized both the stories and our responses to them" (229). No matter how vehemently we argue our individualism, the concept of self we developed is a result of the stories we hear and the stories we tell. Booth also argues that we engage in a social relationship with texts. Referencing Aristotle, he says, "His claim amounts to saying that what makes life human, and what makes human life worth living, are our relations of trust and affection: we are naturally, essentially social animals" (173). Readers, particularly young adults, expect to enter a relationship with a novel with an idea of mutual trust. They expect the stories to be true, if not in plot or setting, then at least in their moral lessons. (While not a YA text, consider the uproar over James Frey's Million Little Pieces.) Therefore, critics, teachers and parents agree that authors need to be acutely aware of the messages they impart.

As previously noted, the YA novel in verse frequently addresses difficult issues. Hopkin's YA series, beginning with Crank, includes drug addiction, teen pregnancy, suicide, homosexuality, rape, illicit student-teacher relationships, and mental illness. Additionally, because of the age of the intended audience, YA novels are often seen as imparting advice or guidelines for how to live. So how do we deal with this difficult subject matter in YA literature? One example is again found in

Hopkins' character, Connor. The reader watches him attempt to reveal his deep secrets and uncover the source of his depression. Yet, despite the medical attention and the companionship he finds in Vanessa and Tony, Connor is unable to defeat his demons. His story ends with a tragically successful suicide during their camping trip. Virginia Burke Epstein questions what the role of morality should be for young adult literature in her article "Moral Reading: Children's Literature as Moral Education." She writes, "But for me, 'moral education' does not mean the inculcation of a particular set of values.... It means, instead, the systematic analysis of differing value positions, the evaluation of purposes, and the proposal of new or alternative purposes and values" (68). The first person perspective of the YA novel in verse aids Epstein's argument. Instead of looking at moral decisions in broad terms with assumptions, the first person point of view helps readers evaluate Connor's mental, emotional, and social position. Cadden reaffirms this saying, "Though the reader may not come to some decisions about the 'rightness' of a particular perspective, the text has not clearly argued for that position and has provided other complete positions to consider" (147). While not condoning suicide, it allows readers to explore the circumstances which drove Connor to such a decision and perhaps to understand what leads to the epidemic of adolescent suicide all the more.

Another YA verse novel that brings morality into question, perhaps even more gruesomely than Hopkins, is Patricia McCormick's *Sold*. This series of poems recounts the story of a thirteen year old girl, Lakshmi, in Nepal who is tricked into the sex slave trade with promises of a city job and the ability to provide for her mother and baby brother. Unlike the issues addressed in Hopkins' works, human trafficking is fortunately an occurrence that most American and British YA audiences will never experience. However, this does not make McCormick's work any less important or any less problematic. Dianne Koehnecke, in her article "Smoky Night and Crack: Controversial Subjects in Current Children's Stories" notes that, "Some critics attack books that deal with these topics as far too nonjudgmental, while others deplore either their explicit, realistic treatment or their didactic tone" (17). I believe that most parents and teachers who object to these novels automatically focus on the controversial subject matter, but miss the goal of these texts. McCormick says in her author's note, "These young women have experienced what many people would describe as unspeakable horrors. But they are speaking out—with great dignity". The aim of these stories is not to expose our youth to "unspeakable horrors". Rather, it is to bring awareness and understanding of events in the world that American and British youth are all too often sheltered from. McCormick writes, "Worldwide, the U.S. State Department estimates that nearly half a million children are trafficked into the sex trade annually" (Author's Note). This is a glaring statistic that should not be ignored by educators, parents, or citizens of the world as a whole. But there still remains the problem of how to keep these novels like Sold and Impulse from seeming overly didactic or remotely judgmental.

A unique aspect of children's literature is the disconnect between authors, publishers, and marketers and the intended audience. Barbara Wall points out that "It is adults who write children's books, adults who choose which books are to be published for children, adults who review, criticize and buy those books. Adults then, as well as children, are readers of children's books" (18). Adult influence is inevitably bound up in every aspect of children's and young adult literature, from production and sales to its reception and reviews. Since the character and narrator become so intertwined, this adult intrusion becomes particularly troublesome for the YA novel in verse. Cadden illustrates this irony saying:

> While any novel is an ideal site for studying the different layers of narrative relationships, the young adult novel that features the consciousness of young characters is especially interesting because of the unique and ironic relationship between author and reader in this age-based genre. Novels constructed by adults to simulate an authentic adolescent's voice are inherently ironic because

> the so-called adolescent voice is never—and can never be-truly authentic. (146)

Again, this is even more crucial for the verse novel because of the reliance on first person perspective. Therefore, how do authors deal with this doubled awareness that they must construct a teen voice in their texts but also acknowledge that their authorial experience and views have moved beyond adolescence?

Hopkins texts are in a distinctive situation. She has repeatedly acknowledged that her impulse to write Crank and the verse novels that follow stem from her own daughter's addiction to methamphetamines. Hopkins, in turn, embodies the role of author and parent. However, her novels seem to escape any overt didacticism and there is little indication of the innate power relationship between an adult author and a teen reader. This results, particularly in Impulse, from the variety of narration and character awareness that Hopkins builds into the text. Cadden writes, "When an adult writer speaks through a young adult's consciousness to a young adult audience, he or she is involved in a top-down power relationship. It becomes important, then, there be equal power relations between the major characters within the text so that the young adult reader has the power to see the opposing ideologies at play" (146). On top of the multiple teen perspectives in Impulse, Hopkins' adeptly uses the portrayal of adults within the story to undermine any hint of moralizing. Each character has at least one parent who either fails to understand their child's dilemma or completely removes themselves from the problem. While Vanessa's mom may have some understanding of what her daughter is going through, her mental illness prevents her from verbalizing it. On the other hand, Vanessa's father is completely removed from the narrative until the end of the text. He is an Army Ranger and therefore rarely in contact with his family and even more rarely present in the home. It is only until he discovers that his wife has become comatose in a mental institution that he transfers stateside (Hopkins 626). While we have already discussed the lack of trust between Tony and his mother, it is his father who actually pays for Tony's residence at Aspen Springs. Tony's father had abandoned him shortly after he was born and has only seen his son once before. However, it is Connor's parents that offer the most glaring portrayal of flawed adults and parents.

Throughout the text it becomes obvious that Connor's family life is the root of his mental illness. He remarks that on the outside they seem like a typical, perfect suburbanite family (Hopkins 187). However, their dialogue with Connor in the mental institution reveals the amount of pressure and expectations they place upon their son:

> Mom picked up the ball at
> a hard sprint. *I just don't*
> *understand how you could*
> *treat us with so little regard.*
>
> *We have standing in this*
> *community, a reputation*
> *to protect. Did you expect*
> *to act with impunity?*
>
> "I'm sure you can't understand
> this, Mom, but everything
> isn't about you." I looked her
> in the eye, willed myself calm.
>
> "What I did had nothing to do
> with you. It was about letting
> myself feel—desire, pain, fear.
> emotions you don't permit." (Hopkins 296)

They have no obvious concern for their son's well-being beyond the repercussions it will have on the family and their image. In fact, his mother is worried about having blood on her own blouse when she finds Connor after his first suicide attempt (Hopkins 8). Moreover, it is interesting to note that while Vanessa and Tony's parents make a conscious effort to help their children while Connor's do not. In turn, it is Connor who is unable to cope with the prospect of life outside of Aspen Springs.

While Hopkins had an intimate connection with the moral dilemmas she encountered, Patricia McCormick is literally a world away from the characters in her text. McCormick acknowledges that "As part of my research for Sold, I traced the path that many Nepalese girls have taken—from remote villages to the red-light districts of Calcutta. I also interviewed aid works who rescues girls from brothels, provide them with medical care and job training, and who work to reintegrate them into society" (Author's Note). A reader may expect the text to be even farther removed from its subject matter and to seem even more didactic. However, McCormick integrates the role of teacher and moral guide into the Nepal society she depicts. She places Lakshmi's mother, Ama, in the role of instructor throughout the poems:

> In the city, says Ama, the people clean the floors with one rag and the dishes with another. Take care not to mix them up, or you will risk a beating.
>
> Get up early in the morning before anyone else in the house and be the last one to bed at night. Never sit down in the presence of your mistress or her husband or even in front of the children. And never eat your meal until they have gone to bed. This will prove what a hard worker you are. (McCormick 50)

McCormick skillfully merges any direct lessons through the mouth of Ama and interweaves these lessons with the cultural expectations of Nepalese women. Thomas Leitch makes an interesting note concerning the disconnect between author and character. He writes, "the requirements for tellability are appreciably relaxed for any story presented as true; or, to put it another way, a truth claim often serves as the primary basis for a story's tellability" (33). Considering the statistics and the interviews that McCormick conducted, her stories are certainly based on true events. Leitch goes on to say that "such privilege was once accorded tellers of fictitious stories when stories were regarded as a mode of wisdom" (33). Sold may not necessarily be considered wisdom but it certainly brings awareness into the consciousness of young adults about deplorable acts being committed across the world.

I would argue that the use of first person narrative and the intimate relationship built between reader and narrator in the

YA verse novel has contributed to its recent rise in popularity. In our continually fragmented world, the YA novel in verse is a reflection of this existence but also a reassurance of the companionship that can be constructed between a reader and a text, and in turn between people. Additionally, Alexander argues that the verse novel mirrors growing trends in the media. She writes, "The evidence suggests that the novel as a text-form is continuing to evolve, becoming more cinematic and kinesthetic and manipulating language creatively and expressively. This is good news for literature and reasons enough to celebrate the new genre of the verse novel" (282). As previously noted, "she also cites Ong's idea that our society craves a certain aspect of orality which we lacks" (Alexander 270). Perhaps this form can serve as a bridge between written and oral discourse even while it maintains the name of young adult novel. Whatever reason one chooses to support, there is evidence enough to assert that the YA novel in verse presents a niche in children's literature that will continue to grow and evolve through the end of the decade.

WORKS CITED

Aczel, Richard. "Hearing Voices in the Narrative Texts." *New Literary History*, 29.3 (1998): 467-500.

Alexander, Joy. "The Verse Novel: A New Genre." *Children's Literature in Education*, 36.3 (2005): 269-83.

Booth, Wayne C. *The Company We Keep: An Ethics of Fiction*. Berkeley: University of California Press, 1988.

Cadden, Mike. "The Irony of Narration in the Young Adult Novel." *Children's Literature Association Quarterly*, 25.3 (2000): 146-54.

Campbell, Patty. "Vetting the Verse Novel." *Horn Book*, 80.5 (2004): 611-16.

Epstein, Virginia Burke. "Moral Reading: Children's Literature as Moral Education." *Children's Literature Association Quarterly*, 11.2 (1986): 68-72.

Hollindale, Peter. "Novels in Verse, For Better or Worse." *Books for Keeps*, 146 (2004): 12-13.

Hopkins, Ellen. *Crank*. New York: Simon, 2004.

——. *Impulse*. New York: Simon, 2008.

Koehnecke, Dianne. "Smoky Night and Crack: Controversial Subjects in Current Children's Stories." *Children's Literature in Education*, 32.1 (2001): 17-31.

Leitch, Thomas M. *What Stories Are: Narrative Theory and Interpretation*. University Park: Pennsylvania State University Press, 1986.

McCormick, Patricia. *Sold*. New York: Hyperion, 2006.

Shahan, Sherry. "A Fresh Approach to YA Novels." *Writer*, 122.2 (2009): 34-55.

Sullivan, Ed. "Fiction or Poetry?" *School Library Journal*, 49.8 (2003): 44-45.

Wall, Barbara. *The Narrator's Voice: The Dilemma of Children's Fiction*. New York: St. Martin's, 1991.

5

Some Aspects of the Children's Literature in Albania

Enkelena Shockett (Qafleshi)

Introduction

The *Children's Literature* in Albania mostly enjoys a wide range of peculiarities accumulated on the basis of two essential aspects noticed so far. The first aspect collocates round the essence they are important and significant for the stylistic and literary peculiarities they take up which directly differentiate them explicitly from books produced for adults; and the second one closely correlates to matters like how basically such a differentiation confines this sort of literature within the parameters of pedagogical requirements which eventually compose the characteristics of children's books as expression of featuring *Children's Literature* genre in total.

To date the posing aspects of this literary genre indeed promotes researches and encourages scholars to undertake such enterprises in order to elucidate the essentials and peculiarities of this genre scholarly.

In pursuit of this stand, I purposefully allow myself to frame this genre under the shape of totally being defined as a progressive phenomenon in Albania that establishes convincingly a harmonious balance between the literary art guidelines in power and morals which are either expressive inheritage of folkloric materials or artistic materials developed periodically in complete terms to the philosophy and aesthetics and policy and pedagogy in power.

And also it is conceived and perceived as an interesting constituted science in itself and a special art as well that irresistibly code on children important didactic elements which doubtlessly and critically transmit esthetic, cultural, religious, instructive, moral values in terms to children's growth and their personality development as well as their role positioning in the Albanian society regarded in its wholeness.

Turning back to the core question of interest, my intentions will be channeled into researching on aspects of this genre, differently known as literature, sufficed within the principles on the basis of which children's books are mostly organized and featured in Albania. With reference to their aspects and characteristics, which of course are various and diversified, I will project the reflection of my research on a few aspects and peculiarities starting with titling in one hand and then I will shift my attention and aims towards certainly a couple of dominant motifs vested under the features of nationalism and internationalism on the other hand. Added to them surely I will attempt to figure out the peculiarities of the translated *Children's Literature* in Albania.

Title of Children's Books

Starting with description of title as an expression of book identity, I will attempt herein to explain generally the importance of it as an indispensable element in literary work be it a drama, a poetry or a novel, because it preserves distinguishably the featuring marker of the book. Otherwise described, it reliably represents the Madre text, which requires to be developed as artistically as realistically with material organized and shaped substantially on the basis of either prose composition, or verse composition.

Noticeably I. Kadare[1] counts the title as something more interesting and challenging than the whole material closely comprehended and envisaged in reading which orients us to shift our critical stand towards the idea that the material endowed in books sometimes really becomes acquired clearly through the title. Yet it is precisely the title, which keeps us hooked on all pages and allows us to proceed with our reading creating our reflective stand to it. Another one named B.

Dedja[2] points out convincingly how the title "The Kids of My Building" displays immediately the life and deeds and adventures also of children's community that live in his building. What strikes most relates completely to the fact that he has used the word *kid* and not at all *children* and I think the effect of this becomes nurtured round the idea that children easily become attracted by this element—title exhibition to provoke childish effects.

Furthermore, it randomly occurs that in children's books we find out that title reflects also directly the structure of the book and it always seems to keep its readers on alert about its style and narration and above all its stylistic figures employed as well, which so conceivably attempt to serve faithfully to the selected material elaborated later on skillfully and masterfully by the author; the material initially is concealed but progressively explained and amplified in reading process. At this point if provided a list of children's books, I would rather prefer to emphasize that the motifs and thematic concerns and woven featuring of narrations simply are exhibited right at the title and so in convergent manner its title mirrors the content of the material depicted from the author and indeed so it explicitly engulfs, of course in advance, what essential material is contained in that particular book. At this point the Madre text inspires the existence of daughter texts (Chapter "organization of the narration") where the characters perform their artistic charges accordingly and the mutual relations title —text in entity make up the uniqueness of the book they both stand for. Positioned as such, titles then deal with all aspects of life and their reference includes all human activities and all possible sources to extract materials from and elaborate artistically later.

Under this track of thinking I allow myself to emphasize the history of the Albanians can yet be explored in reading the followings: *Once Upon a Time in Illyria* (A. Malaj); *The Swords that Always Shine* (V. Muçi); *The Dardanian Knights* (M. Zeqo); *Mic Sokoli with Seven Hearts* (B. Harxhi); *The Struggling Mornings* (Dh. Xhuvani); *The Bravity of Ujkan Gjoni* (P. Koçi); *The Torn off Flag* (S. Vaqari) and so on beside other reading sources which represent real historical fiction. These books illustrate pretty well how practically the historical narrations accompany and orient young readers responsively to historical labyrinths and also approach them to appropriate the included historical elements properly and accurately under the cloak of artistically woven material.

Other examples including the following products: *The Girl who Speaks the Language of Birds* (D. Shapllo); *The Pinocchio in the Beach* (P. Risto); *The King of Giants* (K. Jakova); *The Flying Horse* (P. Zoto) and so many others akin as far as titling composition, explicitly resonate either fairy tale structure or fable structure of them. To proceed with composition of titles, other examples like: *The Adventures of Straw-Headed Girl* (Stavri Pone); *Four Children of the Invisible Pogi* (R. Marku) orient their readers to *waters* confined within fantastic fable.

As it is seen until now, the titles of books taken for examples are composed in a very childish language. From this viewpoint, they should well satisfy the interest of the children and also come to terms with their psychic-physiological development. Consequently, they accelerate the proper development of their imagination and bring them close to their interests in life. *The Rabbit with Five Legs* (R. Kukaj); *Çufo and Curly Bubi* (G. Bushaka); *The Bird Named Pup in the Glassy House* (A. Mamaqi); *The Loyalty of a Dog* (I. Reso); *The Deeds of the Regretful Bear* (K. Kyçyku); *The Kindergarten of Rabbits* (A. Mici); *Seagullish Evenings* (H. Ulqinaku); *A Penguin in Dukagjin* (M. Haziri) *A Squirrel Studies at School* (A. Zeka); *The Lilacs of Mamica* (Xh. Spahiu); *A Man Becomes a Monkey* (O. Grillo); *A Mouse Ate up a Cat* (L. Papa) all are books titled after animals' names as well as flowers' names which range within the authors' tendency to account mostly for the curiosity of children about flora and fauna. And indeed, titles are the very source out of which children's curiosity is nurtured immediately with relevance to exploring deeply and digesting progressively what kind of world they are going to navigate into visually, metaphorically and realistically. It happens not randomly that children's books possess onomatopoeic titles. F. Lamaj is noted to employ this device in his literary products, hence we encounter titles like: *Ham, ham! Kikirikiii!* However, indeed, this apparently constitutes another feature of children's books, which yet counts for more attention.

Nationalism and Internationalism in *Children's Literature*

What chiefly concerns me in this part revolves round the education and civilization of children's character in *Children's Literature*. Perceived so, I strongly express out that children's education has been oriented and developed through the tendency to encourage personal reflections and attitudes towards the following criteria of features that amplify my concerns in this research:

> The love for Albania and all its social, natural and material values in total. A typical example the scholars always revolve themselves to anytime that this peculiar aspect of Children's literature comes forth, confines within the features of N. Frashëri's poem titled "Our Language". In this poem the writer expresses out his stand towards the Albanian language and impressively describes its beauties and along with its particular features also. More poems that evoke values are: "To You Republic" (A. Mamaqi), "To the Party" (S. Çomora), "The Tractor" (B. Harxhit), "The Head of Cooperative" (B. Harxhi), "The Nephew of Miner" (M. Agimi), The Dawn (M. Agimi), "The Unforgotten Year" (Sh. Vreto), "The Broken Arm" (Sh. Vreto), "The Little Icy Planet" (M. Meksi) and so on, which are also recognized for their preserved cognitive archetypes that illustrate the creation of culture of memoria in Children's literature genre as an entity. Nationalistic features predominate and become nurtured gradually and progressively as they define the tendency to educate and civilize children with norms and values specific in Albania with reference to the past and present and future, because communist idealization for the New Man appealed to children's development and formation during communist regime and yet democratic idealization actually attempts the alike address. And the

motifs elaborated by authors prone to problem oriented realism which evokes and deals with all possible concerns and pains of society originating from all levels of cognitive knowledge and beliefs on the grounds of philosophy and policy in power.

The preservation of freedom, independence, integrity, ethnicity, idealization of patriotic and nationalistic feelings as well as engagement to develop lifestyle and cultural heritage in Albania. In this spectrum it is worth establishing a kind of categorization as far as motifs developed by various writers.

In this light a considerable space is taken by those literary creations that evoke all attempts and struggles of the Albanians to survive as a nation with all its own features and characteristics. In this category there are included poems and stories and novels that evoke the Illyrian time, the Ottoman occupation of Albania, the Independence War and World War I and also the National Liberation War along with World War II. The examples considered for illustrating this phenomenon attempt to elucidate what they evoke and express out the contents and motifs right from the titles. Again we see how the titles help a lot in clarifying and addressing the reader to the concerns and intentions of the writers.

Some of examples that serve the above purpose are rendered as follows: *Once in Illyria* (A. Malaj), *The Dardanian Knights* (M. Zeqo), *The Goats with Candles* (M. Gurakuqi), *The Arm of Gjergji* (M. Gurakuqi), *Mic Sokoli with Seven Hearts* (B. Harxhi), *The Deeds of Ujkan Gjoni* (P. Koçi), *Our November* (T. Papuçiu), *Mother, o Party* (A. Mamaqi), *Ilir's Trick* (Q. Bushaka), *Fall Night in Wartime* (Q. Bushaka), *The Hut of Uncle Bato* (J. Karalliu), *Albania, My Homeland* (D. Agolli), *The Struggling Mornings* (Dh. Xhuvani) and so on.

Also this category recalls nationalistic values and stands up towards patriotic and humanist phenomenon perceived in Albania with reference to the past. The idealization of these feelings recalls for strong nationalistic education fostered through *Children's Literature* in Albania either during communist or democratic regime. Both regimes are known to enhance and advance this aspect of *Children's Literature* in

Albania and the scholars perceive and envisage this canon as an important instrument to teach pedagogy and didactics and significant means to foster and sharpen manners towards solid national identity parameters.

The love for the other nations and nationalities which create con-existent relations with the Albanians alongside with the respect to the positive values of national and international history. The literary creations, which attain this sort of feature, predominantly evoke constant struggles against racial discrimination of black people in USA (Negroes called otherwise in Albania). The Little Negro, My Friend written by I. Kadare really describes the tendencies of the author to express out his attitude towards racial discrimination flourished once in USA. This category includes illustrations that refer to the present and also to the past. Other features explored while dealing with idealization of internationalist characteristic dominant in *Children's Literature* in Albania are those that qualify humanism and brotherhood. R. Kukaj's novel titled *The Bird's Stone* is noted for inclusive humanist feelings and stands that cross beyond specific geographic borders and which require displacement of locus and location. Elaborated under this purpose its protagonist named Misha, a German officer, collaborates secretly with partisans to liberate an unidentified foreign country.

Purposefully this is featured in the *Children's Literature* in Albania in order to cultivate to children the feelings of alertness to help and experience what the others do as they also should conceive themselves as members of great human family known internationally apprehended. Kosovo genocide and patriotic feelings to gain freedom from Serbian governing is also situated in the children's books in Albania. They merely provide evidence of historic facts that really embody love for homeland, flag, Albanian language and other markers of Kosovo identity compositional part of the Albanian identity. These attempts are reflected significantly in the development of *Children's Literature* in Albania during either communist or democratic regime in power.

Translated *Children's Literature* in Albania

Briefly referring to this issue although it really matters me a lot, I would like to drive firstly your attention to the fact that nowadays translated *Children's Literature* is encountering certain problems that derive from absence of specific board in charge of controlling and commissioning the translating process and evaluation of the final product by specialists of children's education and psychologists and children's linguists who are able enough to testify the values and significance of final products for the development of intellectual and cognitive formation of children as well as their language level and development. Encouraged by the tendency to translate and develop publications of children's books with problem oriented realism, the publishing houses have forgotten to provide this sort of logistic management of the whole translating process and the products surely in many cases result to be inappropriate for children age they specifically are translatably designed for.

Although strong initiatives and actual innovations are inclined to encompass many problems oriented to realism providing models and to follow and reflect, they yet sound inappropriate as the Albanian children have to digest the new culture transmitted through certain problem with orientation to comprehension as language level found in them really classify them belong to other readership beyond that of children.

Furthermore they have to hamper also the reshaping of that unknown culture transmitted by page reading by means of complicated language not rarely but on the contrary frequently loaded with many loans and calques constructing so a kind of barrier which establishes non-perfect import-export relations as far as text comprehension and interpretation.

In this light the encountered problems lead to organization and disorganization from the part of publishing houses that do not utilize the proper management of children's books translation and do not hire specialists to deal with these barriers which are both cultural and linguistic, or gender based oriented and real age oriented. More the publishing houses should also be very careful to pick out the right translators to work with selected children's books to be translated. They should know well the world of children and why not be even writers involved in this creativity.

It is true that translation of *Children's Literature* in Albania makes a canon within the mainstream of *Children's Literature* as translation policies commenced and yet they are prone to develop strict policies to make out of their products "intellectual hybrids", although they are questioning a lot the identity of children who constitute their readership.

Conclusions

Concluding I could emphasize that yet in Children's literature the titles, the nationalist and internationalist features do constitute some essential aspects of this genre in Albania. They enjoy their own respective features worth discussing about and pose serious questions to be solved in future by either developing them more profoundly as they enjoy the parameters of national identity markers, or adding more colors as Albania is becoming open to the world due to democratic changes. In addition they offer challenges and innovations to the scholars involved in undertakings to deal with these aspects of the *Children's Literature* in Albania. The fostering of tendencies and parameters of these aspects put forth, really resonates to the effects produced to result into a more solid and avant-garde genre even though segments of it are canonized due to the particularities it pertains and preserves faithfully. We assume this in nationalism and internationalism aspects, which accompany children's books in Albania.

Another significant aspect that matters a lot in this research includes the translation of *Children's Literature* in Albania. The posing of problems encountered in the development of this phenomenon really counts for the serious consideration of this genre and tendencies to elaborate distinguished policies in service to adequate and accurate products for children who constitute a particular readership worth regarded.

And furthermore, the discussed aspects of *Children's Literature* in this research, of course, lead to other researches as other aspects request us to pick them out.

NOTES

1. Ismail Kadare is a famous Albanian writer and critic.
2. Bedri Dedja is a famous Albanian writer for children. He is also known for his criticism and reflective researches on *Children's Literature* in Albania.

BIBLIOGRAPHY

Baçi, H. (1996), *Kritika jonë pas luftë së dytë botërore.* Mësuesi, 29 Maj.

Beqja, H. (1954), *Për një pasqyrim më të thellë të jetës në letërsinë për fëmijë.* Nëntori nr. 4.

Bushaka, G. (2001), *Historia e letërsisë shqiptare për fëmijë.* Tiranë: Studime filologjike nr. 3-4.

Çapaliku, S. (1999), *Letërsia e interpretuar.* Tiranë.

Dado, F. (1996), *Proza nëpër teknikat poetike.* Tiranë: TOENA.

Dedja, B. (1971), *Tradita dhe probleme të letërsisë shqipe për fëmijë.* Tiranë: TOENA.

Deva, A. (1977), *Romani ynë për fëmijë.* Prishtinë.

Hoxha, H. (1995), *Teoria e novelës dhe e tregimit.* Shkup.

Kallulli, A. (1965), *Libri duhet të jetë i bukur.* Drita 12 Shtator.

Qafleshi, E. (2004), *Disa probleme që lindin gjatë përkthimit të letërsisë për fëmijë në Shqipëri.* UNIEL nr. 2.

Skëndaj, B. (1982), *Trajtimi i temë historike në romanin për fëmijë,* Drita 22 Gusht.

Sopaj, N. (2000), *Letërsia për fëmijë.* Shkup.

Uçi, A. (1970), *Estetika, jeta, arti.* Tiranë.

Yzeiri, I. (2000), *Poetika.* Tiranë.

Other Sources

The Anthology of Translated Literature for Children in the Albanian Language (1959), V. Bala & B. Dedja. Tiranë.

6

(De) Centering Hierarchies: Programming Children in Hansel Ndumbe Eyoh's *Munyenge*

Kelvin N. Toh

Hitherto, I think the only critique that has been done on Hansel Ndumbe Eyoh's *Munyenge* is that of Edward Ako in "Children's Literature in Cameroon: A Review Essay" where he avers that "in the area of theatre, only Hansel Ndumbe Eyoh has, so far tried to use this medium of expression for children" (1996: 314) and he cites among Eyoh's plays *Munyenge*. This play gets its roots from the popular West African folk tale that tells the story of a village belle about to make a choice of husband. Eyoh's transformation of this oral narrative into dramatic art, tailored for children in this case only stresses on the serviceable purpose of literature for people of all walks of life and ages.

Eyoh's interest on children's and young adult literature was born as an afterthought and fast developed as he explained to Edward Ako in an interview that:

> The child is said to be the father of the man. If literature must grow, if enjoyment of literature should develop, if new creators of literature have to be born, then literature should begin with the child...it expands the child's linguistic competence, develops his creativity, provides him entertainment and provides him with a perception of the world. (qtd in Ako, 1996: 315)

The views of this academic and artist are revealing. He sees literature as an instrument of training and building up of children to understand their culture. This gives children's and young adult literature the function of transforming the child. It is this training that I call, in this paper, the programming of the child to fit in their particular space/place and be an integral part of their community ideology. Thus, it is good to find out what kind of doctrine literature can give a child and, if the child becomes a producer, from where does he or she get his or her programming basing from the fact that Eyoh thinks like Wordsworth that the child is the father of the man. My preoccupation in this essay is not on the child as producer but on what the child has been given to consume as the tool for educational training and upbringing.

The programming of the child is very vital as Eyoh puts it and this implies that the child has to get acquainted to his or her literature to learn his/her culture. I therefore agree with Emily A. Schultz and Robert H. Lavenda in their book *Cultural Anthropology: A Perspective on the Human Condition* that culture is a "set of learned behavior and ideas that human beings acquire" (1998: 3). Yet, it is possible to read Eyoh's text, under study here, as a modernist text that is built on the 'pure' and the dominant 'self' which seems to me, is the ideal that Eyoh's play attempts to build in the psyche of the child. In other words, the *Munyenge* constructs binaries especially built on centre/margin values upheld by precolonial Africa (at least the setting of the play tells us so). Eyoh's view is corroborated by Judy Anne White in "Quest for Selfhood: The Female Hero in Amos Tutuola's *The Brave African Huntress*" who holds that:

> As adolescent boys and girls read these [African] tales, they learn what is acceptable behavoir, often because the monsters demonstrate what unacceptable behavior is. More important, they learn that maintaining a sense of honor and developing psychological toughness, and maybe even learning to acknowledge personal weakness, are all important skills for a man to grasp if he is to function in his world. (1998: 132)

This claim sounds modernist as it tells us clearly that children's and young adult literature should be able to construct the binary between the 'civilised self' and the 'monster other'. This binary, as of course known, is built on false representation for the most part because it is hard to understand what makes the 'other' to be the monster while the self is sane and symbolises virtue, good and the civilised. The discussion we get from White's quote also gives room for the construction of hierachies and thus, the firm implantation of 'high' and 'low' cultures in the mind of the child.

It is therefore true to think that the child will grow up to uphold such binaries. At this point, the young boy and girl are already programmed and cannot think or operate freely as there is a power structure for which they can be trained to grow as agents. My focus in this paper is to demonstrate that modernist meta narratives like Eyoh's *Munyenge* can or may initiate children to be absolutist and eventually stand to defend and protect either their race, gender, creed and political opinion in the most aggressive manner (Said, 1993: XV). This is because they have been trained to see the 'other' from a biased perspective and hardly from a perspective of coexitence and double consciousness to use Paul Gilroy's phrase.

The play, proper, is set in a dominantly patriachal and dictatorial society where the ruling class is projected to be sacred and therefore must be untouched. Any attempt to question this authority, whose costodian is the Chief, is regarded as profane to the existing 'pure' culture and thus, any one who does so is considered the monster that most be feared or eliminated. The discussion between the Town Crier and Villagers is prove of the fact that this society is put under the weight of the Chief, who does not need another opinion. The people must obey him without questioning "lest the wrath of the Chief fall on you" (1990: 4) or they are reduced to silence because the Chief "has ears and eyes everywhere" (1990: 5). This situation reveals the society that is not a plural. Also, it can be seen that the dominant 'centre' cannot be in anyway profaned by the 'periphery'. In this consolidation of dominant space, the masses are prone to live in fear. That is why in that same dicussion between the Town Crier and the Villagers we read:

> Town Crier: And me? Do you think it is fun for me to leave my bed?
>
> 2nd Villager: Then why do you have to be up every morning at cock's crow, beating your gong into people's slumber?
>
> Town Crier: Why don't you ask the Chief that question?
>
> 3rd Villager: Hm! Ask the Chief? You must be joking. We dare not. You know that. Who dares ask the Chief any question? Even if he thought our complaint was justified, he will make us pay dearly, only for complaining. (1990: 5)

What one finds from this discussion is that the masses are a defeated people who live in constant fear. They fear every thing about their leader to the point that they cannot ask question. The town crier in the text and his gong, is not only a communicator of the Chief's messages to the people; he is more of a nuissance to the people. That is why his gong gets into their slumber. This picture is representative of the grim and sordid state that the despote has put the people under his rule. But out of fear, these people choose to be silent so that they can live. Eyoh's presentation of this kind of strong binary which throughout the play, no effort is made to deconstruct seems to be helping children to know that in the face of whatever leadership, their duty is to be silent. The fact that the 'centre' has eyes and ears everywhere is not only a construction of supremacy but that of resistance as well. Frantz Fanon in *The Wretched of the Earth* has argued that:

> The colonized man is an envious man. And this the settler knows very well; when their glances meet he ascertains bitterly, always on the defensive 'They want to take our place'. It is true, for there is no native who does not dream at least once a day of setting himself up in the settler's place. (1967: 30)

From Fanon's words, we learn that in postcolonial societies, resistance is obvious because of the rise of this new elite and the masses. The new elite gradually and carefully programmed to fit into the shoes of the ex-colonialist whose victims are the masses. Here, the 'centre'/'margin' binary is not constructed as colonised and coloniser but as ruled and ruler. The 'centre' in Eyoh's *Munyenge* is the village Chief. This man is conscious of the fact that his position is coveted and as Fanon puts it, creates all the defensive mechanism around and about him. This is to enable him to keep his place that they (the masses) want to take. He says that:

> I told you. Who says the life of a Chief is an easy one? You can't trust any one. You can't believe anyone. Bloody hypocrites all of them. The Chief has his eyes and ears everywhere! What are they complaining about? Before you, everyone is bowing in respect. Falsehood! Behind your back.... (1990: 10)

These words from the Chief show, in the first place, that he understands how the people see their ruler and Eyoh, in terms of characterisation creates a Chief that is capable of disguising and meeting with the villagers as a town crier without them noticing him. At this point, the Chief is presented as one who owns and masters the material of production. Karl Marx and Frederick Engels in "The German Ideology" seem right when they wrote that:

> The ideas of the ruling class are in every epoch the ruling ideas: i.e., the class which is the ruling *material* force of society is at the same time its ruling *intellectual* force. The class which has the means of material production at its disposal, consequently also controls the means of mental production, so that the ideas of those who lack the means of mental production are on the whole subject. (1992: 47)

The Chief's ability to disguise and not be identified is a rare artistic strength that he possesses. The acquisition of such creative potent may be largely attributed to the fact that he is of the rulling class and therefore, like Marx and Engels think, is capable of controlling the intellectual and mental ideologies of his time to fit into his mould. Also, his ability to confront his subjects in a disguised manner shows that he is conscious of the fact that the villagers want to take his place; a place he would not let go so easily. Through this, we find this Chief as a witty fellow who has the tools to outwit his subjects.

The sense of dramatic irony here is only humourous and satirical as it exposes a naïve people that have allowed themselves to be so manipulated by the agents of the power structure in their society. The buffonery of these people is seen even as the Town Crier (the disgiused Chief) pushes them to utter statements which he uses to put them in constant fear and trembling.

> 2nd Villager: Who is shivering? Hurry up. I have some important business in my bed which I did not complete.
>
> 1st Villager: And so do I.
>
> 3rd Villager: And me too.
>
> Town Crier: So, you want me to tell the Chief that you say he is not important.
>
> 2nd Villager: You with your evil tongue. Who ever said that the Chief is not important?
>
> Town Crier: You just did.
>
> 2nd Villager: I?...
>
> 1st Villager: Take it easy man. It is too early in the morning for us to quarrel. We've not even wet our mouths with palm wine. We are sorry that we could ever say any thing bad about our chief. What is the message from the Chief, this time? (1990: 6-7)

This shows a people driven by fear of their ruler and are in no way ready to make an attempt for change. Eyoh's dramaturgy rejects any effort of change since, as we have just seen, the general ideology that governs the age during the production of the text and the world in the text makes the one who questions the order of things a 'subvert' and 'monster'; a representation which seems to me that Eyoh would not want children to be identified with.

Also, the dramatic irony of this disguised Chief reveals the extent to which African systems and leaders do all in their power to remain in the 'centre' and position of power for as long as they can. This is what Terry Eagleton calls the superstructure. According to him, superstructure means:

> Certain forms of law and politics, a certain kind of state, whose essential function is to legitimate the power of the social class which owns the means of economic production. But the superstructure contains more than this: it also consists of certain "definite forms of social consciousness" (political, religious, ethical, aesthetic and so on), which is what Marxism designates as *ideology*. (2003: 421)

It is easy to quickly conclude here that Eyoh's presentation of this superstructure in Africa, as presented in *Munyenge* can be read as satirical. But what is it that is registered in a child's tender mind? The ability to use power to silence and to victimise. The ability to device crooked and dictatorial methods of leadership and above all, making the children to understand that change is not necessary as the Chief remains all powerful and should never be challenged. Such is the programming that is registered in the child's mind. That is the ideology that has been constructed in the mind of the child. The child begins by understanding that society is stratified between the superstructure and the 'base' for this is what forms ideology. I do agree with Terry Eagleton that "To understand an ideology, we must analyze the precise relations between different classes in society; and to do that means grasping where those classes stand in relation to the mode of production" (2003: 421). This may probably justify why this play was published in 1990; a time of political struggle and awareness in Cameroon. The country has remained under the same leadership for close to thirty years and the children and young adults from the period of the 1990s are reduced to silence in the face of this.

Part of the programming that builds a strong centre/margin divide is illustrated in the man's reduction of the woman to the marginal place; thereby, making her to remain in invariable subjectivity. Josephine Donovan in "Beyond the Net: Feminist Criticism as a Moral Criticism" is right when she opines that "usually the critic discovers that the images [attributed to women] are *Other*" (2003: 225). This 'fixity' of otherness leaves the woman in a not too comfortable space, as her otherness is regarded with 'negativity' which, in effect, is saying yes "to reified perceptions, structures, and models that have historically denied full humanity to women" (2003: 225). This means that the patriarchal 'centre' has succeeded for centuries to put the woman in the space of the 'other'. This otherness is better explained by Rosalyn Mutia who describes the situation of women thus, "in the family, women keep reproducing the iconoclastic values of domesticity such as marriage and motherhood, while men handle decision-making, even when these decisions have to do with the destiny of women" (2009: 153). The Chief's decision to have his daughter married is solely his. Not even the daughter, the principal concerned, is consulted. This is, in the first place, a confirmation of the fact that this society rates women as second sex. That is to say people who really do not matter. The Chief's decision, in the second place, shows his dictatorship on all the villagers and family members as well. When his wife tries to persuade him to change the decision as to the marriage of their daughter, the Chief says: "Woman, wife of mine. Why don't you continue with your part of the preparations? Why must you always do things late? I have set up today for our daughter's marriage and that is when you think you should talk to me against it?" (1990: 16). The quote clearly exemplifies how women are seen in this community. The number of possessive pronouns in the words of this Chief shows his authority over his wife. The wife is his and this denotes and conotes that she is his property. By implication, the Chief makes his wife understand that even Munyenge, the daughter concerned, is his property and in that case, he decides for them like he does for the whole village. The Wife of the Chief and Munyenge, their daughter, are seen as objects; without opinion and reduced to silence. This silence is seen in the surprise expressed by Munyenge when her father informs her of the day of her wedding. In fact, her father tells her of his decision, her opinion is not sought:

> ...my darling Princess. You remember what I talked to you about, don't you?
>
> Munyenge: Yes I do.
>
> Chief: Well, today is the day.
>
> Munyenge: Today, father.
>
> Chief: Yes, today.
>
> Munyenge: Well your wish is my command, father. (1990: 10)

This dialogue only emphasises the woman's inability to speak even about the things that concern her. Any viewer in post-modern age will be surprised at Munyenge's stoic submission to her father's will; if we agree with Bill Ashcroft, Gareth Griffiths and Helen Tiffin in *Post-Colonial Studeis Reader* that postmodernism is "the destruction of the centralised, logocentric master narratives of European culture" (1995: 117). The suddenness of Munyenge's wedding may seems a test of her father's power and also his authority as a chief over his daughter, wife and the people he rules.

The only character who, through out the play attempts to speak back is the Chief's wife. That is why the Chief is not happy when she is against his decision to marry off their daughter (1990: 16). She feels she is not treated as a wife and a mother when she says: "If you had sought my opinion before, I'd have told you what I felt" (1990: 16). This view by this woman sounds as though the world is falling apart. In this appalling atmosphere, the Chief, in a stupor wonders "why the hell is everybody suddenly wanting to give an opinion?" (1990: 17). The 'everybody' mentioned here is just a simplification of the woman folk which enforces the notion that women are people of the common place and therefore, asking for their opinion sound more or less eccentric. Judith Butler in *Bodies that Matter* corrobrates this view as she writes that "those who are not yet 'subjects', but who form the constitutive outside to the domain of the subject" (qtd. in Amorelli, 2009: 128). The argument here is that wife, since she is the queen of this community sees herself as subject when she is not in the domain of subjects—men but infront of her husband and men she is an 'other'.

This "difference" built of sex lines shows a careful and well-constructed centre which, unfortunately, no narrative is yet to counter, not even the dramatic ideology of Eyoh in this children's and young adult play. This is because even Wife's resistance can only be read as a verbal wish "I still wish you could listen to me. I'm not sure what she will do if she is not allowed her free will" (1990: 21). In *Munyenge*, no effort is made to dismantle the centre/margin divides that make up the dramatic world. This responds to Hegel's view in *The Phenomenology of the Spirit* where he sees the "conscious self" as that which has built a strong hegemony that gives authority. The authority is that the man's/ruler's wish becomes the command to all. The dramatic world of *Munyenge* is that which "women...have been relegated to the position of 'Other', 'colonised' by various forms of partriarchal domination" (Ashcroft et al., 1995: 249). The construction of this patriarchal 'self' as against the matriarchal 'other' is strongly represented in Eyoh's play and therefore leaves the child to continue to understand that society is programmed and that one need not question hegemonic spaces.

The girl child, in this case, has already been taught to be a silent listener and observer of the things that concern her. This, ironically, may seem to be the foundation of harmony in society. Talking about the Igbo society of Achebe's *Things Fall Apart,* Kristen Holst Petersen writes in "First Things First: Problems of a Feminist Approach to African Literature" that:

> Achebe's much praised objectivity with regard to the merits and flaws of traditional Igbo society becomes less than praiseworthy seen in this light: his traditional women are happy, harmonious members of the community, even when they are repeatedly beaten and barred from any say in the communal decision-making process and constantly reviled in sayings and proverbs. (1995: 253)

This harmony is problematic in that these women do not choose their silence but it seems imposed on them by society.

In *Munyenge*, this standpoint is clear in that no woman in the text seem comfortable though they accept things for the sake of harmony. Munyenge accepts the marriage plan because her father says so, not that she likes it. She complains; "Father, I know that you mean well for me. I know you've planned my life for me and this is in my interest. But I'd loved to have a bit more time before getting married" (1990: 11). What this young woman says seems interesting, especially with regards to the way society has constructed her space. The decision of her father against her will and opinion comes ironically because her father loves her. This dialectic view of demonstrating love is very crucial since one would need to see whether there is a link between interest and love. We see that her father's decision, as we have said, is based on greed and the desire to express his authority. Interestingly, this greed is seen by the child as a form of love that her father has for her. The voicelessness of this girl is also revealed from her words. Her father is very central because she has her life well planned by him. This reveals that the princess lives as a disguised or a programmed product of her father's. She is not seen as amimic girl but one who has been brain washed by her father. That is why her resistance to her father's will seems not to be worth the salt.

Eyoh's play also leads the child to the ensuing problematic of gender stereotypes—the masculine superior and the feminine, for the most part, being inferior. Rosalyn Mutia quoting from Dorenkamp et al. helps us to read this:

> Her flaccid muscles, tender skin, highly nervous organisation, and aptitude for internal injury, decide the question of offices involving hard bodily labour, while the predominance of instinct over reason, or of feeling over intellect, as a rule unfits her for judicial or legislative command. Her power is essentially a silent and unseen influence, her functions are those of a wife and mother. (qtd. in Mutia, 2009: 156)

The reductionist image of the feminine is to buttress the grounds for her otherness as she is simply seen as irrational and at all levels unable to be masculine. Eyoh, it seems to me is a product of this mould of thinking. That is why in the play *Munyenge*, the only time a woman is given the opportunity to choose, she results in making a serious mistake. Munyenge's rejection of real men and going for a ogre is indicative of the fact that women are naïve and need to be guided at all cost. The irrationality of this girl is such that not even the father is capable of calling her to order:

> Munyenge: Father, father, that's him.
>
> Chief: Who?
>
> Munyenge: My husband to be.
>
> Chief: Your husband? But you hardly even know him.
>
> Munyenge: It is love at first sight. He is so handsome. I love him.
>
> Chief: Not so fast, daughter.
>
> Munyenge: Not so fast? See how beautiful he is. (1990: 25)

This naïve posture reveals that women are generally naïve and must always be guided. Interestingly, the hero of this play is far from being Munyenge. The hero is Mukete, Munyenge's twin brother. He is the one who salvages her sister from the dangers of the ghost. Interestingly, when the rescue operation is done, Munyenge thinks she is dreaming. This reveals that the girl child is at the mercy of the her brother who is realitic and has the God-given talent and ability to rule and guide his sister in times of danger. This is the mind set that the child has and seems to be trained with.

In conclusion, I have demonstrated that Eyoh's *Munyenge* (being a story written for children) is built on binaries—the ruler and the ruled, men and women—and these binaries only enforce the myth of the superior 'self' as opposed to the inferior 'other'. Eyoh's play in this context, is a tool to programme the child's mind with emphasis that this 'centre' is a perpetual state and no effort should be made to deconstruct.

WORKS CITED

Ako, Edward. "Children's Literature in Cameroon: A Review." *Epasa Moto: A Bilingual Journal of Language, Letters and Culture* (1996): 310-17.

Amorelli, Delores. "'Neither My Presence nor My Absence': The Crisis of Subjectivity in *The Sun Hath Looked Upon Me.*" Ako, Edward O. *Cameroon Literature in English.* Berlin: LIT Verlag Dr. W. Hopf, 2009. 115-33.

Ashcroft, Bill, Gareth Griffiths and Helen Tiffen. *The Post-colonial Studies Reader.* New York: Routledge, 1995.

Donovan, Josephine. "Beyond the Net: Feminist Criticism as a Moral Criticism." Keesey, Donald. Contexts for Criticism. New York: McGraw-Hill Higher Education, 2003. 224-34.

Eagleton, Terry. "Literature and History." Keesey, Donald. *Context for Criticism.* New York: McGraw-Hill Higher Education, 2003. 419-26.

Eyoh, Hansel Ndumbe. *Munyenge.* Yaounde: BET & Co., 1990.

Fanon, Frantz. *The Wretched of the Earth.* New York: Penguin, 1967.

Gilroy, Paul. *The Black Atlantic: Modernity and Double Consciousness.* Cambridge, MA: Harvard University Press, 1993.

Marx, Karl and Frederick Engels. "The German Ideology." Easthope, Antony and Kate McGowan. *Critical and Cultural Theory Reader.* Buckingham: Open University Press, 1992. 47-49.

Mutia, Rosalyn. "Because of Men: A Feminist Interpretation of Dipoko's Because of Women." Ako, Edward O. *Cameroon Literature in English: Critical Essays on Fiction and Drama.* Berlin: LIT Verlag Dr W. Hopf, 2009. 153-73.

Petersen, Kristen Holst. "First Things First: Problems of Feminist Approach to African Literature." Ashcroft, Bill, Gareth Griffiths and Helen Tiffen. *Post-colonial Studies Reader.* New York: Routledge, 1995. 251-54.

Said, Edward. *Culture and Imperialism.* New York: Vintage, 1993.

Schultz, Emily A. and Robert H. Lavenda. *Cultural Anthropology: A Perspective on the Human Condition.* California: Mayfield Publishing Company, 1998.

White, Judy Anne. "Quest for Selfhood: The Female Hero in Amos Tutuola's *The Brave African Huntress.*" Khorana, Meena. *Critical Perspectives on Postcolonial African Children's and Young Adult Literature.* London: Greenwood Press, 1998. 131-42.

7

Theoretical Framework of Children's Literature Translation

Elena Xeni

INTRODUCTION

Children's Literature Translation (ChLT) theory, being a 'young' strand of translation theory with origins in comparative studies, is not more than four decades old. During this time, certain theories influenced—in one way or another—the translation product and process and the translator's profile, approaches, strategies, and norms in the context of ChLT. In the subsequent lines, key theoretical approaches in ChLT are reviewed with Itamar Even Zohar, Zohar Shavit, and Hans Vermeer and Katharina Reiss referred to as major contributors in attempts to theorise ChLT. These approaches, that were the catalysts for the emergence of the main theoretical developments in ChLT, are presented below chronologically.[1]

MAIN ATTEMPTS TO THEORETISE CHLT

Itamar Even Zohar's Polysystem Theory

The merging of cultural with translation studies in the 1970s gave rise to the polysystem theory. Polysystem theory was developed by Itamar Even Zohar, an Israeli cultural theorist who investigated how literature and translation function in certain contexts or systems. To Even Zohar (cf. 1978a), a polysystem is an entire network of correlated networks—literary or extraliterary—and covers all major and minor literary systems within a society. Every literary polysystem consists of a number of sub-systems that are hierarchically arranged, primary models (innovatory) and secondary models (conservative), canonised and non-canonised types of literature or positions closer to the centre of the system or closer to the periphery (cf. Even Zohar, 1978a). These represent stronger and weaker literatures. The closer to the periphery a subsystem is, the lower its cultural status within the entire system. Literary polysystems are not isolated systems but correlate with other cultural systems that can be encountered in the ideological and socio-economic structures of a society.

Translated literature as a subsystem may hold any position within the system. It can be found either in the centre, representing a significant part of a country's literature, or in the periphery, representing a less influential part. ChL is one of the parts of the literary system and it usually maintains a peripheral position in the literary polysystem, with traditionally low cultural prestige. Similarly to ChL, ChLT upholds a marginal position in the literary system, and remains in the periphery, having little influence. It relies on norms already established by a dominant type with a particular genre. Due to this, ChLT is, according to Even Zohar (cf. 1978), ignored and liable to manipulation. Similarly to ChLT, the translator of ChL is undervalued in society and is subject to bad working conditions. Raising ideological issues, Even Zohar stresses the impact of norms on the translators' role and status. Since translators are expected to obey the rules established in the culture and society of the target text (the receiving culture) they consequently have less freedom of power in the process of translation. However, according to Thompson-Wolgemuth (1998) wherever translators feel completely free to translate, they still have their own opinions regarding the text. This point raises the issue of ideology that intervenes in the translation process.

Zohar Shavit

Zohar Shavit (1981) developed the polysystem theory further and applied it to ChLT. Shavit's key contribution relevant to the present paper is her list of five characteristics that distinguish ChLT as a subsystem from other subsystems (1981: 172-77):

1. Affiliation to existing models: Texts which have the form of a source text model, which does not exist in the target culture, may be changed. Such changes occur mainly by deleting elements, to adjust them to models which exist in the target culture.
2. Integrality of texts: In this context translators are allowed to manipulate the fullness of STs, in order to adapt them either to a child's level of comprehension or to moral norms.
3. Level of complexity of texts: This characteristic is related to the simplification of texts, meaning that if a text consists of two or more levels—as it happens in the case of ambivalence (see 3.7, this paper)—it is simplified in a single level.
4. Evaluative adaptation (ideological adaptation): In this context texts pose a didactic instrument for ideology transfer purposes.
5. Stylistic norms: These norms indicate a high literary style and are important in ChL for didactic purposes as they enrich children's vocabulary.

What can be said from studying these characteristics is that Shavit (1981) adequately summarises the main factors that come into play in the realm of ChLT: the text, the role of the translator, and translation norms and strategies applied during the translation process. Shavit (*ibid.*) also contributed to determining the relation between ChL and literature for adults (AdL) by identifying the subsystems of canonised and non-canonised ChL and AdL. According to her findings, all ChL maintains a similar position to—and behaves similarly to non-canonised—AdL. With these findings Shavit (*ibid.*) raised awareness of the role and status of ChL and contributed to a great extent to its recognition.

Vermeer, Reiss and Skopos Theory

Vermeer and Reiss are scholars whose contribution to Translation Studies theory also had a major impact on the theory of ChLT. Being the first who advocated the theory of text types (cf. 1971), they managed to apply it in ChLT (cf. 1982).

Skopos theory, has significant application to ChLT. Developed by the "functionalists" (Vermeer, Hönig, Kussmaul, Holtz-Mänttary, Nord and Reiss), skopos theory highlighted that translating and interpreting should primarily take into account the function of the source and target text (cf. Vermeer and Reiss, 1971). Having skopos (purpose) as the most important criterion in any translation that depends on the needs and expectations of the target text readers, this group of theorists moved focus from the sourse text, which was regarded as the "sacred original" (Hönig, 1997: 9), to the reader, placing the child-reader in a central position. In addition to advancing the role of the child-reader and the target text, skopos theory assigned a new role to the translation. Being now considered an "expert" (Thomson-Wolgemuth, 1998: 105), with more freedom at hand, the translation is exempted "from the obligation" to reproduce the source text exactly in the target culture (Βλαχόπουλος, 2010: 150). At this point the translator starts to acquire a higher profile and status. Last but not least, in the context of skopos theory, translation is regarded as "a cultural product" and the process of translation as "a culture-sensitive procedure" (Vermeer, 1994: 10)—an aspect which is linked to polysystem theory and the "culture turn" in translation studies.

Skopos theory marked a new era for translation theory and practice. In the context of ChLT, skopos theory introduced changes for all main parties: the child reader, the translator, the translated text and the translation process itself. It also raised important issues such as the status and income of the translator and ideological concerns in the context of Translation Studies. In the context of skopos theory, the translator is given relative freedom in the sense that he is not shackled by Source Text norms. However, as Thomson-Wolgemuth (1998) explains, in real life a translator working under commission, still has limited freedom and cannot really reject a project, due to his low status, profile and income. In this respect he is still subject to source and target culture pressures. In line to this, if the translator does not maintain the norms of the original, the commissioner who has the final word may interfere, thus reducing the translator's freedom.

CONCLUSION

In this paper attempts to theoretise ChLT were critically reviewed highlighting the role of the translator of ChL. A brief analysis of the development of key ChLT theories demonstrates a shift from conservative to more liberal approaches. As a result, thc former focus on the status of ChLT and translation methodology, shifted to settle on the power of the translator as a key player in the translation process and the target readers' interaction with the text. In addition, it was then acknowledged that translation is not a purely linguistic matter but is affected to a great extent by social, cultural, economical and political factors (Fornalczyk, 2007).

Besides issues of concern deriving from its multifaceted missionary role and developments in the theory, ChLT has had to face further issues that have led to continuing debate in the academic and non-academic world (Xeni, 2011). The translator's invisibility, low status, profile and royalties, and the longstanding issue of translatability are some of the issues that come to surface from visiting the main theories of ChLT. The concepts of ideology, censorship and manipulation, and ambivalence are also issues of concern in the context of ChLT (*ibid.*). All these issues form the reality based on what ChLT develops. A reality based on a complex past, developing present and prosperous future as ChL and its translation have been gradually acknowledged as scientific fields in their own right.

Since its beginning, translation theory has undergone major changes as an academic discipline. A brief presentation of the main contributors or instigators of the development of the theories of ChLT hints at the relationship between theories, approaches, strategies and norms in the field. These translation theories reveal some key general changes in the field which affected all of the sub-fields and highlighted a "methodological shift from source orientation to target orientation (Tabbert, 2002: 303) was. Quoting Sas:

> Reiss and Vermeer did not one day wake up and decide to start a new theory based on a Greek word. On the contrary, skopos theory is the result of a development in translation studies where the focus shifted from the source text to the target culture.... (2010: 67)

NOTES

1. In this paper it is not intended to provide an in-depth analysis of these theories, but solely an overview to highlight their relevance for ChLT.
2. Throughout the paper, 'he', 'his' and 'him' when referring to the translator, the student or the subject are used, as opposed to using the following: 's/he', 'she or he', 'he or she', 'his/her', and 'him/her'. This was chosen as a course of action for the purposes of clarity and consistency.

REFERENCES

English

Even Zohar, I. (1971). *An Introduction to a Theory of Literary Translation*, PhD thesis, Tel Aviv: Tel Aviv University.

Fornalczyk, A. (2007). "Anthroponym Translation in Children's Literature—Early 20th and 21st Centuries." *Kalbotyra*, 57 (3), 93-101.

Hönig, H. (1997). "Positions, Power and Practice: Functionalist Approaches and Translation Quality Assessment." In Schäffner, C. (ed.). *Translation and Quality*. Special Issue of Current Issues in Language and Society, 4(1), 6-34.

Sas, I. (2010). *Treacle Triplets: A Functional Approach to the Translation of Children's Literature*, MPhil Thesis, Stallenbosch University.

Shavit, Z. (1981). "Translation of Children's Literature as a Function of Its Position in the Literary Polysystem." *Poetics Today*, 2, 171-79.

Tabbert, R. (2002). "Approaches to the Translation of Children's Literature. A Review of Critical Studies Since 1960." *Target*, 14 (2), 303-51.

Thomson-Wolgemuth, G. (1998). *Children's Literature and its Translation: An Overview*. MA Thesis, Department of Linguistics Language and Culture, University of Surrey.

Vermeer, H.J. (1994). "Translation Today: Old and New Problems." In *Translation Studies: An Interdiscipline*. Snell-Hornby, Pöchhacker, F. and Kaindl, K. (eds.), 3 ff.

Xeni, E. (2011). "Issues of Concern in the Translation of Children's Literature". In Panaou, P. (ed.). "Comparative Approaches in Children's Literature". *Κείμενα* (13). Last accessed at: 1st October 2011 at: http://keimena.ece.uth.gr/

Greek

Βλαχόπουλος, Σ. (2010). Μετάφραση και Δημιουργικότητα: `Ενα οδοιπορικό μεταξύ γνωστικής και εφαρμοσμένης μεταφρασεολογίας. Αθήνα: Κλειδάριθμος

8

Unobtrusive Dissemination of the Didactic Teachings through the Indian Folklore

Devika
Sushila Rathore
Virendra Singh Nirban

Richness of Indian folk lore deeply infused with striking expression has successfully made its way to the hearts of children and elders, boys and girls, learned and illiterate, firmly retaining its individual aura and diffusing its universal appeal, entirely unique and rich in its own way.

> Indian culture is full of wonderful surprises and one of the shining jewels among them is Indian mythology. It is not only unique but is also comprised of richest elements. Different stories in Indian mythology have been passed from one generation to another through scriptures, fables and word of mouth.[1]

Since Indian culture is abundantly profuse in folk lore, its versatility and depth have acquired an unquestionable respect due to its pristine focus on the values to be inculcated in the people. Oral tradition of singing the valour of its soldiers, fidelity of ladies—maids and queens alike, of crookedness, abject plight of treachery, intelligence of well-read scholars, spiritual treasure of monks and saints, inherent goodness of even misguided miscreants, etc. unveil the layers of meaning, so essential for the poised pace of life. The Indian folklores and epics have served varied purposes including didactic, philosophic and aesthetic in several other countries including India in creating, supporting and preserving the indigenous culture of the country. As Finnish Indologist Petteri Koskikallio states, "The Indian epics are totalities of different, or even contradictory ideas about morality or religion, the one dharma. At the same time they are totalities consisting of a massive number of tales, with interdependent teachings and stories."[2] The ways adopted by the narrators have been varied but always profound, never deviating from the single point focus of imparting instructive messages to the masses. These instructions have always been steadily disseminated by rishis, sadhus, monks, teachers, narrators and above all grandparents and mothers. The impact has always been immaculate to convey the teachings in an effortless yet powerful expression to make a permanent mark on the minds of receivers.

An unending array of folk tales is vast enough to accommodate all types of stories beginning from kings and queens, covering demons and monsters, monks and beggars and reaching to animals and birds. Lekshmi has rightly observed the richness of the diversity when she states, "Long before the advent of motivational gurus, life coaches and agony aunts, India had the tradition of summing up all the words of wisdom in the form literary gems. Be it in the form of puranans, *Upanishads*, *Vedas*, the epics like *Ramayana*, *Mahabharata* or the *Bhagavat Gita* or fables."[3]

II

Myriad stories in the Indian folklore illustrate the moral through the relationship between animals and human beings. The animals are believed to possess great wisdom which they generously impart to human beings in times of need. The inclusion of animals in Indian folklores emphasizes the spirit of cooperation human beings share with animals which is exhibited when the aid offered by humans is returned through an act of kindness by the animals, as shown in the story of Mangoose and the Brahmin. David Pickering has rightly summed up his opinion on animals in Indian folklores in his book, "Animals of all kinds feature in folklores, in rituals, legends and folk tales throughout the world culture, reflecting the curiosity humans have always had about other species with which they share the earth, and the desire to share the remarkable powers of other species."[4]

The stories related to monks and munnies help people learn the messages in the most unobtrusive way/s so that the message gets conveyed and also imbibed without any force. All the stories related to Mahatama Buddha, Lord Mahavir or for that matter even unknown sages and rishis open up a new channel of understanding for a long lasting and fruitful acceptance leading to direct and indirect changes in the perception and personality. When Mahatama Buddha asked the bereaved mother to collect handful of mustard seeds from a house where no death has taken place, he very subtly makes her learn the valuable lesson about the certainty of death as the ultimate reality. Her coming back to Buddha after cremating her son helps her accept the truth with understanding; something which seems to be almost an impossible task gets accomplished by a very simple yet befittingly profound manner. The desired transference of messages in the most rewarding way vouchsafe for the irresistible force of Indian culture.

The depth gets intensified not because it has been rhetorically conveyed but by the outcome which wields the force to accept, reject or change the outlook for life and ways of life. Angulimal, after killing nine hundred ninety-nine people warns even his mother to leave him because of his temptation to make it one thousand. The transformation in his life after his encounter with Mahatama Buddha from a brutal murderer to a composed soul sets another example of the power of great personalities and their way of making people understand the essence of their existence in particular and life in general. The accounts of Lord Mahavir's life leave an indelible impression on the otherwise impervious sensibilities of human beings. The mere revelation that thorns use to change their direction so as not to prick the bare feet of the Lord and the premature blooming of the buds on his arrival so as to get his blessings, establishes the faith in the purity of soul. Similarly, the tale where the guru gets angry with the disciple who lifted a lady on his shoulders to help her cross the overflowing river tells about the effort put in to attain the purity of heart. The response of the disciple that he had carried her on his shoulders only through the river whereas the guru was still carrying the lady mentally highlights that age and designation are no parameters of excellence; it has to be duly nurtured by purity of thoughts.

Even Sufis have added an enormous corpus to the already overflowing body of knowledge. They work hard to help people differentiate between genuine and fake gurus and disciples. They use a profound undercurrent to teach the simple but overlooked principles. The famous story of the division of guru's seventeen camels is in reality an attempt on the part of the guru to help his disciples trace a genuine guru who could be unselfish enough to teach them with proper care. The division of the seventeen camels into half to the eldest one, one-third to the middle one and one-sixth to the youngest one at the surface level appears to be an ill-framed division but holds a deeper meaning. The division is mathematically impossible unless somebody is wise enough to add his one camel to the equation to make the division appropriate. The power to be in for the sake of others is one of the qualities of a true master; hence the dying guru made an intricate yet intelligent equation.

The profusion of information just keeps on increasing in an enriching way as the master disciple tales keep on adding. Imparting the knowledge while simultaneously setting the yardsticks for righteous and erroneous patterns adds that extra tinge. The tales of princes and fairies do allow innocent people to be cursed and victimized but ultimately their virtue is openly accepted and acknowledged by everyone. The story of Cinderella and her stepsisters holds its own significance. The fairy helps Cinderella because of her goodness of heart and purity of soul reflected through her deeds. Despite being treated in a very inhumane way by her stepmother and step-sisters, she still loves them. The relationship between humans and fairies are very common where the fairy gets thrown out of the fairyland and her special powers are taken back by the fairy queen as she has stooped enough to love a mortal. However, when the fairy queen herself falls for a common man, then only she realizes the power of true love and returns the power of the fairy. The fairy gets her powers back as she has helped the people in distress and worked for the welfare of others, a message that is strong enough to sustain the urge to help people in real distress. Treading on the simultaneous line of the power of giving, demons, despite being powerful and blessed do get killed by a commoner as the unfair means and barbarous acts never ultimately support the malefactors. Coming to the simple hearted people who have preferred a life of simplicity to a life of luxuries, treasures keep coming to them, fortune seems to befriend them, difficulties automatically get mild, and the happiness seems to be constantly in search of them; obstacles just turn out to be blessings in disguise. The simpletons in the family get the roughest jobs to do, seek nil pleasures, and remain happy and contended.

To keep the interest intact and convey the message, the tales have even animal characters that represent all emotions and impersonate all situations.

> The Panchatantra is the best guide to enroot moral values in children since its each tale has a moral lesson in its end. The Panchatantra is a great book where plants and animals can speak and converse with human beings too. The etymology of term 'Panchatantra' suggests that it is a combination of two words, 'Pancha' (five) and 'Tantra' (practice/principle). So, the five principles or practices illustrated by Panchatantra are 'Mitra Bhedha' (Loss of Friends), 'Mitra Laabha' (Gaining Friends), 'Suhrudbheda' (Causing discord between Friends), 'Vigraha' (Separation) and 'Sandhi' (Union).[5]

No wonder, the animals are intellectually bright with the power to think, argue, question and think beyond the ordinary. Sagacity of animals just makes people appreciate their power. The simple story of a rabbit who made a ferocious lion jump into the well to kill his own shadow assuming it to be another lion overwhelms the senses of listeners or readers. The simple yet profound execution of intricacies adds a unique charm to the tales of India. Vishnu Sharma in his *Panchatantra* weaves a pattern of stories to educate untrained princes. To quote Edgerton:

> ...there are recorded over two hundred different versions known to exist in more than fifty languages, and three-fourths of these languages are extra-Indian. As early as the eleventh century this work reached Europe, and before 1600 it existed in Greek, Latin, Spanish, Italian, German, English, Old Slavonic, Czech, and perhaps other Slavonic languages. Its range has extended from Java to Iceland... [In India,] it has been worked over and over again, expanded, abstracted, turned into verse, retold in prose, translated into medieval and modern vernaculars, and retranslated into Sanskrit. And most of the stories contained in it have "gone down" into the folklore of the story-loving Hindus, whence they reappear in the collections of oral tales gathered by modern students of folk-stories.[6]

III

Whatever may be the outcome of this string of tales on the princes, they hold great value to the readers even today, the chief reason being their universal appeal. Lauri Honko has emphasized the need to document the folklore as a valuable material, in fact as a "grammar bank"[7] which can be significant for the future generations also. The lessons on political, societal and psychological recesses of human life seem as fresh and valid today as at the time of their original creation. For one or another reason the demarcating line between stupidity and simplicity has been made very distinct and powerful. Ignorance of the basics is never excused and knowledge of superficialities is never rewarded. Stupidity is not allowed to bloom to warn people about its short as well as long-term ill effects. Reflection of various themes makes the corpus all the more engrossing.

Unflinching faith in the guiding force is one of the most intriguing yet powerful themes echoed through these stories.

Blessed with simplicity and unaffected by the impurities or vices, the characters are always guided by either humans or fairies or god or even by the circumstances. The guru disciple relationship does take the basis for the spread of this message of the simplicity of the disciple strengthened by the unflinching faith in his guru. The famous story of a disciple who asked his guru the way to visit heaven and his efforts to follow the exaggerated and unthinkable instructions by the guru to stand for six months with his hands raised towards the sky to allow him a visit to heaven finally do result positively. The sham guru on his return finds his disciple flying in the air to move towards the heaven who then gets hold of the feet of his disciple to go along with him.

This idea holds true and gets substantiated further though the famous epic *Mahabharata* where Eklavya, a man of Nishadh tribe which has been considered a low caste nurtures a desire to learn the art of archery. On being rejected by Dronacharya, he commits himself to self-study in front of a clay image of Dronacharya and acquires perfection in the art of archery. Nonetheless, his perfection surpasses even Arjuna, the most immaculate archer and a favourite disciple of Dronacharya. This revelation becomes a cause of worry to Dronacharya, consequently he demands Eklavya's right thumb in return for his fee, the hitherto education he has never imparted to him. Full of admiration for his master, Eklavya happily cuts his right thumb and gifts him. This story signifies the unflinching respect of a disciple for his master which is absent in the present generation. Moreover, it communicates the fact that a strong urge to learn something can make everything possible. Sincere efforts coupled with simplicity or purity of heart can make things wonder sue to the charisma of positivity. To keep oneself focused with no doubts or negative vibes result in success is the theory propounded by the spiritual gurus or influential speakers even in twenty-first century. Roma Chatterji feels about the folklore written by Rabindranath Tagore, "We might turn to folklore in order to prove that there are other kinds of historical sources than the imperial monuments and dynastic or colonial histories."[8]

Sanctity, truthfulness, purity of heart, etc. are some of the other themes ancient yet applicable even today. Parents encourage their child to speak the truth is strongly communicated through Indian epics such as *Mahabharata* through Yudhishthir an epitome of truth and wisdom. The message on the part of the parents to stay away from bad influences is strongly conveyed through these tales. The narration of the pathetic fate of such companies indicates the need for obviating the negative elements that are obnoxious enough to ruin the life in a way leaving no scope for shedding it or getting a chance to untangle oneself from the self-destructive nature of their existence. The humiliating and remorseful end of the thugs, thieves, dacoits or for that matter cheating spouses highlights the need to remain cautious from the very beginning of letting oneself glide into this infernal rut. Sagacity of elderly comes handy to warn the novice souls to understand the ill-effects with great clarity. However, if the faith in the integrity is maintained, there is no dearth of options to redeem oneself. The life of Angulimal clearly highlights that anyone can modulate the current of one life by the sheer power of determination. Of course, the guiding force is always needed, more so in the hour of adversity. Role of experience and sagacity gets supported by the power of vision or common sense. Revelation of the information or knowledge before one is ripe enough to sustain it may result in disastrous outcome as it ended the life of King Parikshit.

The method of imparting knowledge and instructions has always been an integral part of Indian culture but the beauty of it remains in the method of imparting it in the most acceptable form. The role models like Shravan Kumar, Ram, Ravan, Lakshman, Karan, Harishchander, and to quote infinite names, do affect the people in the most desired way so as not to get swayed by the temptations when they lure people. The fear of doing wrong or being punished by God has also influenced the selection between moral and immoral paths of life. The tales associated with God, the incarnation and His or Her blessing people with their friendship goes a long run to fascinate people. Mira, the well-known princess, is saved by Krishna throughout her life. Her corporeal assimilation in the body of Krishna still speaks for the power of faith in the supreme power. How even supreme powers can be at the call of commoners is a morale boosting feeling. The stories of gods coming at the call of their devotees to help them out of distress are not discarded as the mere myths. The relationship with the supreme power is showcased by saints like Ram Krishna Paramhans to make people realize the worth of embracing a life of sainthood, still prevalent and acceptable in India.

The stories not only project the problems but also suggest the possible way out. "In theory, the *Panchatantra* is intended as a textbook of *niti* ("policy," especially for kings and statesmen); the aphorisms tend to glorify shrewdness and cleverness rather than altruism."[9] The coverage through these tales is vast and varied; not only the problems of politics or spiritual matter are dealt with but day-to-day affairs are also focused on with remarkable perspicacity. The focus on the daily dealings covers all aspects with practical understanding and feasible solutions. The messages for masses have always been clear and emphatic because of their easy to understand approach.

The ability to differentiate between true and false friends has been specially focused on to help people nurture and utilize this imperative essentiality, a trait that enabled people to learn it and use it to avoid putting things at stake. The betrayal by friends has been equally balanced by the faithfulness of friends to tell about the presence of both with strong perspectives. To be aware is one of the most significant positives essentially needed to put theory to work, of course with adaptations; the rewards and punishments decide the real worth of the friendship. Along with friendship comes another theme that cherishes a well-settled place in these tales. Faith or trust in relationships has been much talked about not because it attracts more attention but because it cannot afford to be absent in human lives. Its absence unbalances an extremely delicate balance of relationships which may ultimately result in infidelity, treachery or betrayal. Friends keep on betraying friends for money, land and ladies; wives and husbands cheat their spouses sometimes merely for carnal pleasure and sometimes for ego satisfaction; servants, attendants or helping hands murder or indulge in treachery for innumerable reasons.

The tales related to marital disharmony, jealousy, insecurity, indifference, humiliation, and for many other known and unknown reasons have broken the homes of common men and brought down the whole empires. The well-known story of Pinlga and her unsuccessful flirting with her stepson resulted in lot many unpleasant and inhuman decisions only to be equaled by the timely advent of the sage in the story. The tale gives a very strong message about the imbalances and strange combinations in marital life. The betrayal is not because of the absence of money or injustice; it may be guided by many other suppressed or subconscious motives. Treachery coupled with lecherousness has often been talked about with all the effects on the all people with its short-term benefits and long-term losses. The role of society has never been neglected or kept in the background but has always been referred to with proper and specific emphasis, though it may be adverse or supportive but it has always been there.

Wit has always been one of the intrinsic components of these narrations as it adds the much needed spice to enliven the account; it fulfills the void which many people seem to lack and they feel happy when presented with this kind of handling of situations. All the anecdotes related to Birbal seem to vouchsafe for the same, something equally balanced by Mulla Nasaruddin. The famous account of the sweet seller and the poor man highlights the importance of knowing things and putting them in the right perspectives. When the man says that his stomach is filled by the mouth watering smell of the sweets and he is asked to pay for the sweets as he has smelled it really puts the poor man in a real tight situation. Finally, he is suggested very appropriately to let the shopkeeper listen to the tinkling of the coins as he has only smelled the sweets. These kinds of stories prepare the people for very unlikely yet plausible situations from where they have only to save themselves but also to prove their mettle. Another story which highlights the win of wit over imprudence is an excerpt from tales of Birbal, known for his cleverness. On being trapped one day by the courtiers to tell the number of crows present in Agra, his intelligent reply silences the courtiers and Akbar. Such witty remarks not only bring in the wisdom of Birbal, a brilliant minister but also one important idea that for professional excellence he had never harmed anyone and yet had remained successful. The awareness of these kinds of situations mentally prepares the people to think beyond, reason beyond and win beyond. In fact, it directly or indirectly nurtures the latent ability to defend oneself.

Pride has always been talked about only to convey the message about its disastrous repercussions which annihilate not only the very existence but all grandeur of the life-long achievements. To add to the imperativeness about its awareness, all powerful and influential people even gods have been made to pay the price for pride. The sun and moon eclipse and the increasing and decreasing moon positions warn people to keep their egos in proper check. Those who seek forgiveness are, of course, not spared the punishment but are spared with grace to continue their lives whereas those who prefer to nurture their adamant nature get killed and even deprived of all the credit and grace. In the never ending battle between gods and demons heaven is ruled over by who prefers to curb the pride and stand by virtue. In *Mahabharata*, when overpowered by pride, mighty Bhima and chivalrous Arjuna forget the courtesies of delicacy, Lord Hanuman is sent into teach them a lesson. Inclusion of every character of this grand a stature awakens the realization in masses to understand the need of keeping ego in check.

Greed remains an indispensable part of humans but how its excess or distorted version may deprive person of even the wealth he have had opens the eyes of even greedy people. Kings, queens, commoners, even animals are referred to convey the message. The king in his greed to expand his empire loses his original one; the queen in order to attain the love the savant loses the love of her own husband, children wishing to get all the mangoes of the tree is robbed of even the two mangoes in his lap. The fate of the jackal who found a deer to eat, thinking about the whole month food began eating the horns which pierced through and killed him. Greed when allowed to flourish acts as a corrosive and starts working for the deterioration of the relationships only to make them look ugly, unwanted and disgusting. Indian folk tales do impart the message but in an inconspicuous way as clearly reflected in all the stories of *Panchatantra*.

> The morals, therefore, in *Panchatantra* are in sharp contrast to our conventional understanding of the word 'moral'. They are not comforting stories of the victory of good over evil. Nor are they preachers of ethics. They are a manual of administration—of all aspects of one's life, in the complex and varied world of ours. The lessons learnt are applicable equally to the common man's life as to the princes for whom the Panchatantra was originally devised. They try to expose the reader to various occurrences that he could come across in his daily life and prepare him to face them with courage and prudence.[10]

Virtue even dipped in crookedness gets paid and may even result in noble deeds. To understand things with clarity of vision, a direct approach is adopted through very simple yet subtle tales. Basic values that need to be inculcated in children are disseminated in entirety to help children understand in a way that becomes easy for them to implement these also. Feeling of remaining united conveyed through the story of four sons and the old men who in a simple yet profound way made his sons realize the importance of staying united. Similarly, the value of virtue and unselfish acts get rewarded in a direct or indirect way, though it might be immediate or delayed. To be of some use to others may not result in monetary benefits but may provide the contentment to the soul. The story of a thug who in order to rob befriended four merchants who have sewn the diamonds in their thighs results in his death when in order to save four merchants he asks the dacoits to first kill and search his body. He knows that he too would be killed by all means but he offers himself first to save the lives of remaining merchants.

Common sense is always preferred to the skills and knowledge as its absence makes life miserable for everybody. The decision of the four friends who are experts in different arts first recognize the skeleton of the tiger, then arrange it perfectly, provide meat to the whole body and infuse life in it is not approved of by the fifth friend who does not know any of the arts but understands that tiger is a meat eating animal and would kill all of them if brought to life. When they do not listen to him and are bent on making a display of their specialized skills, he requests them to let him climb a tall and sturdy tree. They mock at him and when he safely lands one of the trees start exhibiting their skill one by one; the moment tiger gets alive and they are rejoicing their triumph, it pounces on them and kills them all. The power of the message is too strong to be neglected which allows people to be cautious enough to understand the context as well.

The mere glance at the folklore hints at an opulence of themes. One thing that seems to bind all the links is the didactic thread running through all of them. Whatever takes place in an apparent as well as subliminal way leads to the perfect dissemination of pristine directives. The stories though meant for inculcating a value or teaching a lesson never seem to lose their grip even once. The values these stories focus on are the gems of wisdom delicately crafted and even more delicately passed on from one generation to another one. Some of the prominent themes are adherence to probity, acquisition of power of discrimination, belief in hard work, faith in sanctity of soul, etc. conveyance of the message is imparted in a continuous way either by rishis, munnies, saints or enlightened souls or by grandparents, teachers, gurus, mothers, etc.

Putting all the threads together, these yarns weave an exquisite pattern of pearls of wisdom to be disseminated in the most effortless way. Indian civilization is embedded in a vast assortment of didactic stories expounding morality and blessings of a morally led life though also describing the misery that follows ill deeds. All the stories discussed above have one common yet universal theme which imparts an exquisitely touching and sophisticated reflection of the rich culture of India. The depth never gets dampen by too much or too apparent messages. The portrayal of characters chirurgeonly blended with the execution of narration produces such an enchanting aura that it casts its spell in the most fruitful way. The deep-rooted morality combined with the value of virtues is welcomed with open arms. Their relevance and universal appeal make these tales a gem of rare and its own kind. Needless to say, the fragrance of these exotic flavours is strong enough to waft through the boundaries and affect people for a considerable period of time.

NOTES

1. http://www.indianchild.com/stories/panchatantra.htm retrieved on 30 March 2011.
2. Koskikallio, Petteri. "From Classical to Postcolonial: Changing Ideologies and Changing Epics in India-Honkolauri (Special Edition): Epics along the Silk Roads." A UNESCO Workshop in Turku, Finland. Oral tradition, Vol. 11:1 Slovica Publishers: Columbus Ohio, 1996.
3. Lekshmi. Application of Panchatantra Stories in Today's Context. 28 March 2011. http://www.caclubindia.com/articles/application-of-panchatantra-stories-in-today-s-context-9296.asp retrieved on 30 March 2011.
4. Pickering, David. "Animals". *A Dictionary of Folklore.* New York: Facts on File, Inc, 1999. 10-11.
5. http://www.culturalindia.net/indian-folktales/panchatantra-tales/index.html retrieved on 2 March 2011.
6. Edgerton, Franklin. The Panchatantra Reconstructed (Vol. 1: Text and Critical Apparatus, Vol. 2: Introduction and Translation). New Haven, Connecticut: American Oriental Series, Volumes 2-3, 1924.
7. Honko, Lauri. "Systems of Central and Local Archiving." (Unpublished Paper) In *Finnish-Chinese Seminar on the Collection and Recording of Folklore.* Nanning, China. 1986.
8. Chatterji, Roma. "Emergent Events and the Folklore Archives in Bengal." (Unpublished paper) In *Culture Archives and the*

State. The Centre for Folklore Studies Spring Colloquium. The Ohio State University. May 3-5, 2007.

9. http://www.britannica.com/EBchecked/topic/440899/ Panchatantra retrieved on 5 March 2011.

10. http://www.indiaprofile.com/heritage/panchatantra.htm retrieved on 15 June 2011.

9

Children in Victorian Fiction

Sushmita Bhattacharya

Childhood emerged as the core theme in Victorian fiction and eminent writers of the age gave new inclusiveness and depth to the portrayal of the child-mind. The pre-Victorian artists (Vaughan, Wordsworth, Blake) are imaginative and visionary in their approach, inspired as they are by the divine and ideal child. They lend a mystic dimension to childhood and did not probe into the inner recesses of the child-mind. The universe of Victorian fiction presents children who are vividly alive and intensively portrayed: "The way in which novelists of this period present human character, moreover, also brings the idea of the Real into prominence" (Williams, 1). Dickens' power "can with a phrase make a character as real flesh and blood" (Eliot, 462). Emily Bronte while describing children shows psychological insights which are remarkably modern. Her children are "very realistically drawn...never sentimentalized or conventionalized...are fighting, laughing, squalling, untamed little animals, like real children" (Cecil, 141).

Charles Dickens, however, emerges as a colossus from among his contemporaries because he "captures so unerringly" (Allen, 164) the child's point of view. Dickens' sensitive understanding of the child's mind is revealed with all eloquence and power in *Great Expectations* through the words of Pip:

> In the little world in which children have their existence, whosoever brings them up, there is nothing so finely perceived and so finely felt as injustice. It may be only

> small injustice that the child can be exposed to; but the child is small, and its world is small, and its rocking horse stands as many hands high, according to scale, as a big-boned Irish hunter. (67)

The children in Victorian fiction are both a continuation and departure from the earlier treatment. The inspiration of George Eliot's *Silas Marner* is manifestly Wordsworthian and it is appropriately prefaced by a quotation from his poem *Michael*:

> A child, more than all other gifts
> That earth can offer to declining man
> Brings hope with it and, forward-looking thoughts.

The shaping power of fear on the child's mind as was emphasized by Wordsworth is also found in Dickens. Wordsworth shows in *The Prelude* how the guilty child-mind "Worked with a dim and undetermined sense/of unknown modes of being" which was a "trouble to my dreams" (*Poetical Works*, 499). Dickens' comprehensive genius grasps the tremendous shaping impact of fear upon the child's sensitive mind and Pip reflects that "few people know what secrecy there is in the young, under terror. No matter how unreasonable the terror so that it be terror" (*Great Expectations*, 25). Except for these obvious similarities the scene of childhood in Victorian fiction presents a glaring contrast. On the whole it portrays pictures of difficult childhood—"The Wordsworthian child of Nature survives in the productions of his Victorian successors, but it survives in altered shapes, mutations that call attention to new relations between self and nature" (Knoepflmacher, 304). The Victorian child is the very picture of the lonely outcast who is bewildered and depressed. He is incapable of experiencing the visionary gleam—"Heaven lies about us in our infancy" (Wordsworth, 460). For him it appears like Oliver that "heaven is a long way off, and they are too happy there to come to the bedside of a poor boy" (Dickens, 126). The child is brought up in uncongenial and hostile conditions and there are no guardian angels as in Blake's poems to ease his sorrows and sufferings. Even if he has parents the child is deprived of parental care and affection—"not an orphan in the wide world can be so deserted as the child who is an outcast from a living parent's love" (*Dombey and Son*, 292). "The tension between innocence and experience, sounded initially by Blake, became the main motif of early and mid-victorian literature of child" (Coveney, 92-93).

The industrial revolution which ushered prosperity by leaps and bounds, nevertheless, took its toll of child-labour. "The early nineteenth century was not a good time to be a child" (Orwell, 15). The pressures of the urbanized and commercialized environment aggravated the misery of these children. "In London alone, there were thirty thousand such ignorant children, hunted, flogged, imprisoned; meanwhile, the priests and teachers of all denominations quarreled among themselves—Teach this;—Teach that;" (Collins, 72-73). The malaise was pervasive and grave. The loss suffered in terms of sensibility was too heavy to be compensated by all the material wealth. Human relationships were now viewed solely from the utilitarian perspective. It was only natural in such circumstances that children who had no productive role were callously treated.

Unwanted Orphans

The first thing that strikes us is the fact that the majority of the children in Victorian fiction are orphans—Jane, Helen Burns, Heathcliff, Oliver, Pip, Nell, David, Jo and Esther. They are left to fend for themselves early in life without any loving care and protection. However, their position as orphans gives their authors the opportunity to explore a wide range of situations. "Waifs pursue their own ways through life, threading the solid world of statesmen, generals, bishops, bankers, philosophers and economists, twisting and slipping through that world like quicksilver" (Cruikshank, 3). These children are left entirely at the mercy of their guardians.

Jane Eyre presents Jane's disgraceful position on a winter night when she is excluded from the family circle of her aunt and cousins. Mrs. Reed, her aunt, shuts out Jane "from privileges intended only for contented, happy, little children" (Bronte, 1). She finds the child, to whose responsibility she is bound by her husband's promise a "truly forbidding child" and cannot tolerate even her presence. Her situation is that of "a child without status or adult protector" (Tillotson, 29). Mrs. Reed expressly forbids her children to associate with Jane. It is the presence of the apothecary Mr. Lloyd which makes Jane feel "sheltered and befriended" (13) in such oppressive and unjust surroundings where even the servants dare not take her part for fear of offending the mistress. Jane feels "an inexpressible relief, a soothing conviction of protection and security," on finding "a stranger in the room, an individual not belonging to Gateshead, and not related to Mrs. Reed" (13).

Heathcliff, in *Wuthering Heights*, is presented as the "dirty, ragged, black-haired child; big enough to walk and talk" (40) who is brought home by the warm-hearted Earnshaw from his business trip to Liverpool where he finds the orphan "really half-dead with fatigue, starving and houseless" (41). The child is named 'Heathcliff' after one of his sons who died in childhood. The entire household is hostile to the orphan child. Mrs. Earnshaw is "ready to fling it out of doors" (40) and exclaims how her husband could bring that "gypsy brat" (40) when they have children of their own. But at Mr. Earnshaw's insistence she "grumbled herself calm" (41). Hindley who finds that his fiddle is crushed "blubbered aloud" (41) and Cathy on discovering that her father "had lost the whip in attending on the stranger, showed her humour by grinning and spitting at the stupid little thing" (41). Even the good-hearted Nelly Dean "put it on the landing of the stairs," that night after the children "entirely refused" to allow him in their room, "hoping it might be gone on the morrow" (41). Heathcliff is "as uncomplaining as a lamb; though hardness, not gentleness, made him give little trouble" (42). Mr. Earnshaw's unwise favouritism proves a disadvantage to the lad. Hindley's treatment, after his father's death is "enough to make a friend of a saint" (67). Emily Bronte seems to have been obsessed with the vision of a young, lovely, happy child growing up to a life of misery and/or crime. Death for the child would clearly be better than life (Bradner, 129-46).

Dickens, in *Oliver Twist*, shows how Oliver's mother dies soon after his birth and he is "enveloped in old calico robes which had grown yellow in the same service, he was badged and ticketed, and fell into his place at once—a parish child—the orphan of a workhouse—the humble half-starved drudge—to be cuffed and buffeted through the world—despised by all, and pitied by none" (47). He is presented as "the item of mortality" (45) who is "rather unequally poised between this world and the next" (45). This precisely is the orphan's position in this world. Oliver's ninth birthday finds him "a pale thin child, somewhat diminutive in stature, and decidedly small in circumference" (49) and it is his "sturdy spirit" which "had plenty of room to expand, thanks to the spare diet of the establishment" (49) which allows him to survive. When Oliver asks for "more" there is a "general start" (68) and the gentleman in the white waistcoat declares "That boy will be hung" (58). Oliver is flogged as a "public warning and example."

Pip, in *Great Expectations* is the victim of the Victorian attitude towards illegitimacy. Though his hard-hearted and shrewish sister has brought him up "by hand" nevertheless this has "established a great reputation with herself and the neighbours" (19). Her hand is so hard and heavy that Pip's childish mind fancies "she must have made Joe Gargery marry her by hand" (10). He is frequently thrashed with Tickler "a wax-ended piece of cane, worn smooth by collision with my tickled frame" (20). Pip is made to feel that he is an unwelcome burden and "was always treated as if I had insisted on being born, in opposition to the dictates of reason, religion, and morality, and against the dissuading arguments of my best friends. Even when I was taken to have a new suit of clothes, the tailor had orders to make them like a kind of Reformatory, and on no account to let me have the free use of my limbs" (33). Mrs. Joe's companions have a high regard for her for bringing up the orphan child. Mr. Pumblechook tells Pip to be especially grateful "to them which brought you up by hand" (35). He points out that but for them he would not be "rolling in the lap of luxury" and gives a frightful picture of his destination "You would have been disposed of for so many shillings, according to the market price of the article, and Dunstable the butcher would have come up to you as you lay in your straw, and he would have whipped you under his left arm and with his right he would have turned up his frock to get a penknife from out of his waistcoat pocket, and he would have shed your blood and had your life. No bringing up by hand then. Not a bit of it" (36). Joe is too meek and simple to protect the child from the abuses and insults of Mrs. Joe.

The helpless and dependent position of these children is fully exploited by their guardians who use them as instruments to further their own ends. Miss Havisham is "dreadfully fond" of Estella but Pip learns gradually that there is a specific motive behind this fondness and that Estella "was set to wreak Miss Havisham's revenge on men" (279). Pip is educated by Magwitch but here also the criminal's motive for revenge on society is stronger than his feeling for gratitude.

Ineffectual Parents

Even if the parents are living the child is deprived of their loving care and protection which makes the situation more terrible. A noted historian has highlighted this fact "For it was not only bad employers but bad parents living on their children's labours, who required watching" (Trevelyan, 543). The parents show little understanding of the child's needs and their concern for the child is inevitably linked with their ambitions and interests. The onlookers describe Gaffer Hexam's arrival in Our Mutual Friend thus "Here comes the man as ain't good enough for his own son" (120), Steerforth laments in David Copperfield "I wish to God I had had a judicious father these last twenty years! I wish with all my soul I had been better guided!" (296).

Mrs. Reed in *Jane Eyre* is incapable of exercising any restraint on her children with the result that they fail to derive any happiness in their later lives. John grows up to be a reckless, dissipated young man who commits suicide to end his frustrated life. Jane also feels acutely the need of "a good home and kind parents" (49).

Mr. Earnshaw's partial treatment of the orphan Heathcliff in *Wuthering Heights* makes Hindley regard his father "as an oppressor rather than a friend" and Heathcliff as "a usurper of his parents affections" (42). In fact, Mr. Earnshaw jealously attended to his favourite "petting him up far above Cathy," who was "too mischievous and wayward for a favourite" (42). He has no understanding of his children's natures—"Mr. Earnshaw did not understand jokes from his children: he has always been strict and grave with them..." (45).

George Eliot has truthfully shown in *Mill on the Floss* how the Tullivers are incapable of paying attention to the particular needs and abilities of their children. The principle illustrated here is that "Each sex receives a different kind of upbringing" (King, 74). But the Tullivers are blind to this fact and Maggie's aptitude for learning is not encouraged whereas all attention is given to Tom's education though he "hasn't got the right sort o'brains" and is "a bit too slowish" (12). Despite Maggie's obvious superiority she is compelled to accept her brother as master.

Mr. Dombey's frigid nature in *Dombey and Son* is described "as hard and as cold as the weather" (44) which is governed by his lust for money. This lust governs his whole character, his attitude towards his children and his attitude towards life. He tries to shape his son's life as the heir of his prestigious firm "Dombey and Son". He cruelly neglects his daughter Florence for "girls have nothing to do with 'Dombey and Son' and regards her as "a piece of base coin that couldn't be invested—a bad Boy—nothing more" (2). Mr. Dombey is impatient for his son to grow out of childhood, to make "a man of him" though Paul pleads "I had rather be a child" (145). All Dombey's efforts to instill in Paul a high sense of pride and power of money fail completely and the child becomes "even more strange, and old and thoughtful than before" (128). He turns for love and affection to his sister Florence which Dombey vehemently resents. Finally, he succumbs to this oppressive atmosphere. Edith, under no condition allows her mother Mrs. Skewton to keep Florence Dombey for she "will have no guileless nature undermined, corrupted, and perverted, to amuse the leisure of a world of mothers" (364). She laments "O Mother, Mother, if you had but left me to my natural heart when I too was a girl—a younger girl than Florence—how different I might have been" (365).

Arthur Clenham in *Little Dorrit* is "the only child of parents who weighed, measured and priced everything; for whom could not be weighed, measured and priced had no existence" (59). His parents had been at variance from his earliest remembrance. His "hard father and mother" have blighted his childhood; "will, purpose, hope? All those lights were extinguished before I could sound the words" (17). He grows up to be "a retiring man, with a sense of many deficiencies" (165).

Mr. Gradgrind with his friend Bounderby in *Hard Times* tries to educate his children Tom and Louisa according to his strict code which has no room for the child's sense of wonder, imagination or curiosity but the entire emphasis is on facts—"Facts alone are wanted in life" (47). His aim, as he later tells Louisa, is "to educate you, as that you might be, while still in your early youth be (if I may so express myself) almost any age" (15). But both children are unsuccessful and Louisa laments in the end "if you had only neglected me what a much better and much happier creature I should have been" (239).

The parents in Dickens' novels, if unable to impose their views, are weak, helpless parasites who have to be looked after by their children. "The Father of the Marshalsea" Mr. Dorrit could be no father to his own children. While discussing his wardrobe with *Little Dorrit*, he who ought to have fulfilled her wishes tells her "that when she could afford it, she should buy him a new one" (193). He is utterly unheedful of her requirements—"All this time he had never once thought of her dress, her shoes, her need of anything" (193). And extreme example is Jenny Wren in *Our Mutual Friend*, the crippled, haunchbacked child, the poor doll's dressmaker who is "dragged down by the hands that should have raised her up" (249).

It is interesting to note that Dickens' children, especially the ones who are really significant, are motherless. Pip, Oliver, Nell, Esther, Little Dorrit are all motherless. And even if the mother is allowed to survive she proves to be hopelessly inadequate and unsatisfactory. The Pardiggle and Jelly by children are made unhappy rather by their mothers than their fathers. The reason for this literary matricide can partly be traced back to Dickens' childhood days when his mother insisted that he should continue his degrading job "...but I never afterwards forgot; I never shall forget, that my mother was warm for my being sent back" (Forster 1: 49). The divine, angelic mother of early childhood "died for Dickens beyond all hope of recovery in the crisis of his misery at the blacking warehouse, when she was warm for my being sent back to that place of despair" (Johnson 2: 679). Quoted in the same volume is his similar observation made to friend Thomson in 1884 that "the greater part of the parents who came under his observation seemed to him selfish in their behavior to their children" (685).

Aware of Bitter Realities

Childhood for the Victorian children is no period of bliss and extraordinarily observant that they are, they fully comprehend their deplorable and dependent status. They envy the love, care, protection and happiness of more fortunate children. Jane's childhood is no period of divine bliss but is spent amidst the abuses, insults and taunts not only of her aunt and cousins but even their servants. John tortures her not only verbally but physically treating her as "bad animal". He is enraged to find Jane reading books: "You have no business to take our books; you are a dependant, mamma says; you have no money; your father left you none; you ought to beg, and not to live here with gentleman's children like us..." (5). Miss Abbot, the lady's maid reveals her humiliating position: "No; you are less than a servant, for you do nothing for your keep..." (6). Jane's first recollections of existence comprised of this reproach of her dependence which "had become a vague sing-song in my ear" (7). The children in *Wuthering Heights* wage a grim struggle against guardians who are obsessed with a desire to kill them. Heathcliff is despised and scorned by all: "a little Lascar, or an American or Spanish castaway" (53). Mrs. Linton is shocked and calls him "a wicked boy" "quite unfit for a decent house". Uncomplaining and indifferent though he is, yet he feels bitterly the difference the Lintons make in treating Cathy and himself "she was a young lady, and they made a distinction between her treatment and mine" (54). Though he despises Edgar he cannot help wishing "...I had light hair and fair skin, and was dressed and behaved as well, and had a chance of being as rich as he will be" (59). The world of *Wuthering Heights* is brutal where "Normal emotions are almost completely inverted: hate replaces love, cruelty replaces kindness, and survival depends on one's ability to be tough, brutal and rebellious" (Thompson: 97).

Oliver's childhood is spent in penury and chill in the appalling conditions of the workhouse where the children suffer slow starvation. He goes to sleep depressed at the Undertaker's, after being fed with the dog's victuals and wishes that his bed were a coffin where he could be lain in a calm and lasting sleep "with the tall grass waving gently above his head, and the sound of old, deep, bell to soothe him in his sleep" (75). After leaving that place Oliver finds himself in the toils of the terrible London underworld. The wily, old Jew spares no effort to instill poison into his soul hoping to "blacken it, and change its hue forever" (185). He is paralyzed with fear in Fagin's den reading books of "dreadful crimes," "secret murders" and "dreadful bloodshed" (196). Unlike the children of pre-Victorian literature who show their inability to even comprehend the reality of death, these children are amidst death.

Pip's first impressions in *Great Expectations* are formed in the graveyard. His first ideas regarding his parents "were unreasonably derived from their tombstones" (15). David also has early acquaintance with the mystery of death by his father's grave "my first childish associations with his white gravestone in the churchyard, and the indefinable compassion I used to feel for it lying out alone in the dark night" (2). He suffers mental and emotional torture when his mother marries

Mr. Murdstone who does all he can with the help of his sister to alienate the mother and child. He describes the influence of the Murdstones "like the fascination of two snakes on a wretched bird" (50). Very soon he becomes acquainted with the ways of this world so much so that he "almost lost the capacity of being much surprised by anything" (142). Though a supremely gifted child "of excellent abilities and with very strong powers of observation, quick, eager and delicate" (142). He has to provide for himself by working as a laboring boy in the degrading conditions of Murdstone and Grinby.

Florence suffers intensely in *Dombey and Son* when her father's cruel indifference becomes prolonged and all her efforts to win him are unsuccessful. She thinks of "children who were as frank and happy with fathers and with mothers as those rosy faces opposite home. Children who had no restraint upon their love and freely showed it" (288). She earnestly wishes to learn from them the art of winning a father's love. Jo in *Bleak House* lives in Tom all-alone's a "foul existence" worse than the lower animals. He painfully succumbs to indifference, malnutrition, and disease in this sickening atmosphere.

Amy in *Little Dorrit* takes charge of her "fallen family" and bears in her heart "its anxieties and shames--"At thirteen, she could read and keep accounts—that is, could put down in words and figures how much the bare necessaries that they wanted would cost, and how much less they had to buy them with" (60). Maggie, the retarded daughter of Little Dorrit's nurse is left to fend for herself despite her invalid condition—"She earns her own living entirely" (86). The only comforts she has ever enjoyed were in the hospital which she delightfully narrates: "But what a nice hospital: So comfortable, wasn't it? So nice it was. Such a Ev'nly place.... Such lemonades: such oranges; Such d'licious broth and wine; Such chicking; Oh, AIN'T it a delightful place to go and stop at" (86). Jenny Wren's vision in *Our Mutual Friend* is a powerful expression of the feelings of the deprived child: "...the children that I used to see early in the morning...were not like me; they were not chilled, anxious, ragged or beaten; they were never in pain.

They were never like the children of the neighbours; they never made me tremble all over, by setting up shrill noises, and they never mocked me" (290). Life for these children is a grim battle for survival. Childhood is a dreadful and trying period to which memory is reluctant to return.

Isolation and Fear

Exposed as they are to all brutality the Victorian children are haunted by deep-rooted fears and feelings of isolation and insecurity. Their childhood is deprived of all company and recreation. Jane dreads her cousin John because neither Mrs. Reed nor the servants protect her—"every nerve I had feared him, and every morsel of flesh on my bones shrank when he came near". For the child the terror is too real "because I had no appeal either against his menaces or afflictions" (4). When Jane is unjustly condemned in the chill, silent red room for knocking John, all sorts of ides and fears oppress her. The only thought that checks her sobs is that her violent grief might cause Mr. Reed's spirit to quit its abode for she had heard of "dead men, troubled in their graves by the violation of their last wishes, revisiting the earth to punish the perjured and avenge the oppressed" (11). In such a state of mind the quivering of a streak of light terrifies her and she screams for help. Her aunt refuses to show any mercy and Jane falling unconscious develops fever. For three months she is isolated "restricted so long to the nursery, the breakfast, dining and drawing-rooms were become for me awful regions, on which it dismayed me to intrude" (25). The heart of this lonely, solitary child pleads to the servant "Bessie, you must promise not to scold me any more till I go" (33). She can hope to find some sympathy only from this servant.

One remembers Maggie's attic in *The Mill on the Floss* in which she takes refuge from her brother. She sobs aloud and is depressed "with a crushing sense of misery". George Eliot aptly remarks "These bitter sorrows of childhood. When sorrow is all new and strange, when hope has not yet got wings to fly beyond the days and weeks, and the space from summer to summer seems measureless" (37). On leaving Mrs. Mann's wretched establishment Oliver feels "a sense of loneliness in the great, wide world sank into the child's heart for the first time" (53). Oliver is confined to a dark and solitary room for "the impious and profane offence for asking for more" and mercilessly treated—"He only cried bitterly all day; and, when the long, dismal night came on, spread his little hands before his eyes to shut out the darkness,...drawing himself closer and closer to the wall, as if to feel even its cold hard surface were a protection in the gloom and loneliness which surrounded him" (59). Oliver's dismal feelings are vividly described when he is depressed at Mr. Sowerberry's house with the smell of coffins and its frightful scenes "drive him mad with terror" (75). When Oliver is recaptured and brought to the Fagin's gang, the wily Jew prepares the boy's mind "by solitude and gloom, to prefer any society to the companionship of his own sad thoughts in such a dreary place" (185). Dickens' describes with great power and subtlety the impact of fear on the child's mind. While enjoying care and security in the Maylies household Oliver is startled out of his wits even in his sleep by what appears to him as Jew and Monks, which sight "sent the blood tingling to his heart, and deprived him of his voice, and of the power to move; There—there at the window—close before him—so close, that he could have almost touched him before he started back.... It was but an instant.... But they had recognized him, and he them; and their look was as firmly impressed upon his memory, as if it had been deeply carved in stone, and set before him from his birth" (311).

Nell, when she suddenly encounters Quilp and barely manages to escape notice, in one of her night walks, is so terrified "Notwithstanding these protections, she could get none but broken sleep by fits and starts all night, for fear of Quilp, who throughout her uneasy dreams was somehow connected with the wax-work, himself, or was Mrs. Jarley and wax-work too, or was himself, Mrs. Jarley, wax-work, and a barrel-organ all in one and yet not exactly any of them either" (278-79). Nell is distracted when her grandfather again takes to gambling. The indifference and isolation which they feel in their wanderings on entering a big city is powerfully described. They are "stunned and bewildered by the hurry" and felt "amidst the crowd a solitude which has no parallel but in the thirst of the ship-wrecked mariner..." (413). They are "desolate" and wonder why did they ever come to this "noisy town" where "they were but an atom, here, in a mountain heap of misery..." (414).

Florence Dombey, when she leaves home deeply hurt by her father's behaviour, is terribly alone. She is frightened by strange voices which enquired where she went. She is miserable and lost. "Where to go? Still somewhere, anywhere; She thought of only other time she had been lost in the wide wilderness of London—though not as lost as now—and went that way" (558). Even during her stay at her father's house this motherless child is painfully alone: "And oh the desolation of the solitary house again, with the evening coming on and no one there" (269).

David, after he bites his stepfather is soundly thrashed and locked in his room for five days. He is treated as "a most atrocious criminal" and wonders "whether I should be taken into custody and sent to prison? Whether I was at all in danger of being hanged?" (54). As has been aptly put "about any early disaster there is a dreadful finality. A lost child can suffer like a lost soul" (*Chesterton*, 24). These five days prove to him more dismal than anything and are permanently etched in his memory—"...the uncertain pace of the hours, especially at night, when I would wake thinking it was morning, and find that the family were not yet gone to bed, and that all the length of night had yet to come—the depressed dreams and nightmares I had..." (55).

Dickens vividly illustrates the shaping power of fear in *Great Expectations*. Pip's encounter with the convict, and the fear he inspires, remain the most formative influence of his life. It has been pointed out that Dickens' "adapts for his purposes the terror that plays such an important role in *The Prelude* (Knoepflmacher, 416). It may be recalled that the child after the bird stealing episode in *The Prelude* is haunted by "Low breathings coming after me and Sounds/ Of undistinguished motion" (*Poetical Works*, 498). Pip, after robbing the pantry is haunted in a similar way "everything seemed to run at me", the gates and dykes and banks seemed to accuse him "A boy with Somebody's else's pork pie; stop him;" and a black ox stares at him in "an accusatory manner" (27). Pip is "guilty yet innocent" (Leavis, 380). His association with the convict haunts him with inexplicable fear—"I could not have said what I was afraid of, for my fear was altogether undefined and vague, but there was a great fear upon me...it was the revival for a few minutes of the terror of childhood" (215).

The stranger who stirred his rum with the file appeared to Pip "as if he were expressly taking aim at me with his invisible gun" (79). The file continues to haunt him—"A dread possessed me that when I least expected it, the file would reappear...and in my sleep I saw the file coming at me out of a door, without seeing who held it" (82). The file proves ominous, and Pip's sister is attacked by it. The scenes in which Pip resorts to a series of outrageous lies describing his visit to Miss Havisham reveal intensely the loneliness of a deprived child. "All the isolation of childhood is there. And how accurately he has recorded the mechanisms of the child's mind, its visualizing tendency, its sensitiveness to certain kinds of impression" (Orwell, 14).

Dickens has been singled out as his collection is incomparably subtler than his contemporaries. But some of the significant child-portraits by Charlotte Bronte, Emily Bronte and George Eliot have been considered keeping in view the pattern which emerges and completes the Victorian picture of child. It would perhaps not be an exaggeration to say that it is also comprehensive in as much as it explores various possibilities given the major motif of misery. An attempt has been made to establish Dickens primarily as a creative artist against the modern readiness to dismiss his works as sentimental and exaggerated. Nor can he be viewed merely as a social reformer. His novels transcended the requirements of his age and audience and can be relevant for coming generations for different and perhaps profounder reasons. No period in English literature has perhaps shown as much concern or understanding of the child as this age, nor so insightfully dwelled into the soul of the child.

WORKS CITED

Allen, Walter. *The English Novel.* Harmondsworth: Penguin Books Ltd., 1973.

Bradner, Lecicester. "The Growth of Wuthering Heights", *PMLA,* Vol. XLVIII, 129-46.

Bronte, Charlotte. *Jane Eyre.* London: Dent & Sons Ltd., 1908.

Bronte, Emily. *Wuthering Heights.* New York: Airmont Publishing Co., 1963.

Cecil, David. *Early Victorian Novelists.* Ludhiana: Kalyani Publishers, 1972.

Chesterton, G.K. *Charles Dickens.* London: Methuen & Co. Ltd., 1949.

Collins, Philip. *Dickens and Education.* London: Macmillan, 1963.

Coveney, Peter. *The Image of Childhood.* Harmondsworth: Penguin, 1967.

Cruikshank, R.J. *Charles Dickens and Early Victorian England.* London: Isaac Pitman & Sons Ltd., 1949.

Dickens, Charles. *Bleak House.* London: Pan Books Ltd., 1976.

———*David Copperfield.* New York: Bantam Books, 1981.

———*Dombey and Son.* London: Oxford University Press, 1982.

———*Great Expectations.* Delhi: Rupa & Co., 1982.

———*Little Dorrit.* London: Oxford University Press, 1982.

———*Our Mutual Friend.* Harmondsworth: Penguin, 1971.

——— *Oliver Twist.*

———*The Mystery of Edwin Drood.* Harmondsworth: Penguin, 1974.

———*The Old Curiosity Shop.* Harmondsworth: Penguin, 1972.

Eliot, George. *Silas Marner.* Harmondsworth: Penguin, 1967.

———*The Mill on the Floss.* London: Oxford University Press.

Eliot, T.S. *Selected Essays.* London: Faber and Faber, 1951.

Forster, John. *The Life of Charles Dickens.* Two Volumes. London: J.M. Dent & Sons Ltd., 1966.

Johnson, Edgar. *Charles Dickens His Tragedy and Triumph.* Two Volumes. London: Victor Gollancz Ltd., 1953.

Knoepflmacher, U.C. "The Counterworld of Victorian Fiction" in *The Worlds of Victorian Fiction.* Ed. J.H. Buckley. Harvard: Harvard University Press, 1975.

Orwell, George. *Critical Essays*. London: Secker and Warburg, 1960.

Thompson, Wade. "Infanticide and Sadism in *Wuthering Heights*". *Critics on Charlotte and Emily Bronte*. London: Allen and Unwin Ltd., 1968.

Tillotson, Kathleen. *Novels of the Eighteen Forties*. Oxford: Clarendon Press, 1954.

Trevelyan, G.M. *English Social History: A Survey of Six Centuries—Chaucer to Queen Victoria*. New Delhi: Orient Longmans, 1968.

Williams, Ioan. *The Realist Novel in England*. Plymouth: The Bowering Press Ltd.

Wordsworth, William. *The Poetical Works of Worrdsworth*. Ed. Thomas Hutchinson. London: Oxford University Press.

10

Violence in the Schoolboy Stories of Sukumar Ray

Saurav Das Thakur

The fact that children's literature across cultures has more often than not been imbued with elements of violence is commonplace today. Critics have already drawn attention to the moral and psychological implications of violence in narratives from fairy tales to *The Famous Five*, from *The Hostile Hospital* to the *Harry Potter* series, from *Panchatantra* to *Password to Larkspur Lane*, form the children's versions of the *Ramayana* and the *Mahabharata* to that of *The Arabian Nights*. Such critiques have led to the question of the desirability of representation of violence and sexuality and that of censorship in books—and other cultural texts, like movie—for children. One can profitably refer to such essays as G.K. Chesterton's "The Fear of the Film" and Charles Lamb's "Witches and Other Nightfears" to acquire an idea of the length of the history of such criticism.[1] Yet it seems that this history has not paid adequate attention to an exploration of the complex political and ideological significance of violence in children's literature in the modern context. The questions that are commonly raised and addressed are mostly associated with the effect—physical, psychological and moral, and to that extent social and cultural—of such violence on the tender reader: how far the representation of violence is suitable for children, how far it contributes to their 'ideal' development into individual and social beings, whether it cripples their psyche through a traumatising impact, or if it serves as a necessary textual exposure of the child to prepare him/her for the big bad world, how far violence constitutes an innate human impulse and finally, how the use of violence is associated with a didactic desire, how certain moral lessons intricately connected with the idea of justice are imparted and imprinted through the creation of binaries like good/bad, reward/punishment and so forth.[2]

Although nobody can deny, or even underestimate, the broad validity of such questions, violence in children's literature today, especially in texts produced in the modern period,[3] I believe, can be read in a more critical fashion, with an eye on its political-ideological implications. What role violence plays, for instance, in the endeavours of the state to produce the 'desirable' subject through institutions of ideological control, like the school and the family and in what ways the subject, through producing spates of counter-violence, confronts and negotiates this desire, can be useful questions to ask in this context. The relationship between power and knowledge and their discursive functioning through certain modes and institutions of ideological production, dissemination and circulation in a specific socio-cultural context are not certain seamless and straightforward phenomena. They are invariably fraught with several counter narratives, disjunctures, moments of strife and bickering and eloquent silences that often take the form of violence in the content or form of a narrative that is on the one hand a product of this broad cultural paraphernalia, and on the other hand vitally contributes to the shaping and functioning of the forces that produce it. Schoolboy stories are posited in a complex fashion at the point of convergence of certain crucial categories of ideological dissemination and resistance like the school, the adolescent male psyche, the parent (mostly father)—like teacher whose paternalistic impulses often coalesce the school and the home/family, the textbook, language, sports and games and in a related fashion the body/ corporeal geography and above all the omnipresent state. They can thus be seen as a literary genre that dramatises the multi-dimensional conflict between suppression and subversion, desire to discipline and punish and the counter-desire to interrogate the politics of such disciplining, compulsion to impose order and passion for throwing everything into disarray, internalisation and interpellation. The traditional categories of 'morals', 'justice', 'virtue' and 'vice'—as used in 'pre-modern' children's literature like fairy tales and so on—thus need to be revaluated and applied in the modern context in order to understand the politics of representation in schoolboy stories.

The aim of this small article is to understand this politics of foregrounding and silencing on the one hand and modes of subversion of that politics on the other as practised by the 'authority' and the 'others' in Sukumar Ray's Bangla schoolboy stories, anthologised in *Pagla Dashu*. It will seek to explore how the discursive functioning of power—and the various forms of violence it produces—in the urban schools in the age of colonialism as represented in this volume can be seen as a microcosmic literary evocation of the power-politics (and essentially violent practices) in the adult world. It will also try to discuss how such 'violent' politics of subjugation and subversion was not something peculiar to the colonial institutions like the school alone, but also affected certain traditional indigenous institutions, like the family, which were effectively enmeshed in the larger cultural politics of colonialism. Finally, it will try to argue, in spite of certain differences in approach, style and technique from 'pre-modern' children's narratives, the 'modern' stories of *Pagla Dashu* are marked by a broad continuity of some patterns and tropes that featured in such narratives. For one instance, the simplistic, straightforward didacticism in the earlier tradition is replaced here by a more complex attitude to the question, but the basic binary of desirable/undesirable, prescribed/proscribed is often retained. Power-structures are at times questioned, but at other times they are subscribed to, with only a change in the locus—for instance from kingship to family, from king to father—according to the demand of contemporaneity.

One of the most important institutions through which colonial rulers sought to establish their hegemony—by adopting coercive measures and manufacturing consent through ideological control—over the indigenous masses was the school. The project of affirmation of absolute imperial control—physical, mental, psychological, moral, cultural—behind the facade of reformation and 'redemption' of the 'barbaric' masses by bringing them into the light of civilisation led to the overlapping of several apparently unconnected spheres. Administrative, educational and religious 'reformations' in India in the age of colonialism, thus, were often different but coterminous wings of the same basic ideology. Producing the 'ideal' subject/citizen for the state/empire for a smoother functioning of the administration demanded a thorough colonisation of the mind and culture, and the school was one of the most conducive institutions to do that. In fact, the entire colony was seen as an extended school, for the imperial ideology considered the colonial people only as juvenile and feminine—physically weak, morally deprave and intellectually half-grown—and therefore in need of complete reformation through all-round 'schooling'.[4] The Evangelical leader Charles Grant, who was one of the intellectual forces behind the 'Permanent Settlement', for one example, wrote a tract in 1792 (published 1797) titled "Observations on the State of Society among the Asiatic Subjects of Great Britain, Particularly with Respect to Morals, and the Means of Improving It," which showed the close relationship of the three spheres of administration, education and religion in the imperial ideology. One of the first major thinkers to write about the potentials of Ideological State Apparatus in strengthening the imperial machinery, Grant was followed by luminaries like Jeremy Bentham, J.S. Mill and T.B. Macaulay, who emphasised the necessity of the 'right' kind of education in India, an education that would create a class of hybrid comprador Indians with firm faith in the discipline, order and hierarchies imposed on them by the colonial masters.

If school was one of the most effective institutions of imperial ideological control, family emerged in the nineteenth century nationalist discourses in India as the most congenial site for the preservation of the 'pure' and 'authentic' Indian culture in the face of the colonial cultural onslaught and rampant hybridisation. The hugely problematic questions of 'modernity' and 'nationhood', 'identity', construction of the 'self' and the 'other', the right to self-determination of the nation and its 'fragments' were often being debated over with the discourse of the family looming large as the microcosm of the nation. Both school and family, thus, emerged as sites of intense ideological battle, breeding grounds of discourses and counter-discourses where dominant ideologies fought with residual and emergent ideologies for supremacy in the nineteenth and early twentieth century India. The notions of order and disorder, right and wrong, desirable and undesirable, as constructed, discussed and practised in school and family during this period—and even later, in the age of 'neo-colonialism'—were thus not only ideologically loaded. Given the larger political-ideological canvas against which such questions were being thrashed out, they were necessarily implicated in certain violent practices. One way of reading schoolboy stories of Sukumar Ray—and violence in them, manifest and latent—thus, is to look for marks of that 'violent' phase of Indian history in them, in their aesthetics and politics.

Sukumar Ray (1887-1923), a Kolkata-based poet, writer and playwright in the first two decades of the last century, is widely considered as the greatest writer of 'nonsense' literature—and arguably of children's literature at large—in Bangla. The twenty tiny stories collected in *Pagla Dashu* (inadequately translated, *Loony Dashu*) were originally published in the Bangla children's magazine *Sandesh*, founded by Ray's father Upendrakishore Ray Choudhury and subsequently taken up by Ray himself. The stories mark a refreshing departure from the sentimentalism, moralising impulse and simplistic didacticism of the nineteenth century tradition of Bangla primers and schoolboy stories. They are marked instead by elements of fun and laughter, friendly leg pulling and light hearted banter, revelry and a spirit of carefree, simple celebration. And yet one cannot but feel the undercurrents of tension, rivalry, jealousy and even anger, seething frustration and strong urge for revenge that often find outlet through acts and speeches of violence of various forms, sense of deprivation and marginalisation that leads to aggressive measures, mostly on the part of students who are the major contingent of characters in schoolboy stories. Ideas of norms, code of conduct, legality and authority, hierarchy, discipline and punishment that are ceaselessly associated with the notions of desirable and undesirable (to positions of power), centripetal and centrifugal movements in the form of empowerment or exclusion and so on occupy the mindscape of the characters inside the narratives and the readers outside them. The history of the internal feuds and conflicts among students can be traced back to the functioning of certain larger ideological forces in the age of colonialism. We are once more reminded of Frantz Fanon's seminal argument that the colonial mission of civilisation was fundamentally a violent process that bruised and battered both the body and the mind of the colonial masses, who often responded to the adverse reality around through feats of inter-personal violence.[5]

The subterranean existence of modes of violence under the benign surface of the stories at one level points towards the politics of any form of closure that is associated with generic nomenclatures like 'children's literature', 'nonsense literature' and so on. It only reminds us that the second part of these generic names, literature, is of far greater importance than the first part—children's nonsense and so on—that not just unnecessarily limits, but at times deliberately misleads. At another level, so far as various forms of violence and counter-violence in these stories act only as symptomatic of the ceaseless battle between hegemonic impulses and forms of resistance in contemporary culture, they often show how discourses are necessarily exclusive, and how the power of specific discourses is often derived from its ability to suppress alternative positions, voices and ideologies. For the battle between ideologies takes shape—even comes into existence—through discourses.[6] Violence here thus amounts to a mode of confrontation between the dominant and alternative discourses and practices of education, morality, justice, 'ideal' studentship/citizenship, normality/abnormality and so on.

The fact that the eccentric Dashorothi alias Dashu acts as the protagonist of four of the stories in *Pagla Dashu* and also lends the volume its title is itself suggestive. Dashu by no means is a 'normal', stereotypical 'good boy', one who can serve as a conventional role model, or as a 'hero'. And yet he serves as the anti-hero of the volume precisely because he presents an alternative idea of 'goodness' as student and human being—irreverent of bookish learning that does not lead to an all-round holistic development, and of 'sacrosanct' power-structures—in the tales. Such an alternative model of the 'desirable' student and future citizen would never be encouraged in the school (and society) which acts as a powerful institution of ideological dissemination and formation of 'ideal' individuals. Dashu's violation of the discourse of the 'ideal' student hero thus takes refuge in the authorial strategy of eccentricity, as does the 'lunatic' Bishan Singh's critique of the logic of Partition in Sa'adat Hassan Manto's short story "Toba Tek Singh". The third paragraph of the first story of the volume, that introduces Dashu to the readers in the first two paragraphs, establishes this major conflict over ideas of a 'good boy' through verbal violence: "When 'Dashu' or Dasharothi got admitted to our school, Jagabandhu was the 'good boy' of the class. Though he was good at studies, we never saw a more jealous and hypocritical creature than him. Dashu had once approached Jagabandhu to ask the meaning of a certain English word. For no apparent reason Jagabandhu started shouting at him and said, 'Have I nothing better to do than explain English words to one, solve the sums for another and fulfil somebody else's demand with something else—is that what I do all day?' Dashu got furious and blurted out, 'you are a mean little rascal, you rotten egg!' Jagabandhu marched off to the teacher and complained, 'that new boy is abusing me,' at which the teacher gave Dashu a good scold and poor Dashu went totally off." But not to be outwitted, Dashu avenges his insult in the very next paragraph, in which he plots a savoury detailed verbal thrashing that

Jagabandhu receives from the teacher who liked him the most: "...the teacher snapped at him [Jagabandhu] and said, 'now stop, don't try to look so innocent—enough of that.' Jagabandhu turned red in shame and humiliation—we all were so happy."

The same pattern of rejection/exclusion followed by revenge can be traced in the next two stories, "Dashur Khyapami" (crazy Dashu) and "Chinepotka" (peppery little crackers), in the former of which Dashu forces himself into a play acted by the students, changes its colour beyond recognition and leaves others frustrated and furious. In the course of doing so he manages to get three of his classmates beaten by the teacher. In the latter while avenging his personal insult by Rampada, a co-student, he not only exposes his classmates—who were caught playing book-games during a class—to the teacher, but also unmasks the teacher whose habit of napping during classes was revealed to other teachers who came rushing down into the classroom after a "huge furore of five minutes" plotted by him frightened and confused everybody in the school. The anarchy behind the facade of discipline and apparent sanctity of the classroom is exposed; the unquestionable authority of school as an institution to discipline and punish is challenged, the ideal code of conduct in the essentially hierarchical relationship between teachers and students is flouted so as to temporarily topple the power-ladder upside down. And all this becomes possible, the subaltern manages to speak from the fringes, because of the shelter of 'madness'. Thus, "the teachers departed to their respective classes after some mild rebukes. Dashu went unpunished for he was 'mad'." Order is thus eventually restored, but not before exposing the ills under the apparently benign surface and registering ripples of protest at the individual as well as institutional levels.

The last Dashu-story of the volume, "Dashur Kirti" (Dashu's Antics), involves all-round harassment—physical, mental, verbal—of Nabinchand through an intrigue invented by Dashu who hires fake 'goons' from his classmates to make life miserable for him for a few hours. Here again everybody in the class was very happy in the heckling of Nabinchand, for he was "as arrogant and show-off as anything—nobody liked him". And Dashu caps it all by engaging in a verbal and physical duel with Nabinchand's elder brother Mohanchand—senior to him by a few years—the day after when he came to enquire about the incident. Again the theme of revenge is prominent: Dashu on behalf of almost everybody in the class avenges the feeling of inferiority created by the lordly attire and behaviour of Nabinchand. And in doing so he flouts another code of behaviour prescribed for the 'good boy' of the nineteenth and early twentieth century colonial Bengal—unquestioned respect for elder people.

In three other stories of the collection—"Chaliyat" (show-off), "Sobjanta" (know-all) and "Detective"—arrogance and show-off of the central characters have their source in the superior social/class position in the colonial urban set up. Interestingly, all these three stories introduce the class-character of their protagonists in the very first sentence, and introduce the 'problems' in them in the following sentences in the first paragraph, thereby making the narratorial position obvious. For example, "Chaliyat" begins thus: "Shyamchand's father was a top-notch officer in a British concern, so in attire and behaviour he would miss no chance to show off. When he would come to school in a wide collar, a colourful umbrella over his head, his new shoes would make a squeaking sound as he walked with a grave air with his head held high. And the turbaned and uniformed bearer would follow, armed with his books and tiffinbox; he would then look just as amazing as a peacock in full bloom. The younger boys of the school would gape at him in absolute awe, but all of us unanimously muttered: 'the little big show-off'." The beginning of "Sobjanta": "Our know-all Duliram's father was the editor of some newspaper. So, many of us would believe blindly in all that he said. And he had something to say on every damn subject in the world, the war in Germany or football matches of Mohun Bagan, private life of celebrities or intricacies of deadly diseases. A section of the students would listen to him mesmerised. Even some of the teachers showed signs of believing in him. He would deal with all possible knowledge under the sun, this is why our master named him 'know-all'. But I always had a strong suspicion that he was a big show-off." Again, in "Detective": "Jaladhar's maternal uncle works for the police force, and some other distant uncle of his is a writer of detective novels. This is why it was his firm belief that the only people at par with him in detecting and punishing criminals and fraudsters are those uncles of his." One cannot possibly miss the element of disgust, jealousy, bitterness, sense of inferiority and even anger in the voice of the narrator, especially in the first two quotations in this paragraph, not just about the arrogance, and one-up-man-ship of the characters concerned, but more importantly, about their superior class and social location itself, which is at the base of their surface behavioural disorder. The material ground of violence thus is already there, which is about the growing class distance between the English-educated, colonial servant, comprador bourgeoisie and the poor colonial masses, living in the fringes in the age of colonialism. According to Fanon, colonial reality is based on violence, for it is characterised by an almost geographically marked economic segregation between the rulers and the ruled: obscene affluence on the one hand and inhuman poverty on the other. Fanon's insightful analysis can be extended to understand the economy of relationship between sections of indigenous people itself: the babus and the commoners. For Fanon, thus, decolonisation cannot but be a violent process, for it attempts to overthrow a violent reality, and revenge of various sorts always lurks in the mind of the poor colonised. The narrator of the stories in *Pagla Dashu* cannot possibly think of any sort of eradication, or even amelioration, of the class reality of his existence (and many others' that he represents) even in his wildest dreams. All he can wish for is the 'punishment' or chastisement of Shyamchand, Duliram and Jaladhar, which would give him somewhat a sense of revenge, of an incomplete 'justice'. No wonder the pleasure that 'we'—the majority of students—derive in the harassment of each of these three characters at the end of these stories, would seem to the reader vicarious, sadistic, almost on the verge of cruel.

Through his adoption of violence of various forms, Dashu challenges various positions of authority—school as a disciplining institution, teachers, seniors, haughty and snooty boys from rich families and so on—and the hierarchies imposed by them. Through his own 'eccentricity' or 'abnormality', he seeks to ruffle the apparently 'normal' order of the disciplined society and to create a parallel alternative world where 'disorder' reigns. Not only does this passion for disorder brings a sense of justice, empowerment and 'happiness' to many of his marginalised and fuming classmates, it also comes down heavily on those classmates when they start assuming the role of authority and practise exclusion, as in the story about the play acted in the school. Dashu does not even spare himself; he makes fun of himself and encourages others to have a good laugh at his cost in a non-hierarchical spirit of innocent mirth. Thus in the span of four small stories Dashu succeeds in creating an alternative discourse of life at school, and life at large, a discourse of life invoked in Mikhail Bakhtin's idea of the 'carnivalesque' in Rabelais and His World. The carnivalesque suggests a festive atmosphere in the medieval European life in which all sorts of social hierarchies would be temporarily shelved and replaced by an egalitarian, non-hierarchical existence. Fun and laughter at the cost of one's social superiors and even self-directed laughter is a major component in the carnivalesque. 'Carnival laughter'—as Bakhtin calls it—has a distinct communal character in which everybody laughs and is reduced to an object of others' laughter, and thus comes closer to others. It "is the laughter of all the people. Second, it is universal in scope; it is directed at all and everyone, including the carnival's participants" (Bakhtin, 200). The aim of such impersonal laughter is not to attack individuals, except as representatives of institutions. Dashu's self-directed laughter in the introductory story of the volume evinces his democratic spirit: "We would always make fun of Dashu", the narrator tells us, "and make unpalatable comments on his appearance and intelligence right before him. But he never, even for once, took offence at that. Rather at times he himself would merrily join us and cook up strange and colourful stories about himself." Interestingly, the self-directed, spiteless, carnival laughter of the Dashu stories is absent in "Chaliyat", "Sobjanta" and "Detective", where laughter is mostly satirical. The virtues of eccentricity are lost here, but again the characters in these stories are attacked less for their personal idiosyncrasies than for their representative class character.

The democratic atmosphere created by carnival laughter is similar in spirit to that of Bakhtin's idea of 'dialogism' or 'polyphony' that challenges any hierarchy between voices, languages and perspectives in a work of fiction. 'Polyphony' creates an atmosphere of play of equally powerful languages or discourses. The carnival anti-institutional critique of the serious 'monologic' discourses of hegemonic institutions that strive to perpetuate the existing power-dynamics, therefore, voices the destabilizing desire of the marginal spaces. The most effective instrument Dashu makes use of in creating a carnivalesque spirit in an otherwise extremely ordered institution like school—and in challenging authoritarian discourses—is language, or verbal violence. He creates almost a different linguistic universe which accommodates enough firepower in it to unsettle everybody. He calls a spade a spade, does not stoop to be euphemistic, and thus easily uses 'illegitimate' and proscribed words and expressions revolting in the bhadralok code of decency. Bakhtin analyses linguistic practice not as an abstract universal exercise, but as a concrete and materially shaped enterprise. Linguistic and philosophical enterprises, thus, are tools of mediation of the ideological conflicts on a material plane. Bakhtin goes on to suggest:

> Languages are philosophies—not abstract but concrete, social philosophies, penetrated by a system of values inseparable from living practice and class struggle. This is why every object, every concept, every point of view, as well as every intonation found their place at this intersection of linguistic philosophies [during the European Renaissance] and was drawn into an intense ideological struggle. (Bakhtin, 204)

If language is one of the realms through which discourses are manufactured and kept in circulation, ideologies are brought into play, 'knowledge' is produced and disseminated and power is exercised, Dashu's use of 'inappropriate' anti-institutional language has radical implications. Can it then be suggested that Dashu's use of 'indecent' words or expressions to Jagabandhu or Nabinchand is not merely a personal response in a specific situation, but has larger ideological significance vis-à-vis the class-distance between Dashu and many others on the one hand and students like Jagabandhu and Nabinchand on the other? Ray thus creates a 'polyphonic' universe where multiple languages lock horn with each other—the 'sanctioned' language of the always already powerful teachers, that of the 'good' boys and that of Dashu, the 'mad' marginal, who speaks on behalf of the voiceless so-called 'bad' boys in the school.

So far as the four Dashu stories make use of violence—physical, linguistic or any other—on behalf of the marginal, in order to challenge powerful institutional discourses, their use of violence differs fundamentally from that in a whole lot of children's literature of 'pre-modern' origin, for example, fairy tales, mythological narratives, religious stories and so on, which use violence primarily on behalf of the powerful—like the king, God, religious or social authority and so on—in order to prove a point. Violence in such stories is used as means, a mode of punishment, to establish or uphold a law, to impart a moral lesson, or in other words, to perpetuate and strengthen the existing power-structure. Walter Benjamin in "On the Critique of Violence" understands the nature and operation of such violence thus:

> ...the function of violence in establishing law is in a sense twofold: while this operation seeks to achieve *what* is established as law as its end, using violence as its means, in the moment of establishing what it is aiming at as law it does not repudiate violence but only now, strictly speaking, turns it (directly, this time) into a law-establishing agency; this it does by establishing as law not an end that is free of violence and independent of it but one that is necessarily and intimately bound up with violence, calling it power [*Macht*]. Establishing law

> equates to establishing power, and to that extent it is an act of direct manifestation of violence. (Benjamin, 22)

While establishment of power is the final implication of such violence, interrogation of power of various sorts is the ultimate motive of violence in the narratives we have briefly discussed so far. There are other stories in the same volume dealing with student-characters with specific peculiarities—Jagyidas in "Jagyidaser Mama" (Jagyidas's Uncle) and Bholanath in "Bholanather Sardari" (Precocious Bholanath)—who are disliked by everybody because of their behavioural 'abnormality' of sorts. Jagyidas's one-up-man-ship and Bholanath's precocity make them objects of chastisement with a narratorial consent and everybody seems to rejoice in their misery. So far as these are tales of minor 'crime' and 'punishment' in a very general sense, the violence involved in their chastisement carries some broad moral lessons. Even the existence of such a moralistic impulse implies a tacit social agreement between the narrator and the readers of the tales, who, it has been taken for granted, believe in the same social code of conduct and behavioural pattern. The institution of school does not play any role in the pattern of conflict and conflict-resolution in these tiny stories, and yet the binary of good boy/bad boy keeps figuring in both of them. And interestingly, unlike in the earlier stories, the narrator in these stories turns into a mouthpiece of power, of the majority who determine the definitions of right/wrong, appropriate/inappropriate, desirable/undesirable and rewardable/punishable. He thus adopts the perspective of the majority and shares their vicarious pleasure in—almost gloats over—the 'punishment' of these 'abnormal' characters for their 'wrongdoing'. Thus, the author sheds light on the complex, relative and discursive nature of power: one who is powerless, feels deprived, bitter and jealous and thus seeks revenge against his social superior in one context, turns powerful, marginalising and herd-minded within his equals in another context. It is almost an adult world where themes of revenge, sadistic celebrations of the snubbing of others create an air of 'justice'. Some invisible, but omnipotent, already existing 'law' is upheld; establishment of such 'laws' is an inherently violent phenomenon. Individual 'violation' or 'infringement' of that law is met with collective 'counter-violence', or exhibition of power. Functioning of the categories of 'law' and 'justice' in the modern secular societies therefore has fundamental affinities with that in pre-modern societies governed by kings and religious authorities. Thus, invoking Georges Sorel, Benjamin suggests:

> ...in the early days all law [*Recht*] was the prerogative [*Vorrecht*] of kings or magnates—in short, those in power [*die Machtige*]. So it will remain, *mutatis mutandis*, as long as it exists. For from the standpoint of violence, which is the only thing that can guarantee law, there is no equality but at best equally great violences. However, the action of setting bounds is important for the recognition of law in another respect as well. Rules and defined bounds remain (or at least they did in primeval times) unwritten laws. A person may overstep them unawares and so fall into moral debt. Because every intervention of law that is occasioned by infringement of an unwritten, unknown rule is called not punishment but a state requiring expiation. (Benjamin, 23)

Atonement for the 'crimes' Jagyidas and Bholanath commit comes through withdrawal and tears respectively. It is not clear whether they were received back into the fold after their 'expiation', but one can be reasonably certain that in future they would be afraid of any further 'infringement' of the unwritten laws which they transcended. Once more it is a children's world which hardly differs in any way from the world of the adult. The stories can easily pass off as modern fictional versions of morality plays and questions can once more be raised about the validity of the generic nomenclature 'children's literature' with respect to such narratives.

The idea of 'guilt' and 'expiation' takes its most formidable form in a story—"Jatiner Juto" (Jatin's shoes)—that shifts the locale of the narrative from school to family, another institution of ideological control and shaping. There are three other stories in the volume—"Byomkesher Manja" (Byomkesh's Kite-string-powder), "Gopaler Pora" (Gopal's Study) and "Petuk" (The Glutton)—in which paternal figures in the family try and transform 'bad boys' into 'good boys' through punishment—verbal and even physical. But the inculcated feeling of 'guilt' and the resultant trauma is nowhere as terrible as in "Jatiner Juto", where the entire narrative takes place in the dream—rather nightmare—of Jatin. The power of surveillance of the 'panopticon' called family has spread its tentacles to capture even the unconscious of a 'naughty' boy who is disciplined through punishment in his dream. Jatin's is not merely a case of indiscipline, but one of moral failure to obey the dictum of the father, whose overarching presence is felt in the very first sentence of the story. Byomkesh in "Byomkesher Manja" can temporarily escape the authority of the teacher in the classroom, but not that of his eldest brother who snubs and beats him up. This incident of punishment, of course, does not contribute to the final outcome of the story, as it does in "Gopaler Pora" and "Petuk". In the former Gopal's kite-making stuff is forfeited by his maternal uncle as a punishment for not studying enough in the summer vacation, and in the latter an elaborate intrigue is invented by Haripada's maternal uncles—to the effect of creating a fear of death by poison in him—to cure him of his gluttony. "When Haripada got released [from his sick bed] after three days", the narrator assures us in the last paragraph, "Haripada was no more his earlier self, he was a thoroughly transformed person", just as "we snubbed Jagyidas to tears. Then he admitted that...", or as "[Jatin's] mother would say, 'my poor boy!' Where is that jest, that energy!" Certain unwritten laws about the life of a good boy in the family are upheld through a reaffirmation of the social and moral authority of the father or the father-figure in these stories. This happens with such fluency—in spite of the presence of physical and psychological violence—as to establish unquestioned submission to the authority of the father itself as one of the laws in the life of a good boy.

Such 'legally sanctioned' violence of the modern times has close similarity with the law-establishing or law-upholding violence of the pre-modern era of myths and fairy tales. Benjamin distinguishes such 'mythic violence' from 'divine violence' on the ground that

> justice is the principle of all divine end-establishment, power the principle of all mythic law-establishment. The latter principle finds a hugely momentous application in constitutional law.... It is in the area of constitutional law that the kind of drawing of frontiers undertaken by the 'peace' that settled all wars in the age of myth is the archetypal phenomenon of law-establishing violence altogether. (Benjamin, 22)

Benjamin's analysis of law-establishing 'mythic violence' helps us understand not just the actual nature of 'peace' in pre-modern (and modern) times arranged and ensured by kings (and states), but also the nature of the 'peaceful' colonial mission of enlightenment, civilisation and redemption of colonies. It also sheds light on the functioning of Ideological State Apparatus—like school, family and so on—that sought to shape the child (and adult)-psyche in 'peaceful' non-coercive means in the age of colonialism. Does not it also help us reflect on our own (neo-colonial) times, when dominant social groups (class, gender, religion and so on) and discourses continue to engage in hegemonic practices within legal boundaries, even with the help of law? Sukumar Ray's schoolboy stories tell us as much.

NOTES

I am grateful to Champa Ghosal, Associate Professor of English, Jogesh Chandra Chaudhuri College, Kolkata, for her generous help in translating some of the passages from the Bangla original of *Pagla Dashu*.

1. These two, along with other interesting articles on the subject, are anthologized in Nicholas Tucker ed. *Suitable for Children?* (Berkeley and Los Angeles: University of California Press, 1976).
2. All these questions can be summed up by the title of a small article by Megan Creasey that I recently came across in the internet, "Does Violence Have a Place in Children's Literature", a question the author raises in the article and

answers in the affirmative in the concluding paragraph, arguing for "an effective and careful" use of violence in the literature for children. Creasey's idea of an ideal book of children's literature, one that can be taught in the classroom, takes into account most of the questions that have been enlisted above, and thus can be considered broadly representative of the critical concerns of a substantial body of works on violence in children's literature: "While violence in literature can have many benefits for the young readers, certain criteria must be taken into account before one can deem a book 'worthwhile' for the classroom. Those choosing literature with violent aspects should carefully assess the material to check that the violence portrayed serves a purpose, such as showing the consequences of violence or alternatives to violent actions. Unfortunately, violence is not likely a part of human nature that can be entirely eradicated, although if children are familiar with relevant and useful literature that teaches them about violence, they have a better chance of facing a world of violence and conflict responsibly."

3. I use the word 'modern' here to loosely signify a world after the emergence of the idea of nation-state, a post-medieval 'rational' world where it became increasingly difficult, if not impossible, to find any 'realistic' basis for the fantastic, the mythological and the legendary and for such 'children's narratives' as fairy tales.
4. The gendering impulse of the hegemonic imperial discourse also considered the West virile and "masculine", exploring and penetrating virgin lands waiting to be rescued in the margins of civilisation. Ashis Nandy's book *The Intimate Enemy: Loss and Recovery of Self Under Colonialism* explores in detail the politics of age and sex-based construction of the colony and its repercussions in the Indian social, political and psychological life.
5. Frantz Fanon's "Concerning Violence" in his *Wretched of the Earth* is one of the seminal critiques of the colonial framework as basically dependent on intense application of strategies of physical and psychological violence. Fanon's suggestion that resistance movements aimed at any degree or form of decolonisation cannot bypass this network of violence can also have important implications for us in the context of understanding resistance, revenge and subversion in *Pagla Dashu*.

6. Michel Foucault's "The Order of Discourse" in Robert Young ed. *Untying the Text: A Poststructuralist Reader* (London, 1987), pp. 48-78 for a detailed discussion of the relationship between power and discourse.

WORKS CITED

Bakhtin, Mikhail M. *Rabelais and His World*. Trans. H. Iswolsky. 1963. Anthologized in *The Bakhtin Reader*. Ed. Pam Norris. London: Arnold, 1994.

Benjamin, Walter. *One-Way Street and Other Writings*. Trans. J.A. Underwood. London: Penguin, 2009.

Creasy, Megan. "Does Violence Have a Place in Children's Literature." www.oneofareadingjournal.com, accessed on 27.05.2011.

Fanon, Frantz. *The Wretched of the Earth*. Trans. Constance Farrington. 1963. New York: Grove Press, 1968.

Ray, Sukumar. *Samagra Shishusahitya*. Eds. Satyajit Ray and Partha Basu. Kolkata: Ananda Publishers, Bangla 1383 (1976), rpt. Bangla 1392 (1985).

Young, Robert. Ed. *Untying the Text: A Poststructuralist Reader*. London, 1987.

11

Fairy Tales and Fantasy as the Upholder of Values in Children's Literature: A Visit to *The Winged Horse: Fairy-tales from Bengal*

Saurabh Kumar Singh

I

Children's literature has always been associated with the elements of fairies and fantasies. These fairies and fantasies contain in themselves the seeds of basic values, principles, and certain positive associative factors which in turn help a lot in the pruning and nurturing of children, and at the same time offering young readers ways to negotiate their place in the world. Human society, since its origin, has been a cradle of problems, worries, and tensions. Human mind amidst all these problems, worries and tensions tries to transform these harsh and crude realities of life into beautiful things with the help of imagination, i.e. fairy tales and fantasies. These fairy tales and fantasies have been mediating us from the very beginning as the means through which we can discuss not only human conflicts, but basic cultural ideologies pertaining to growing up, maturation and most important a sense of self also.

In connection to realism, fairy tales and fantasy in children's literature in general, has been considered serious. This aspect has been well highlighted by contemporary scholarship. It has recognized that the genre of realism has no exclusive authority over claims to truth. Now it can safely be affirmed that fairy tales and fantasy have shifted radically from their previously undervalued position as somehow less significant than other genres of literature which employ realism (Stephens, 1922: 241-42; Hunt and Lenz, 2001: 2), to negotiate questions related to values, morals and principles that are at the foundation of cultural tensions and anxieties. In this connection Reynolds rightly observes that fantasy is considered "one of the most important genres" in its ability and capacity to allow authors and readers both deep engagements with "disturbing material" (2005: 42-43).

II

Kamal Sheoran has rightly commented that "India is country of many contradictions. Contemporary children's literature is one of them" (1975: 127). To be very precise, India is the second most populated country of the whole universe. India has millions of children and unfortunately thousands of them are doomed to be in the clutch of demon illiteracy. India does not have enough schools for its children. Teachers! With the due course of so-called growth of industry and cities, the very basic structure of India as a nation has crumbled down. Perhaps this bitter truth is known to every sensitive person so I need not to talk about this. What I need to talk is to facilitate our children with certain basic textbooks and other basic needs which can fulfill their rudimentary need of education. At this crucial point, to speak of children's literature as a specialized field is far-fetched and fanciful. This sad aspect is well-conjoined by the fact that India has the greatest living oral narrative tradition in the world. This narrative tradition in the form of myths, folks, fairy tales, legends, and histories fulfills and feeds the needs of every young and growing child in that he gets his complete "story" quota orally in the form of story passed down through the generations where the children would flock to their grandmothers in the evening to receive wondrous fairy tales and fantasies brought alive through gesture and mimicry. And in this context children's literature in India remains perhaps the greatest paradox of all.

Indian treasure of fairy tales, folklore, and fantasy is rich and imaginative and remains the most interesting source for children's literature. Chief among them are the *Panchatantra* (Five Principles), written in Sanskrit in 200 B.C., the *Hitopadesh*, the *Brihatkatha*, Kshemendra's *Brihatkatha Manjari*, Somadeva's *Kathasarit—Sagra*, the *Jatakas*, the *Puranas*, the *Ramayana* and the *Mahabharata* epics as well as a large number of ancient Indian Sanskrit classics. Like the Norwegian collection of folklore, the Norske Folkeeventyr, Indian mythology is not specifically for children but it is most popular with children. The *Panchatantra*, an ancient Indian collection of animal fables in verse and prose both, is the most important book of Indian fables. It has greatly influenced the folktales not only of east but of the west also. It is the main source of Indian folktale literature. The original Sanskrit work is attributed to Vishnu Sharma. However, it is based on older oral traditions, including animal fables that are as old as we are able to imagine. Animal fables from this source are predominant and remain as always society's traditional vehicle of social and moral instruction. Tales of animal wisdom, cunning, and foolishness, in which conventional animal characteristics are ignored, are peculiar to India. Thus, it is not at all surprising to find a clever quail, a smart jackal, an intelligent crow, or a stupid tiger; though the owl is regarded as an ill omen, yet not the raven; the peacock, far from being vain, is said to weep because he has such ugly feet, and the snake is not considered dangerous and vile but a protector of the innocent. These fables are retold in many languages not only within India but throughout the universe.

Indian folklore and fairy tales, much of which has yet to be printed, remain a curious mixture of tradition and pure fantasy. In these we find plethora of stories populated with ghosts, ogres, restless spirits, and other such representatives of the underworld as, angels, demons, Yama the God of Death, and holy sages, "rishis", and "munis" who are gifted with supernatural powers to curse a whole kingdom to ashes or bring alive the dead with a mantra. These exploitations of supernatural and fantasy are not merely to pass the time but must be understood in terms of the chronicles of timeless concepts that assume authentic dimensions not only with children but also with adults to this day. Fantasy, as represented in myths, legends, folk/fairy tales, and epic forms, is stimulating and unusual enough to keep even the 21st century child wonderstruck for hours. Story concepts are imaginative and are best put across to a receptive audience in oral narrative, which provides full vent to the storyteller's interpretations, according to the mood and expectations of the audience. Fear and excitement go simultaneously. This phenomenon is quite opposed to the prevalent modern storytelling tendencies which shun situations that create unwanted tensions tend to be jejune because they not only lack the natural pace of the folklore but also fail to keep up with the imagination of the child, for whom nothing is impossible, nothing implausible, and nothing so strange that it cannot be enjoyed. This is particularly noticeable in the children's story hour programs on All India Radio which broadcast songs, ballads, and riddles for children. Although oral narrative is still a tradition in every home in India, story forms are changing. The old grandmother, wizened with age but full of stories, is an institution still found in most houses where the joint family system exists. Stories of gods and goddesses engaged in a battle of good and evil, the ideal love of the brother Lakshman for his elder Ram, the devotion of Hanuman to Ram and Sita, Kaikeyi, the wicked stepmother, the pranks of Krishna when he was a child, Yudhisthir as a man of truth, Eklavya as the symbol of ideal disciple, and numerous others are such stories which have not gone stale with repetition. In many cases, the tone of the story remains amoral and free of inhibitive tendencies which most adapted versions exclude. The settings of most myths and epics are, however, woven into the fabric of the story and the content perforce remains unchanged. Thus, polygamy is the rule rather than the exception where kings were concerned, and wicked asuras (demons) who carry off girls to their dens are as much a part of traditional lore as children born out of wedlock. Oral rendering of such lore is common to every regional language and dialect, i.e. Bhojpuri, Bengali, Marathi, Gujarati, Malayalam, Tamil, Telugu, and

Hindi. In the English language, imaginative and inspired translations are found in such collections as Tales from Indian Classics, the Panchatantra Tales, and many others in a series of hardbound volumes brought out mainly by the Children's Book Trust, Jataka Tales published by Echo, Lalvani Brothers, India Book House, Somiaya Publications, Thompson Press, Oxford University Press and many other regional publishers.

Children's literature in Bengali has deep ancient roots both orally and in the written form. Translations of Indian classics and mythology into Bengali language appear as early as the beginning of the eighteenth century. Middle Eastern literature specially the tales of Arabia and Persia has been imported and adapted to such an extent that a Bengali child considers it part of his own rich heritage. Children's literature in Bengali language was well-disciplined by publication of a children's magazine by two brilliant writers: Ishwarchandra Vidyasagar and Aukhoy Kumar Dutta. They can well be hailed as the architects of children's literature in Bengal. These established writers also contributed a number of small books for children. These books, albeit written in an archaic style, are still sought after today by parents and teachers alike. A period of prolific creativity in poetry followed, and fresh, lively renderings of the rules and laws of arithmetic in humorous verse appeared for the first time. Needless to say they are popular with children to this day. Bengali children's literature is marked by the keen interest taken in it by every man of letters. This interest has given it a status and style enjoyed by none of the other regional literatures for children. This feature is quite exclusive to Bengali children's literature. The association of such names as Rabindranath Tagore, Keshav Chand Sen, and Shastri with juvenile literature has raised it to the pinnacle. Although the production of books in terms of illustration, typography, and design is not of high standard, the extraordinarily well-written texts often lead the reader to overlook the physical appearance of the books.

In the beginning of the twentieth century, a noted man of letters Upendra Kishore Roy brought out the highly reputed monthly children's magazine *Sandesh*, which still enjoys the privilege of being the most popular magazine. Apart from *Sandesh*, numerous children's magazines appeared in print and a few have survived so far. A multitude of gifted writers like D.R.M. Majumdar and Yogindranath produced a rich and diverse literature for the children. Their themes and plots are striking in that they touch upon common and basic problems of life like sickness, hunger, work, and loyalty in the form of fantasy in a way that is appreciated by children of all ages. Satyajit Ray, Lila Majumdar, Kishore Bharati, Sukhatara, and Ananda are other major personalities who contributed a lot in the proper growth and nourishment of children literature.

III

The late Daksshinaranjan Mitra Majumdar (1877-1957) was arguably the most well-known and popular writer of children's books in Bengali during the first decades of the 20th century. His range was wide and varied, his output was prolific, and his métier was I the genre of fairy tales and fantasy. The 'jewel in the crown' of his large volume of work was undoubtedly his *Thakurmar Jhuli* (*Grandma's Bag of Tales*) published around 1907. It has remained in continuous print, adored by children and adult alike. In the olden days, when we had the abundance of joint families, it was somewhat customary for the grandmothers to round up the children in the evening and tell them the stories full of wondrous elements and fantasy, employing appropriate gestures and mimicry to transport the listeners to the make-believe world of fairies and demons, of winged horses and talking birds, of daring prince and adorable princesses. The unique quality that marks the stories of *Thakurmar Jhuli* is the preservation of the oral style; an attempt to recover the fast-disappearing heritage of fairy tales that were once an oral legacy of every Indian child. These stories are not merely to amuse and entertain children. They serve a greater purpose. Behind these wondrous elements and fantastic world, we without any fail discern some rudimentary morals, values, and principles which operate deeply in our day-to-day modern and postmodern life. These small bags of fairy tales and fantasy contain in themselves something which any school teacher in any school cannot render to his/her students.

This bag of grandma is full of gems like common sense, humility, decency, bravery, discipline, loyalty, and many other positive values for our own small children which are essential for the betterment any civilized society.

The Winged Horse: Fairy-tales from Bengal is a beautiful collection of fairy tales, rendered into English by Sukhendu Ray from Daksshinaranjan Mitra Majumdar's *Thakurmar Jhuli*. There are six stories. Each one of them is unique. I have selected some of them to show how the elements of fairy and fantasy have the capacity to deliver some useful and valid observations on elementary values, morals, and principles. The very first story of this collection *Kiranmala* in its opening, talks about the responsibilities of a royal king. A King should not merely involve himself in hunting and idle chatting, but he should assume a disguised form to roam around the kingdom to feel the real pulse of the subjects. This story talks about permanent presence of certain human feelings like craving of money and power, greed, and envy. When the youngest sister and now the queen of the king is on the verge of delivery, her elder sisters are full of venom and befool the king thrice by telling him that instead of delivering actual sons and daughter she has given birth to a puppy, a kitten, and a wooden doll respectively. By God's grace these three issues of her are sent to a rich Brahmin. Now pure fantasy comes in full force and we find how these brothers (Arun and Varun) and sister (Kiranmala) perform wonderful deeds. They build a colossal palace which becomes the object of envy even for the king. With the suggestion and help of a holy man they set out to bring diamond branch for the bird of gold, fruits of gold on silver trees to decorate the palace even more. The brothers fail to achieve this but a girl (Kiranmala) succeeds. In this way the very first story of this collection makes a very bold and pertinent statement regarding the high status of girl child in a patriarchal society. This story also talks about the proper employment of common sense by making the king realize how a woman can deliver a puppy or a kitten or even a wooden doll.

Sheeth and Vasanth is a story of a king and his two queens. It again talks about the presence of common human frailties like anger and envy. The younger queen has two sons and the elder has none. Isn't it enough to breed the feelings of envy and anger? Yes, it is. The elder queen with the help of a magical pill turns the younger queen into a parrot and then pretends to have a fatal disease which can only be cured by the blood of parrot queen's sons. By now she has her own three sons but as "thin as bamboo reeds, as frail as bamboo leaves!" (19). This is adding fuel to fire. The poor king would do nothing but orders his servant to kill Sheeth and Vasanth. The executioner turns out to be a man of mercy so he frees them. Now the role of fantasy is in full swing. Sheeth with a miracle becomes the king of a kingdom and Vasanth receives education from a saint. Meanwhile the dictum as you sow so shall you reap turns out to be true as the elder queen now becomes a beggar and the king has lost his kingdom.

Now the parrot queen is with a princess who is grown enough to be married. She has everything except the Ivor Gem. So she takes a vow to marry only that prince who could bring her the Ivor Gem. Now the old hermit's place has two birds: the male bird Sook and his wife Sari. One day Sari is talking to Sook: about a Sea of Cream on a milk-white peak where the Ivor Gem plays hide and seek. Beneath it on the sea there are a thousand lotus flowers of gold. There is also an elephant white crowned on the head by the Ivor Gem bright. With the help of hermit in the form of his trident and Simul tree in the form of his princely robe and coronet he successfully obtained his desired object and three gold fishes which later on turned out to be his cousins.

Then the parrot queen reveals the truth that the man with Ivor Gem is nobody but her own son. Out of joy the princess strokes the parrot queen gently and orders the attendant to bring fresh milk and turmeric paste for she will gives her a bath. With the bath the magical pill comes unstuck and she turns into a beautiful and younger queen. Now Sheeth, Vasanth with his wife Roopavati, their mother and old father, and three sons of elder queen meet and they live happily ever after. In this way we see that this story beautifully spreads the message for love sympathy, kindheartedness, and humility not only to human beings but to animals and birds also.

Neelkamal and Lalkamal is a beautiful fairy tale dealing with the clash between good and bad; virtue and vice in the form of fantasy. It is an archetypal clash in which good and virtue ultimately obliterate bad and vice. The good ones are the king, his younger wife, his elder son Ajit (the son of elder queen, a Raksashi), and his younger son Kusum. Though Ajit is the son of Raksashi queen, he is not altogether devil. He is man of virtue and goodness. He loves his cousin too much. He knows the ill desire of his mother to drink the blood of Kusum, that's why he never leaves the company of him. One day it so happens that a huge male demon picked up Kusum. Ajit fought very well to save his brother but could not help him as the demon has made him a ball of gold. In the utter fury the Raksashi queen eats her own son up and turns him into a ball of iron. Then she buries both the balls under a bamboo. In the morning a farmer fins the balls and throws them on the ground. The balls break and out of them two princes Lalkamal and Neelkamal come.

They, by the passage of time, reach to a kingdom which is deeply ridden with the terror of Khokkash—ogres. By the nightfall these ogres arrive and gobble up some people. The princes assured the king to relieve him by killing these ogres. They massacre all the Khokkash by their courage, bravery and intelligence. Now two demons Aye and Kye report it to the Raksashi queen, the mother of Ajit. She sends Aye and Kye to kill them. Aye and Kye assume the form of two human soldiers and ask the princes to bring the fat from the brain of a Raksash. The princes set out for this. After a long journey they meet a pair of birds—Bengama and his wife Bengami. The princes give their chicks some blood as they cannot see. Now the chicks open their eyes and help the princes by mounting them on their back to fly all around the world. After a long journey they reach the land of demons. After a long battle they successfully obliterate even a single existence of demon from the universe.

Princess Kalavati is another beautiful story full of wondrous elements. It talks about the story of a king and his seven queens who fail to deliver any child. By the grace of a holy man and his root of a tree five of the queens managed to have one son each, but as the fourth queen and the little queen do not take the root in its prescribed form they simply give birth to owl and monkey respectively. The five princes are named Hira, Manik, Moti, Sankha, and Kanchan. The owl is named Bhutum and the monkey is named Buddhu. This story nicely employs maximum of fantastic elements as Bhutum and Buddhu talk in human language, Kalavati lives under water, peacock boat, three witches, huge python, the golden bird, and so many others. The whole story is about the mad pursuit of five princes after Kalavati without involving any sense, and the sensible behaviour of two non-human beings as one is owl and other is monkey. This story is reverberating with teaching/value that it is not necessary for all human beings to be sensible, ardent, intelligent, and wise. While an owl and a monkey who do not have enough brain to judge the things, if given chance and opportunity, can excel any human being in the performance of sensibility and sagaciousness. Throughout the story we find how ungrateful the five princes are as Bhutum and Buddhu always save them out of fraternal love, while they always cheated on them. They show their full disrespect for Bhutum and Buddhu. This story rightly pictures human beings as nothing but the bundle of all the earthly shortcomings.

The Winged Horse as a collection of fairy tales and fantasy is potential enough to deal with elementary and rudimentary aspects of those philosophies of life which are essential in the formation of a healthy civilization. Children and adult alike can easily identify themselves with the multidimensional landscapes of these stories. These stories beautifully raise the question of true essence of life and its true identity whether inclusive or exclusive. They make very valid commentary on our place in the world, the culture in which we live, about why we suffer, and give us some mantra to live a balanced life. It can only be performed when we are beyond our daily hardships of life and transport ourselves into the world of wondrous elements and fantasy. Through this willing suspension of disbelief we can earn panaceas to live a fulfilling life in real world. And as Loy and Goodhew suggest that consciously or unconsciously stories weave a complicated, often confusing world and give us models how to live in it, then certainly children's literature in the garb of fantasy might offer some truths that mainstream realism cannot (2004: 1). After all each of us need a story to survive; or don't we live in fantasy stories? Yes, we do live.

WORKS CITED

Hunt, P. and Lenz, M. (2001). *Alternative Worlds in Fantasy Fiction.* London and New York: Continuum.

Loy, D. and Goodhew, I. (2004). *The Dharma of Dragons and Daemons*. Somerville, Massachusetts: Wisdom Publications.

Majumdar, D.M. (1997). *The Winged Horse Fairy-tales from Bengal.* Selected and Translated by Sukhendu Ray from *Thakurmar Jhuli.* Oxford University Press.

Reynolds, K. (2005). *Modern Children's Literature: An Introduction.* London: Palgrave Macmillan.

Sheoran, Kamal (1975). *Contemporary Children's Literature in India.* Children's Literature, Vol. 4: The John Hopkins University Press, 127-37.

Stephens, J. (1992). *Language and Ideology in Children's Fiction.* Essex and New York: Longman.

12

The Place of Books for Children and Adolescents in the Literary System

Vandana Singh

Fiction has always had a positive impact on the psychology of the children and adolescent and in turn it has a positive reflection on the society. With emphasis on visual effects and applications used in the present age of globalisation literature becomes more effective with use of modern technology. The oral narration of epics and mythology being sung to generations took a back seat as the children in globalised world tend to become more competitive and face psychological stress and problems. Another reason was that the narrators of oral tradition lost its value as the familial bondages fragmented into small nuclear units.

It is very surprising that a two year old today can identify with the cartoon characters more than the adult counterpart who have not been in touch with literature for a larger part of their life. The adolescents are more inclined to watch the animated version which inspires them to read the original text as they grow up. Books become a haven where they relate themselves to the stress and problems they face in reality. The heroic action of the protagonists can be closely identified with.

The time spent on going through musical picture books of Cinderella and Fairy tales remains afresh in mind. Though the stories were transformed into films and animated movies replacing the oral technique of narration. Stories of dancing princesses escaping to an underground world of music and balls, the finding of a magic ring baked in a cake, the agony of a sister trying to free her brothers from a spell that has changed them into swans—these elements of fairy tales is still etched on the minds and imagination today. The child's mind is very malleable and the fantasies of the illusory world makes them enchanted.

The place of literature in a child's and adult world has importance• because somewhere one finds a release while reading and sometimes one can identify with the characters as they are something which one wishes to be. Superman, He-Man, or for that matter Spiderman, take on a very large readership because they are projected as a commoner endowed with superpowers which helps them to incarnate as the Ultimate power. The superhuman that can turn the world upside down to regain the power of the distressed and poor. The life-size protagonists would help the readers to rejuvenate releasing them from the world of realistic dreariness.

But the other side of the story could be that the youth or the child who could not differentiate between the real and the illusory world could also face the psychological problem of disassociation and reality monitoring. The children facing traumatic childhood or the youth facing traumatic experiences tend to find relief in literature which takes them away from their real world and they fantasise a world which is free of the problems that they face. Yet the positive effect cannot be denied as literature helps individuals to overcome the problems in life if they are able to identify the reality from fantasy.

Children books were written keeping the different level of understanding. The books written for the young learners were more of illustrative genre in which use of languages and animations like cartoons and pictures accompanied with colourful drawings and art work that would interest children. Children between the ages of four and eight have books that have fewer words and more pictures. The musical picture books attracted more children to create a world of their own where they could use their imagination and associate with the story.

"In a child or an adolescent, the unconscious is a powerful determinant of behaviour. When the unconscious is repressed and its content denied entrance into awareness, then eventually the person's conscious mind will be partially overwhelmed by derivatives of these unconscious elements, or else he/she is forced to keep such rigid, compulsive control over them that their personality may become severely crippled. The importance of books and good literature gets authenticated as it creates the fictional world where the unconscious mind can release the fears and insecurities in the mind of children and adolescents."[1]

Freud's interpretation of dreams is based on the philosophy of unconscious. For Freud, the unconscious is the storehouse of instinctual desires, needs, and psychic actions. While past thoughts and memories may be deleted from immediate consciousness, they direct the thoughts and feelings of the individual from the realm of the unconscious.

The fairy tales introduced the theme of death, aging, loss of parents and other stresses in much milder way than the realistic fiction of 21st century. Yet the stepmother concept in fairy tales has and will always scare the child. But the good winning over the evil simplified the situation allowing the child and adolescent realize the real life problems in its essence. The characters, each one of them, are characterised in a unique form that makes an impact on the readers mind. Evil is as common as any virtue personified in the form of a figure or their actions. Evil is not without its attractions symbolized by the power of the crafty queen in *Snow White*. One can hardly forget the lines:

> Queen: Slave in the magic mirror, come from the farthest space, through wind and darkness I summon thee. Speak! Let me see thy face.
>
> Magic Mirror: What wouldst thou know, my Queen?
>
> Queen: Magic mirror on the wall, who is the fairest one of all?

Magic Mirror: Famed is thy beauty, Majesty. But hold, a lovely maid I see. Rags cannot hide her gentle grace. Alas, she is more fair than thee.

Queen: Alas for her! Reveal her name.

Magic Mirror: Lips red as the rose. Hair black as ebony. Skin white as snow.

Queen: Snow White![2]

The heroic element and the qualities which were rendered through fictitious character helped the children and adolescents to form a role model to follow. The characters illustrate the consequences of their choice and can easily influence the young minds to apprehend the cause-effect and effect-cause principle in the real world. The moral values drawn from the fiction could mould the character of the child and adolescents. Cinderella and the rest of the characters have contemporary issues dealt in a way that it can have impact on the young minds. Literature inculcates value system in child and adolescents primarily.

Albrecht (1954) cites three main socio-literary theories:

(a) Literature reflects society in terms of depicting significant social norms, values, culture, class struggle and documented social facts such as births and deaths, marriage trends.

(b) Literature shapes society by influencing social and cultural developments.

(c) Literature controls society by stabilizing and strengthening existing social and economic norms.

"Access to Literature becomes a good way to get knowledge, history, and to shape people's thoughts. Literature is essential component to develop linguistic and communicative skills. Children's literature allows us to acquire communicative competence, to study all the areas of the curriculum and to understand many aspects of life. We can define it as a group of productions which have artistic qualities and share aspects with other literary texts. Children access these productions during the early years of their education. Teaching language and literature from a communicative model involves an important change of mentality with respect to educational structures, because it gives more importance to development of linguistic skills rather than testing academic knowledge."[3]

Very few children books were published during the 16th and 17th century. They were part of the old educational system and the major purpose of production was to teach behaviour appropriate to their status in society. These books became more of a part of conceptual cultural framework during 18th century because they did not contribute much in the growth of the children.

Only towards the end of 17th century, with the rise of Puritan writings for children did children literature become culturally recognized field. However, the Puritan establishment was eventually forced to accept entertainment as one of the essential components for books at the beginning of the 18th century. The scope of children's reading interests developed beyond the Puritan literature, particularly as new models of writing for children based on different educational views developed during the Age of Reason and was firmly based on the writings of Locke and Rousseau. New changes and transformation from homogenous to a heterogeneous system was a consequence of new creations and not regeneration of the old models.

There are so many famous characters in Children's Literature which have been contemporary to any age, and have interesting values. One can hardly forget *Cinderella, Little Tom Thumb* besides Snow-white and the Seven Dwarfs. In *Ugly Duckling* much wisdom and humour has been ingratiated in the theme to make the book attractive for the children. Important works such as *Gulliver's Travels* (Swift), *Peter Pan* (Barrie), *The Wonderful Wizard of Oz* (Baum), *Momo* (Ende), *Matilda, Charlie and the Chocolate Factory* (Dahl), *Alice's Adventures in Wonderland* (Lewis Carroll) have found place in the literary system of children and adolescents. The adolescent novel became more popular in the 1950s such as *Huckleberry Finn* by Mark Twain and *Little Women* by Louisa May Alcott. Though these novels were not written specifically for the adolescent but the theme, plot, dialogues and vocabulary were carefully chosen specifically with young minds in focus. The works presented in the fictitious form for the children and adolescents were in reality personified expression of the experiences of the authors. *Charlie and the Chocolate Factory* is a 1964 children's book by British author Roald Dahl. The story features the adventures of young Charlie Bucket inside the chocolate factory of the eccentric Willy Wonka. The story was originally inspired by Roald Dahl's experience of chocolate companies during his schooldays when Cadbury would often send test packages to the schoolchildren in exchange for their opinions on the new products. At that time (around the 1920s), Cadbury and Rowntree's were England's two largest chocolate makers and they each often tried to steal trade secrets by sending spies, posing as employees, into the other's factory.

When we overview the historical background of the fairy tales for children most of them reflects the socio-economic attitudinal nuances of society towards children and death. Many of the fairy tales originated in the seventeenth century as oral entertainment for children and adolescents. They always had the backdrop of the custom and culture of the particular societal norms developed and transcribed specifically for the children in order to inculcate the value system in the younger generation. Over the centuries there has been a significant transformation given to the changing times. In the early twentieth century until the 1970s, topics considered disturbing to children, including death, were excluded or toned down and removed. Although late twentieth-century works began to reverse this trend, many children today are insulated from discussions of death in their literature. Fairy tales and other stories with fantastica as its theme were formulated in a way that the children were confronted with the realities of life without the negative impact on their psychology. Though the Puritans had given more emphasis on inculcating religious faith in child, yet strangely religion is still considered a taboo and has been excluded from child, adolescent and adult literature.

"Fairy tales, unlike any form of literature, direct the child to discover his identity and calling, and they also suggest what experiences are needed to develop his character further. Fairy tales intimate that a rewarding, good life is within one's reach despite adversity—but only if one does not shy away from the hazardous struggles without which one can never achieve true identity.

This is a basic tenet of the Bible as well: that those who want to please God and obtain his favour need to endure difficulties; that these trials produce endurance, character, and hope, and that the hope does not disappoint (Romans, 5: 3-5)."[4]

In the 21st century, the children and teenager have more knowledge of the Sindars, the Noldors and the Silvanos (a kind of elves, defined by Tolkien). These characters share space along with *The Rock Chewer* and other characters that are the inhabitants of fantastica. These fictional characters could help people to widen reality thus broadening their perspectives, which forms a major element of literature. Harry Potter, the most popular character with children and adolescent all over the world, suffers the loss of his parents and the books reflect Harry's quest to overcome the evil dark wizard Lord Voldemort, whose aim is to conquer the wizard world and subjugate non-magical people, and who seeks to destroy all those who stand in his way, such as Harry's parents. A series of seven fantasy novels written by the British author J.K. Rowling, the books chronicle the adventures of the adolescent wizard Harry Potter and his best friends Ron Weasley and Hermione Granger, at Hogwarts School of Witchcraft and Wizardry.

The technique of introducing stories within other stories, which is more of a part of adult literature, but is something interesting to create an atmosphere of illusory environ and stimulate the mind of the readers and their imagination. The Ivory tower where Atreyu must return to free the Child-like Empress from the nothing, has a correspondence to the Emerald city, where the Wizard of Oz lives, to Minas Tirith, or the white city, in which the kings used to live, or to Neverland, which is shown to Wendy by Peter Pan. All these utopian places are significant as the human beings wish to be in such places.

The dichotomy which exists between fantasy and nothing needs to be deciphered as the same dichotomy exists between illusion and the real world. The question arises where the line has to be drawn so as to create a balance between the two dimensions. The unreal world of Narnia and the adventures of the princes with her siblings keeps the adult mind busy when they enter that world to release themselves from the world of reality. The fiction in the literary system for children and adolescents provides solution to the search for a balance between both dimensions of Neverland and Reality. *The Neverending Story*, a German fantasy novel by Michael Ende which was later adapted into several films, has the backdrop of the parallel world of Fantastica, a world being destroyed by the Nothing, which represents and constitutes people's lack of imagination in the real world. The first protagonist is a young warrior, who is asked by the Steward of The Empress of Fantastica, to set off and find a way to stop The Nothing. The other protagonist is a boy from the real world, a reader of the novel, for whom the story gradually becomes more and more realistic. Like other works by Ende, *The Neverending Story* is influenced by anthroposophy, a religious philosophy developed by Rudolf Steiner which believes that spiritual development should be humankind's foremost concern.

The Chronicles of Narnia is a series of seven fantasy novels for children by C.S. Lewis. It is considered a classic of children's literature and is the author's best-known work, written by Lewis between 1949 and 1954 *The Chronicles of Narnia* has been adapted several times, complete or in part, for radio, television, the stage, and film. Set in the fictional realm of Narnia, a place where animals talk, magic is common, and good battles evil, the series narrates the adventures of various children who play central roles in the unfolding history of that world. With the exception of The Horse and His Boy, the protagonists are all children from the real world magically transported to Narnia, where they are called upon by the lion Aslan to protect Narnia from evil and restore the throne to its rightful line. The book covers the entire history of Narnia, from its creation in The Magician's Nephew, to its eventual destruction in The Last Battle.

The question arises if the modern realistic fiction for children and young people present alternate lifestyles and views of society. The canonized system of books for children began to develop almost a century after a stratified system of adult literature already existed. How well does children's and adolescent literature deal with sensitive issues like terrorism after September 9/11, AIDS, Death, in the lives of young people? In the Age of Information, i.e Age of Globalisation, the information communicated to children should be monitored. The narrative forms are as important as the accuracy of the information in informational narratives. Does the informational content of the children and adolescent literature take into consideration as it was done in the earlier Ages? The literature has naturally transformed given to the problems dealt in this Age of Information where the children and adolescent are faced with more psychological problems and undergo stress. In the Age of Information child tends to enquire more than the earlier ages. With the media playing a major role in generating information, the child needs to be mentored at the same speed. Majority of information uncensored filter to the child and adolescent aggravating the psychological stress. The books need to be published and should be used as tools to reveal a respect for the child's ability to inquire and to know.

One wonders how important are books and reading in a media-saturated environment. How can adults learn to make connections between the current interests of young people and potential future reading? Then comes the examples cited of Harry Potter and contemporary books which hold the attention of the children and adolescent authenticating the timeless importance of books and literature. The transtextual and translated texts from all over the world helps the readers to acquaint and identify with the problems among the children and adolescents and find solution. As it is, the children in the 21st century are confronted by a constant stream of visual images from their earliest consciousness and the problems around the world. In this environment, picture books are often a child's first introduction to fine art as well as to popular culture. The transformation from picture story book to film change the nature of that story depends on the technique used in the films, i.e. iconographic as contrasted with animation or realistic footage. Modern media brings real life characters into our homes. Only since the late 1970s and early 1980s this trend began to reverse. Children's books of the twenty-first century frequently deal with feelings, divorce, sex, and death. But the terrorist attacks of September 11, 2001, taught children that the world is not a safe place. *The New York Times* best-seller list for September 30 revealed that the new Lemony Snicket book, *The Hostile Hospital*, outsold any of the *Harry Potter* titles that week. For many years, modern realistic fiction has been considered the most popular genre among young readers, which is closer to the lives they know and, therefore, easier to read. If horror is overtaking realism in popularity, the causes for this change need to be identified. Yet in the age of realistic literature there is the continual appeal of such series as Nancy Drew, Dana Girls, and The Hardy Boys. It's because the protagonist provides the adolescent readers a world of adventure, team spirit and the elation of finding solution to any problem. The young mind is diverted from the pain and stress of the real world and also identify their own problems through the characters. The adolescents acquire these novels from library and bookshops which help them to inculcate reading habits and gradually move to more mature books.

The trend and place of books in literary system changed as per the genre prevalent in different centuries. It involved the perception, psychology and social concern of that particular age. Obviously the books reflecting the socio-economic and cultural situation in 1950s might not be of much relevance in the 21st century but the fact remains that books have the universality which cannot be denied and have always been an important and significant catalyst in development of society. Particular books aforementioned might not be the right channel for disseminating realistic information and imbibing the ethical values appropriate to family expectation, yet it is a channel which can fulfill the social and developmental growth of an individual, family and society.

NOTES

1. Bettelhein Bruno, *The Uses of Enchantment: The Meaning and Importance of Fairy Tales*, Vintage, 1989, p. 7.
2. Enchanted Tales Follow: http://www.movieclubblog.info/enchanted-tales-follow/ Snowhite and the Seven Dwarfs: Disney Platinum (ed.) Motion Picture by Walt Disney http://tinyurl.com/moviesmax123
3. Widdowson, H.G., *Aspects of Language Teaching*, Oxford University Press, 1978.
4. *Bible: New International Version*, 1995.

WORKS CITED

Enchanted Tales Follow: http://www.movieclubblog.info/enchanted-tales-follow/

Motion Picture: *Charlie and the Chocolate Factory* 2005; Director Tim Burton.

Motion Picture: *Chronicles of Narnia* 2010.

Motion Picture: *Neverending Story* (Film: directed by Wolfgang Peterson).

Motion Picture: *Harry Potter Movies in Order 1-7: Hogwarts Through The Years*.

Reading the Star Fisher: Toward Critical and Sociological Interpretations of Immigrant Literature. Lowery, Ruth McKoy 2003, p. 143.

13

Roald Dahl—The Hyberbolic Fantasist

Saloni Prasad (Mrs. Kumar)

> Do you know what breakfast cereal is made of? It's made of
>
> All those little curly wooden shavings you find in pencil sharpeners!
>
> —*Roald Dahl*

Roald Dahl is an author who is able to capture the wonder of a child's imagination, mix it with bizarre and add some elements to it to create stories that children adore. A British novelist, short-story writer as well as a screenplay writer, he is more known as a 'children's author'. Belonging to a big family of six children, he was given education in an English school, according to his dying father's last wishes. Roald describes his memories of Llandaff Cathedral School, in 'Boy'—where his mischiefs earned him and his friends a savege caning by the headmaster. The naughtiness of a child could be seen in Roald from the very beginning, which he himself has described in 'Boy', about him being so homesick that he even faked the symptoms of appendicitis, from which both his sisters—Astri and Ellen suffered and which earned them a trip home. Unfortunately, Astri died of appendicitis in 1920. Though he was eventually able to adjust to school life, school was something which Roald never liked which comes out explicitly in 'Boy', where he describes savage beatings, sadistic headmasters, prejudiced teachers and an abusive matron. Being an ardent fan of Rudyard Kipling, H. Rider, Haggard and G.A. Henty, their heroism and masculinity later influenced Roald's life and his writings. His accounts at boarding schools, especially the famous Repton Public School—faggings, beatings tortures and miseries to the extent that Dahl doubted even the existence of God, when one of his headmasters of Repton—Geoffrey Fisher, known for his vicious beatings, later crowned Queen Elizabeth II in Westminster Abbey. But not all memories of Repton was bad, as Dahl himself fondly recalls in 'Boy':

> Every now and then, a plain grey cardboard box was dished out at each boy in our House, and this, believe it or not, was a present from the great chocalote manufacturers, Cadbury.[1]

This gift of chocolates made Roald dream of working in a chocolate company:

> It was lovely dreaming those dreams, and I have no doubt at all that, thirty-five years later, when I was looking for a plot for my second book for children, I remembered those little cardboard boxes and the newly—invented chocolates inside them and I began to write a book called 'Charlie and the Chocolate Factory'.[2]

Working with the Shell Company in England and then in East Africa, on his two-week sea voyage, made Dahl end his book *Boy* and start with *Going Solo*, which describes many of the existing adventures that he lived through. Another dimension of Dahl's adventurous character is his joining the Royal Air Force, and while flying a glaidator, in 1941, was forced to attempt a land-crashing, fracturing his skull and blinding him for days. But this did not undermine his spirits and he was fit to resume flying. The battles that he fought for months are described at length in *Going Solo*. Later on he became an 'assitant air attache', and on his first duty in America, he struck an immediate friendship with a newspaper owner—Charles Marsh. When famous English author C.S. Forestes wanted Dahl to relate his experiences, Dahl thought it easier to put it on paper himself. The result was so good that in August 1942, it was published under the title

'Shot Down Over Libya'. This was the emergence of Dahl as a writer which was furthered by another story called 'Gremlin Lore' which was passed on to Walt Disney, who turned Dahl's story into an animated feature called *The Gremlins*. The book, *Walt Disney: The Gremlins: A Royal Air Force Story by Flight Lieutenant Roald Dahl* published by Random House is considered a prized book. By 1944, Dahl had become a literary agent, having a number of stories to his credit—'Shot Down Over Libya', 'The Sword', 'Katina', 'Only This' and 'Beware of the Dog'. Of these, 'The Gremlins' and 'Katina' were written especially for children. In 1946, a collection of Dahl's war stories 'Over the You' saw the light which was followed by his first novel *Sometimes Never*. He renewed his friendship with Charles Marsh, got publicity as well as money for his stories which made him settle down as a permanent American citizen, meeting his wife, Patricia Neal in 1951. By this time, Dahl was an established story writer and Alfred Knopf, published some of his collections which included, 'Taste', 'My Lady Love', 'My Dove', 'Skin', 'Dip in the Pool' and 'Someone Like You'—which received some very good reviews, one of which is:

> At disconcerting long intervals, the complete short story writer comes along.... Tension is his business; Give him a surprise denouement, he'll give you a story leading up to it. His name in this instance is Roald Dahl.[3]

Roald Dahl's collection of short stories has been translated into many languages and been the best sellers all over the world. His stories are mostly fantasy and full of imagination. They may seem to be a little cruel sometimes, but never without humour—a thrilling mixture of the grotesque and comic. A frequent motif present in his stories is that people are not, what they appear to be like Mary Maloney, in *Lamb to the Slaughter* is not a friendly widow, but a clever murderess. In his stories, the background is perfectly worked out and details are very close to reality.

> Her husband, he told her, had been killed by a blow on the back of the head administered with a heavy blunt instrument, almost certainly a large piece of metal. They were looking for the weapon. The murderer must have

> taken it with him, but on the other hand he may have thrown it away or hidden it somewhere on the premises.[4]

Dahl has an amazing style and a peculiar sense of creating the unusuality which is peculiar to him. For example, in *William and Mary*, he writes about the brain and eyes of William kept in a basin, giving a sense of chill as Mary, the wife, is all the time aware of her tyrannical husband's eyes watching her forever, but slowly, she really starts enjoying the idea of punishing him by letting him see everything which he hated during his life, and will now won't be able to do anything about it.

> It was a queer sensation peering into her husband's eyes where there was no face to go with it. All she had to look at was the eye, and she kept staring at it and gradually it grew bigger and bigger, in the end it was the only thing that she could see—a sort of face in itself.[5]

In 'Royal Jelly', when the baby refuses to eat anything, the father who is a bee-keeper, feeds her with Royal Jelly—the baby loves it, puts on weight in an alarming amount, the body does not grow in proportion and her skin gets yellow and hairy. These kinds of stories, written for the general public, adults as well as children, seem to fascinate both.

Dahl rose to prominence in the 1940's with works for both the children and adults, and became one of the bestselling authors of the world. He has been referred to as 'one of the greatest storytellers for children of the 20th century.' His short stories are known for their unexpected endings, and his children books for their unsentimental, often dark humour. The crisis in his own life comes out beautifully in his books. When his four-month old son suffered from hydrocephalus, Dahl, the father, became involved in the development of 'Wahe-Dahl-Till' valve, a device to alleviate the condition. When his daughter, Olivia Dahl, aged 7, died of measles encephalitis, he again became a proponent of immunization and dedicated his 1982 book, *The Big Friendly Giant* to her. So, in every phase of his life, he has been directly or indirectly, concerned with children. Dahl's influence has thus extended beyond literary figures and he is said to have a mixture of light and darkness, and not speaking down to kids and regarding them with that politically incorrect humour that kids get.

Dahl went on to create some of the best-loved children's stories such as *Charlie and the Chocolate Factory*, *Matilda*, *James and the Giant Peach*, *The Witches*, *Charlie and the Great Glass Elevator*, *The Big Friendly Giant*, *George's Marvellous Medicine* and *Fantastic Mr. Fox*. Roald's chilren's fiction are usually written and told from the point of view of a child. They typically involve villians who hate and mistreat children, and features atleast one 'good' adult to counteract the villians. These stock characters are probably a reference to the abuse that Dahl experienced in the boarding schools he attended. They usually contain a lot of black humour and grotesque scenarios, including gruesome violence. *The Witches*, *George's Marvellous Medicine* and *Matilda* are examples of this formula. *The Big Friendly Giant* follows it in a more analogous way with the good giant, representing the 'good adult' archetype and other giants being the bad adults. This formula is also evident in Dahl's film script for *Chitty Chitty Bang Bang*. Class conscious themes—ranging from the thinly veiled to the blatant—also surface in works such as *Fantastic Mr. Fox* and *Danny, the Champion of the World*.

Dahl also features in his books characters who are fat, usually children. Augustus Groop, Bruce Bogtrotter and Bruno Jenkins are few of these characters, although an enormous woman named Aunt Sponge is featured in *James and the Giant Peach*, and the nasty farmer Boggies in *Fantastic Mr. Fox*, who is again an enormously fat character. All of these characters are either villians or simply unpleasant gluttons. They are usually punished for this: Augustus Groop drinks from Willy Wonders chocolate river, disregarding his adults who tell him not to, and falls in, getting sucked up a pipe and nearly turned into fudge. Bruce Bogtrotter steals cake from the evil headmistress, Miss Trunchbull, and is forced to eat a gigantic chocolate cake in front of the school. Bruno Jenkins is turned into a mouse by witches who lure him to their convention with the promise of chocolate, and it is speculated, possibly disowned or even killed by his parents because of this.

Dahl's mother used to tell him stories about trolls and other mythical Norwegian creature and some of his children's books contain references or elements inspired by these stories such as the giants in *The Big Friendly Giant*, the fox family in *Fantastic Mr. Fox* and the trolls in *The Minpins*. *James and the Giant Peach* in 1961 was the first result of his inclination towards children's literature, which was followed by *Charlie and the Chocolate Factory* in 1964—the story dealt with one small boy's search for the ultimate prize in fierce competition with other highly unpleasant children, many of whom come to sticky ends as a result of their greediness. It presented the central theme in Dahl's fiction for young readers: virtue is rewarded, vice is punished. In the end, the fabulous chocolate factory is given to Charlie, the kind impoverished boy. Mostly all his children's stories were inspired by the tales that his mother told him. In an interview, he once mentioned:

> My mother was a great teller of stories. Her memory was prodigious and nothing in her life that ever happened was forgotten.[6] He created a special grandmother character in *The Witches* as a tribute to his mother.

It is difficult to describe Dahl's books because they are so different from the typical children's books. The author's own childhood experiences, the death of his near and dear ones, his unhappy years in boarding school influenced his work as did his vivid imagination. They can be described as modern fairy-tales, sometimes violent or grotesque but at the same time well-written, humorous and entertaining. Puns, word coinages and neologism are found in abundance in his stories. Goodness triumphs, revenge is sweet, evil is punished—no wonder that children have continued to enjoy Dahl's stories for decades. He had some very definite ideas about what children liked to read which were supported by the success of his books. Though his life was not an easy one but through it all, he always kept a wonderful perspective on his life which shines through his writings. He had quite a distinguished career for a person who started out having no thoughts of being an author as he himself said, after the birth of his daughter Olivia:

> If I didn't have any children of my own, I would have never written books for children, nor would I have been capable of doing so.[7]

The view of society revealed through his books—his implied criticism of adults and his contempt for social institutions have made his works popular. His *Big Friendly Giant*, *The Witches* and *Matilda* have young protagonists and are in the stage of their psychological development, where they experience the crisis of 'identity versus role confusion'. But his protagonists illustrate to the readers the capacity of young people to accomplish great things and to exhibit an independent spirit. The main character in *The Big Friendly Giant*—Sophie, is an eight year old orphan who is kidnapped by the Big Friendly Giant. Fortunately the giant is not interested in eating humans, as other inhabitants of the giant country. So they together develop a plot to stop the giants from eating children around the world. In *The Witches*, the protagonist is a seven year old boy, who, along with his guardian grandmother, accidently observes the annual meeting of the witches and is turned into a mouse by them. He manages to escape with the help of his indomitable grandmother to stop the witches' evil plot to kill all the children in England. The title character of *Matilda* is a five year old genius whose corrupt parents are oblivious to her existence. In school, she meets Miss Trunchbull, her headmistress, who refuses to acknowledge her genius and promote her, but Matilda finds that she can channel her brainpower to manipulate objects. She then develops her plan to use her power to get rid of Miss Trunchbull for good. These three books of Roald Dahl, with their young heroines and heroes are great success, due to the high level of commonality that his protagonists share with the readers.

Dahl remembered his school days as:

> Days of horror, of fierce discipline, of not talking in the dormitories no running in the corridors, no untidiness of any sort, no this or that or the other, just rules, rules and

> still more rules that had to be obeyed and the fear of the dreaded cane hung over his life like the fear of death all the time.[8]

All this has an impact on his writings. Dahl's moral universe was one in which there would be no question without an answer, no battle without victory, no irresoluble complexity —this was true of his writing also. He, through his writings, establishes a common bond with all the young people who have been oppressed or unfairly disciplined. Adults are dealt with harshly in his books if they dare to cause trouble for his young heroes and heroines. In the introduction to *Children's Literature Review* in 1997, a comment on Dahl's writings explains much:

> The morality of his writings is simple, usually a matter of absolute good versus absolute evil—with no shades of grey—and those who fall into the latter category are sure to meet with a swift and horrible end.[9]

Not all adults are portrayed negatively, but only those that abuse their authority over young people are severely punished. With the exception of Matilda, family members are willing to support, even against the rest of the world. This is evident in *The Witches*, where the protagonist has been turned into a mouse and shares his plan with his grandmother to eliminate all the witches in England, and her immediate reaction is:

> We shall check it out immediately. There's not a second to waste.[10]

Dahl's treatment of adults thus has a very positive effect on children because it closely reflects their own perspective. This is all because, he appeals to their 'gut-punching and slapstick sense of humour' as well as their 'crude sense of fun and delight in jokey phrases'. His philosophy too appeals to the children because of their belief that good triumphs and evil is punished. For example, when the child eating giants are captured in, *The Big Friendly Giant*, they are thrown into a pit where they are imprisoned for life, without attempts to befriend them. Belief in the destruction or punishment of evil appeals to children and provide an incentive for them to read Dahl's books. Another positive feature of his works is that they encourage young people through positive presentation of their peers at a time when they are struggling with low self-esteem.

Literary critic Linda Ray notes that Dahl's main characters are known for their "wit, solitariness, independence, tenacity, intelligence and resourcefulness". His female protagonists, like Matilda and Sophie, are independent and not intimidated by authority figures. For example, Matilda does not allow herself to become a helpless victim by refusing to let her poor home life deny her a sense of self worth. When her parents refuse to buy her books, she finds the public library on her own, at the age of four. This independence characteristic of all Dahl's main characters, allows them to take revenge against their oppressors. Matilda's revenge comes when her parents are going to force her to leave the country with her, but she manages to stay behind with her beloved teacher. However, Dahl offers encouragement too, in *The Witches* when the main character, thinking about his grandmother, comments:

> It doesn't matter who you are or what you look like so long as somebody loves you.[11]

The results of these positive elements appeal too and offer encouragement to young readers. Roald does not concern himself with criticism, but concentrates on entertaining his readers.

The young people/children find in Roald Dahl something that they could not find anywhere else—distrustful of authority figures and firm in the belief that good will triumph. His view of society, his contempt for corrupt authority figures, and his distrust of the system have made his works popular with the children. An expression of such values in the disguise of fantasy and humour is a rare find and one that young adolescents should be encouraged to read. Dahl has certainly achieved his goal as an author because his books have provided a way for many young people to become readers, as he himself once remarked:

> If my books can help children become readers, then I feel I have accomplished something important.[12]

NOTES

1. Dahl, Roald, *Boy: Tales of Childhood*, Puffin Books, 1984, p. 147.
2. *Ibid.*, p. 149.
3. Kelly, James, quoted in Treglown, p. 119.
4. Dahl, Roald, *Lamb to the Slaughter*, Classic Short Stories, 1953.
5. *Ibid.*, *William and Mary*, Classic Short Stories, 1960.
6. *Ibid.*, *Going Solo*, Jonathan Cape, 1986.
7. *Ibid.*, as quoted in www.nytimes.com.
8. *Ibid., Matilda,* Puffin Books, 1982.
9. Pendergast, Tom, *Dahl, Roald: Contemporary Authors New Revision Series*, Vol. 37, Gale Research, 1992.
10. West, Mark 1, *Roald Dahl*, Twayne's Author Series 492, New York, 1992.
11. Dahl, Roald, *The Witches*, NY, Puffin Books, 1982.
12. West, Mark 1, Roald Dahl, Twayne's Author Series 492, New York, 1992.

14

Salman Rushdie's *Haroun and the Sea of Stories*: A Postmodernist Fairy Tale

Reena Mitra

Literature today may be approached through innumerable aspects of study and may offer routes of access through texts, contexts, genres, historical eras and controversies trailing the subject. Children's literature, too, may be written variously and a proper understanding of the type as it has emerged now is possible only by examining the history of the form and the characteristic traditions that have crystallized over the last three hundred years or so. M.O. Grenby in his book, *Children's Literature*,[1] has referred to seven identifiable genres within the macro structure, namely fables, poetry, moral and instructive tales, the school story, the family story, fantasy and the adventure story. What we specifically need to explore is how particular texts and authors fit into the comprehensive general design as we conceive of it in the present times. The term "children's literature", taken in its widest sense, covers such an unimaginable variety of material—fiction, verse, text books, picture books, computer games, folk lores, fairy tales, etc.—that for any study of this category of literature one needs to delimit oneself in terms of subject matter and chronology. In this context most researchers and critics would perhaps subscribe to Peter Hunt's vehement assertion that children's literature comprises only texts that were "written expressly for children who are recognizably children, with a childhood recognizable today"[2] and texts of no interest to the librarian or child of the present times would be of greater relevance to the historians and bibliographers, Hunt rightly observed that concepts of childhood have changed over the years and hence the intent and objectives of children's literature have changed.

The major characteristic that distinguishes children's literature from other branches of academic literary study is that the former is the only category that is defined in terms of its conceived and proposed readership. It is not always about children, nor written by children; it is professedly written for children. Also children's literature was initially looked upon with condescension, but in the 1960s, perceptible scholarly critical attention was showered on it with the thrust then being more on texts in context than on literary achievements in isolation. Today, children's books including J.K. Rowling's *Harry Potter* series have become the bestsellers of the late twentieth and early twenty-first century. They have made inroads into the reading options of adults, into cinema, theatre, computer games and several other media. They provide simple and effective ways to introduce concepts like the postcalomel, for example, to younger individuals.

It is Rousseau and other social philosophers like him who first introduced the concept of the child and the need to provide it with social consciousness and this idea was effectively translated into the Romantic poems of Wordsworth, Coleridge and Blake. Since the child now was to be endowed with an environment for a healthy, multifaceted growth sincere attempts were made to make available suitable reading material for children. This "encyclopedie or encircling of the child with knowledge"[3] began with the revamping and retagging of oral folk tales as reading material for children though some believe that not all folk tales are fit for children to read as they are at times characterized by violence, sex and crime. Yet, by and large, people from all cultures converge on the belief that folk tales are appropriate reading material for children. The book, *Children's Literature* in India published by the Children's Book Trust, in a chapter titled "A Historical Survey" corroborates the above view:

> Every publisher looking for material to publish draws upon this unquestioned resource material so that the Indian epics, ancient lore, classical tales, folk tales, the 'Panchatantra' form the bulk of children's literature today. These stories are full of timeless worldly wisdom and play a recurring role in stimulating the imagination.[4]

With the swelling interest in psychology and specifically. child psychology, the question of what should constitute literature for children has become more challenging. Also, the essential contradiction lies in the fact that children as such have no role to play in the production of this kind of literature, which, in the ultimate analysis, reveals more about the adult writers than about children's preoccupations and fears. The morals conveyed in terms of social and political principles and practices that prevail are more revelatory of the grain of the society than of children and their propensities.

Generally, children's stories, though they often have an element of fantasy in them, are straight and explicit in their communication of the social values that the writer seeks to disseminate. Rudyard Kipling's tales for children, his Mowgli stories, often reflect many involved and abstruse angles of the connection and strained relations between the colonizers and the colonized, particularly in the context of the British rule in India but for children they are primarily animal stories. Sue Walsh's essay, "Reading the Child and Translating the Animal in Rudyard Kipling's Mowgli Stories",[5] though pre-eminently a representative constituent of children's literature suggests the idea of the basic hierarchical set-up in the India of the calonial times.

In the nineteenth century, the thriving publishing industry in Bengal and subsequently elsewhere in the country was able to identify a specific genre of children's literature. In nearly all the Indian languages the earliest books produced for children during the British era were either translations of the *Panchatantra* or revised versions of Aesop's Fables. In post-Independence India, catering to a modern readership was Anant Pai's *Amar Chitra Katha* series which remains till date the most vibrant and markedly extant example of an Indian children's literature as compared to a regional bulk of writing. Writers in the West, too, have started conceiving of the child as a potential reader and viewer and hence, literary classics of the nineteenth and early twentieth centuries like Lord of the Rings and the Narnia series were restructured for a contemporary audience. Thus, children's literature today cannot be ignored in any recounting of a history of literature and is worthy of study as a discrete branch of literature.

John Newbery is now celebrated as the founder of publications for children. One of his earliest successes, "A Little Pretty Pocket Book", (6) and most subsequent works combined instruction and delight in providing a pleasurable way of learning. Newbery was followed by Christopher Smart, Mrs. Barbauld and the Taylor sisters, the unknown authors of "Twinkle Twinkle Little Star" (7). Next in the lineage of children's literature came the chapbook containing romances, ballads, controversial, political or religious comments and other short texts which were sold just for a few pence by travelling pedlars or "chapmen". The chapbooks, close to the folk tales of the people, became very popular with adults as well as children. They drew much from the myths and legends re-narrated by successive generations of ordinary folk. Enclosing within their fold varied subject matter like witchcraft, superstition, street cries, ogres, fairies, dragons and whatever qualified as magic and defied the Age of Reason, the chapbooks gave children accessible and tractable reading matter and immortalized the fairy tale and the nursery rhyme.

In the present times, our world is unrelentingly adultcentric and the intellectual consumption of children, too, is defined and delimited by grown-ups who display absolute disregard for the predilections of a child. Few consider and relate to the world view of the latter, the window through which he/she looks upon the world outside. To understand a child better we need to develop sensitivity towards children and the way they look at things.

Certain recent works of children's literature and more specifically the unconventional novels of Joanne, K. Rowling have revealed the significance of children's literature. With reference to the Harry Potter series Esterino Adami states that "these texts try to detect the intricate relationship between the process of growing and the handling of fantasy."[6] These stories adopt the modes of folk-tale and romance rather than those of the depiction of social realism. Moral values obliquely incorporated in these have to be decoded and understood not in terms of life around but with regard to inner processes of growing and living by way of metaphors and clichés. These processes of growth are given form and direction by prototypes presented through fairy tales. This is amply corroborated by Samina Mishra in her review of the Lebanese writer Hanan Al-Shaykh's *One Thousand and One Nights*, a collection of tales from the Middle East, Persia and India which comprises stories of desire, power and magic. Referring to the author's own particular interpretations of the selected stories of Shahrazad (a version of Scherherzade) in the anthology, Mishra elaborates,

> ...in her reimagining of these tales, she brings to us their sensuality—the sights, sounds and smells, the gardens of abandonment and the palaces of intrigue, the surreal magic in the everyday...but most of all they are wonderful stories of adventure and daring, stories designed not just to alter the king's course of action but also to alter the way we look at the world.... Stories are a way of making sense of the world.[7]

Echoing a similar view point, Manorama Jafa, when interviewed by Rudroneel Ghosh, averred:

> .... Through children's literature a child learns to use imaginative powers to make sense of the world. Emotional development is another key facet...children's literature is not just entertainment. It's a vital tool for shaping the future of society.[8]

India's narrative art from the early *Panchatantra* and *Jataka* tales is characterized by oral traditions but the challenge before Indian publishers of children's literature is to incorporate in its bulk books, traditional as well as contemporary, representing the various aspects of Indian reality in matter, form, concept, visuals and production. Books for children have undergone a sea-change—from the earlier simple stories promoting traditional values and principles we have shifted to those mirroring the newfangled emergent society and the quandaries of children in everyday life. The mode of communication however is very often one of fantasy and magic realism as in the works of Salman Rushdie.

Rushdie's *Haroun and the Sea of Stories* is a typical example of a novel which enchants and fascinates children but is also relevant in the adult world of today and carries within itself a cryptic message demanding uninhibited and unsmothered liberty to express oneself. The introductory reviews of the book cited in the Penguin-Granta publication of the work itself are transparently indicative of the nature of the text. The multilevel communication in the novel is unmistakably implied in Granta's remark about the story of the novel being "so accessible that each reader is certain to get something out of it...."[9] The review adds the vital observation that "there is an underlying message about the importance of free speech and independent thought, but the message never overwhelms the story, it enhances it".[10] The Publishers' Weekly that has been quoted also refers to the novel being as eloquent a defense of art as any Renaissance treatise...saturated with the hyperreal colour of such classic fantasies as *The Wizard of Oz* and *Alice in Wonderland*.[11]

What is most relevant, however, in the context of the present assertion regarding *Haroun and the Sea of Stories* being a postmodernist fairy tale is the substantiation and validation that comes from the review of the novel posted by *Library Journal*, which defines the work as "more a postmodern fairy tale...than a traditional novel"[12] and draws ones attention to its allegorical rather than realistic content and to characters, too, that demonstrate themselves to be symbolic and "flat".[13]

Salman Rushdie, a man of varied sensibility, caught amidst the cross-currents of the individual and the historical, set the trend for autobiographical writing in modern Indo-Anglian fiction with his *Midnight's Children* which won him the Booker Prize in 1981 and later, the "Booker of Bookers" title in 1993 and 2008. The novel, however, is an autobiographical work with a difference—it offers a peculiar blend of the factual and the fantastic which characterizes the microcosmic reality of the novel and provides for the varied nuances and contours of individual experience. Rushdie's book of children's stories, *Haroun and the Sea of Stories*, which was published in 1990, and won the Writers' Guild Award for the Best Children's Book, is a similar concoction of the real and the fanciful. Meenakshi Mukherjee, in her essay, "Politics and Children's Literature: A Reading of *Haroun and the Sea of Stories*", which makes an elaborate comparison between the children's writer and film maker, Satyajit Ray and Rushdie, draws our attention to "Rushdie's personal predilection for Ray's work, particularly for the bizarre and fantastic aspects of his imagination."[14] Rushdie seems to have been largely inspired by the strange, weird and imaginative aspects of Ray's children's stories and has unmistakably incorporated these traits in his own works, specifically in his novel, *Haroun and the Sea of Stories*. Like Ray's 'Goopy Gayen and Bagha Bayen' to which there is an almost explicit reference in terms of the Plentimaw fish that are named Goopy and Bagha, Rushdie's novel, too, has been seen by many as a tale of aesthetics and morals in the garb of a children's story. And again Rushdie, too, like Ray, sees no conflict between the two narrative modes of fantasy and fable and fully subscribes to the latters assertion in this context: "Fantasy...meaning the use of the supernatural and the magical can be part of the fable and the two can merge naturally."[15]

Haroun and the Sea of Stories tacitly argues that life is never absolutely rational and that if the real world happenings can be punctuated with instances of magic, the magic world also may in many ways, be real and "fearsome too" as we are warned by the dedication to the novel. Ingenious adult readers appreciate the magic realism of Rushdie's fiction whereas children display an intriguing readiness to lap up the miraculous, the supernatural and the magical and do not hesitate to accept both the symbolic as the real and the actual as metaphoric as offered to them in this novel.

The text of Rushdie's novel, *Haroun and the Sea of Stories*, evokes a vision of the co-existence of multiple streams of narration and the title itself refers to atleast two of the traditional narrative modes, namely that of the West-Asian Arabian Nights to which we can trace the origin of the name Haroun and that of the Sanskrit Katha-Sarit-Sagar an anthology of stories attributed to Somadeva, who is believed to have lived in Kashmir in the eleventh century Haroun-al-Rashid, the name of the caliph of Baghdad has been cleverly split to give the names of both father and son and the two together suggest a recurrent round of tales representing a never-ending repertoire of stories. Rushdie's lack of faith in the literal and his predilection for the "epic-fabulist mode"[16] as Meenakshi Mukherjee calls it is seen being re-demonstrated in *The Moor's Last Sigh* when the painter Vasco tells Aurora not to depict things in the naturalistic vein which destroys creativity: "The real is always hidden...inside a miraculously burning bush! Life is fantastic! Paint that....[17]

Haroun and the Sea of Stories communicates to the reader not only Rushdie's personal predicament at the time of writing, but also the general prevalent temper of the society of the times swaddled in the term "postmodern consciousness". This state of mind is a bundle of negative and disaffirmatory moods comprising a profound yearning for the past, a fear of the amorphousness and intractability of the present, a feeling of despair and ineffectuality, and a sense of pertinacity in the efforts to resolve the confusion and a kind of commitment to making order prevail over anarchic conditions. All these aspects of displeasure and dissatisfaction are concealed behind an apparent state of balance and concord. In this situation one cannot fail to register the characteristic nature of the postmodern sensibility of father and son, the two together confronting the chaos in life and for some time trying ineffectually, to impose direction on the prevalent disorder. The sense of deprivation and anarchy is there in the novel at the very outset when Rashid, the Shah of Blah, is first deserted by his wife and then deprived of his gift of the gab. There is in him a great longing to see himself re-endowed with the power to produce an innumerable number of stories and the son feeling strongly for his father makes all efforts to retrieve the felicity of storytelling for his father. The situation, it is believed, can be resolved only by commitment to work logic and order on the one hand and on the other, by establishing, a link with creation, destruction, vitality and disorder. Recognizing this creative flux in life is one of the basics of postmodern art. The distinction of Rushdie's *Haroun and the Sea of Stories* lies in its realization of this creative flow in terms of form and thematic content as compared to the static form of the so-called modern novel. The characters in the novel, in keeping with the particular attributes of postmodern literature, give rise to "the dynamic interplay of order and chaos",[18] and the structure of the work is meant to emphasize the plugging of the springs of creativity and the sources of inventive fecundity which eventually are restored to the protagonist, Rashid is initially equipped with oceans of notions but is then deprived of them through the machinations of Khattam-Shud.

Haroun and the Sea of Stories is a novel about stories in which events are recorded through the exploits and escapades of a boy, Haroun, who ventures into a hazardous journey to re-establish his father's lost genius of storytelling. The essential allegorical interpretation of the narrative brings to the fore the tension that prevails between those who delight in imagination and those who are apprehensive of it. The principal villain, Khattam-Shud, who resembles Mr. Sen Gupta, is wicked in his plan of demolishing all stories. When asked by the fearless Haroun why he hates stories so much he replies that the World is not for fun as stories are and needs to be controlled; the story world, however, is beyond anyone's jurisdiction and hence, cannot be ruled. This antithetical positioning of art and power alone, whether political or religious, cannot hold the narrative which needs to be fortified with a series of comic events and verbal ingenuity. The names of the characters in the novel are themselves evidence of the remarkable fertility of the author's mind. Butt and Iff, Chattergy the King, Princess Baatcheat and Prince Bolo, Blabbermouth, etc. are all suggestive of lengthy and tedious sequences of words that are characteristic of the city of Gup. On the dark side of the incredible world of Kahani is the contrastive land of Chup which is typically defined by words representing silence; the field of Baat-mat-karo, Cult-master Bezaban, the intimidating blackguard, Khattam-Shud, etc. As it is words that comprise stories all nuances suggest this textuality in the Guppee Society; in their Army establishment, too, the soldiers who are called "pages" are organized in "chapters" and "volumes" and are dressed in laminations. When General Kitab summons the infantry for a meeting, there is a rustling of pages till "pagination" and "collation" bring order.

Any attempt at an analysis of the novel leads one to a textual approach, or more specifically an alphabetical one. The country referred to is Alifbay, the name being derived from the first two letters of the Arabic alphabet. The places in Alifbay have alphabets for names like the Valley of K and the Tunnel of I. The disturbed and vexed valley of Kashmir from where Rushdie himself originates is evoked in the text by very obvious hints like the Dal Lake being alluded to as Dull lake.

To emphasize the significance of language in the narration of a story Rushdie resorts extensively to a figurative use of words and this verbal dexterity fascinates children while reading *Haroun and the Sea of Stories*. The idiosyncrasies of the characters in the novel, the adventures of Haroun when trying to save his father and restore to him his gift of story-telling and the undertones of a science fiction quest seeking the way to relocate a planet are all sources of delight to young readers and hence the novel irrefutably qualifies as children's literature.

The mythology in the novel as conceived by the author refers to Kahani, the so-called second moon of the earth which has a dark and a bright side to it. The dark side Chup, is characterized by silence and the bright one Gup by loud voices. Comparing the two, Haroun observes their diametrically opposed traits,

> Gup is warm and Chup is freezing cold....
>
> Guppies love the ocean; Chup walas try to poison it.
>
> Guppies love stories and speech; Chup walas, it seems, hate these things just as strongly.

The Chupwalas were polluting the clean ocean with the virus of anti-stories produced by the poison factory in the Dark Ship with the ultimate target of trying to block the well-spring, the original source of all stories situated just below the ocean bed. *Haroun and the Sea of Stories* may primarily be an allegory depicting art and its enemies but it also conveys the message of the need to attend to matters of ecological interest by mention of saving the ocean from being defiled.

In Rushdie's novel Khattam-Shud's poison factory with its means of "converting mechanical energy into electrical energy" and Haroun's bird, Butt, the Hoopoe with a brain-box containing a memory-cell and command modules may establish claims of the work being a piece of science fiction, but more importantly, it is the bottle of "wishwater", a typical fairy-tale ingredient, that saves Haroun and Princess Baatcheat and decontaminates the ocean. The "wishwater" from the domain of magic finally establishes its supremacy over the field of science fiction as it possesses a force beyond [their] power to imagine, let alone control" (172).

It is the bottle of "wishwater" still half-full of the magical golden liquid which the Water Genie, Iff, had given Haroun that works wonders when the boy with his eyes closed pronounces, "I wish this Moon, Kahani, to turn, so that its no longer half in light and half in darkness..." (170). Eleven minutes elapse and then with "a mighty shuddering" Haroun's wish comes true—"The Moon Kahani turned...and the sun rose, at high speed and zoomed up into the sky until it was directly overhead; where it remained" (171). Once the moon begins to move, shadows melt and along with them evil, too, disappears. Haroun's determination combats the wicked designs of Khattam-Shud till the Dark Ship of the Cultmaster melts away leaving the Source of Stories totally clear and unimpeded for fresh stories to roll out of it.

In *Haroun and the Sea of Stories* the conflict between Haroun and Khattam-Shud has two more relatvely underplayed frames of reference that are almost equally significant in the novel—that of the individual and of the state. Before concluding the book in a manner that satisfies children who like the loose ends of a story neatly tied together at the end one needs to see how the tale of Gup's victory over Chup is parallelly enacted in the other two frames mentioned. The novel begins in the Sad City from where Haroun and his family move to the Valley of K where he and his father go at the invitation of Mr. Butto, whose unpopular government tries to misrepresent facts while campaigning for the next elections. The parallel stories in the text are interwoven through pairs of very similar characters like Sengupta and Khattam-Shud and Butt, the bus driver and the Hoopoe bird. Another mode of interlacing employed is the entwining of incidents where one episode leads to several consequential occurrences that bring the novel to a convincing end; for example, the bottle of "wishwater" empowers Haroun to make Kahani recommence the lunar activity, to prevent the well-head of stories from being blocked and to revive the imbibing of story-water by his father. At the state level, the story that had been stifled at the political demonstration in the Valley of K is eventually related at the close of the novel to show that stories can bring people together to fight against injustice and repression. The personal aspect of the narrative, however, is witnessed at the very outset in Rushdie's dedication of this book to his son, Zafar, who is about Haroun's age. Also Haroun's father's name, Rashid, is close to that of Zafar's father's, i.e. Rushdie. The voices of both the fathers are gagged and their power of expression muzzled. Rashid's, however, is soon restored and on returning from Kahani his wife too, comes back to add to his and Haroun's joy. For Rushdie himself, the world of the novel remains a phantasmagorical experience and a mode of wish-fulfilment. For children, nevertheless, the story remains a fable, a tale with a moral tag proclaiming that the world of evil lacks the substance and robustness of the good.

NOTES

1. Grenby, Mathew O., *Children's Literature* (Edinburgh: Edinburgh University Press, 2008).
2. Hunt, Peter, *Criticism, Theory and Children's Literature* (Oxford: Blackwell, 1991), p. 67.
3. Gupta, Nilanjana and Rimi B. Chatterjee, eds., *Reading Children* [Essays on Children's Literature] (New Delhi: Orient Blackswan, 2009), p. 2.
4. Menon, Navin and Bhavana Nair, eds., *Children's Literature in India* (New Delhi: Children's Book Trust, 1999), p. 24.
5. Walsh, Sue, "Reading the Child and Translating the Animal in Rudyard Kipling's Mowgli Stories", *Reading Children,* eds. Nilanjana Gupta and Rimi B. Chatterjee, pp. 18-40.
6. Adami, Esterino, "Harry Potter and the Magic of Growing up through Fiction", *Children and Literature* ed. Shubha Tewari (New Delhi: Atlantic, 2006), p. 98.
7. Mishra, Samina, "Long, Long Ago", *The Indian Express,* Lucknow, September 03, 2011, p. 17.
8. Jafa, Manorama, Interview by Rudroneel Ghosh *The Times of India*, Kanpur, April 01, 2011, p. 10.
9. Rushdie, Salman, Introductory Reviews—"Praise for Salman Rushdie", *Haroun and the Sea of Stories* (New Delhi: Penguin-Granta, 1990).
10. *Ibid.*
11. *Ibid.*
12. *Ibid.*
13. Forster, E.M., *Aspects of the Novel* (Penguin International edition, 1970), p. 75; Forster distinguishes between "round" and "flat" characters.
14. Mukherjee, Meenakshi, "Politics and Children's Literature: A Reading of *Haroun and the Sea of Stories*", *Post Independence Voices in South Asian Writings* eds., Alamgir Hashmi, Malashri Lal and Victor Ramraj (Islamabad, Pakistan: Alhamra, 2001), p. 163.
15. Ray, Satyajit, *Ray in the Looking Glass: Two Interviews,* Introduction by Jyotirmoy Datta, Trans. Kankabati Datta and Vidyarthi Chatterjee (Calcutta: Badwip, 1993), p. 33.

16. Mukherjee, Meenakshi, "Politics and Children's Literature: A Reading of *Haroun and the Sea of Stories*", *Post Independence Voices in South Asian Writings*, p. 168.
17. Rushdie, Salman, *The Moor's Last Sigh* (London: Jonathan Cape, 1995), p. 174.
18. Betsy Draine, "Nostalgia and Irony: The Postmodern Order of *The Golden Notebook*", *Modern Fiction Studies*, Doris Lessing Number, Spring 1980, Vol. 26, No. 1, p. 31.

15

Panchatantra, Ramayana and Kamishibai—The Adaptation and Transition of Tales

Ramendra Kumar

According to scholars five literary masterpieces originated in India and reached other countries throughout the world. These are: *Panchatantra,* Gunadhya's *Brihatkatha,* Buddhist *Jataka-kathas, Ramayana* and *Mahabharata.* Here I shall be taking up Panchatantra and Ramayana as two near perfect examples of adaptation and transition of tales across linguistic and cultural boundaries.

The Adaptation and Transposition of Panchatantra

Long, long ago a learned Brahman, Vishnu Sharma was asked by a king to teach his three sons *niti* (the wise conduct of life). Rather than resorting to the tried and tested methods of teaching, Sharma, an inventive and creative scholar, decided to tutor them by telling value based stories. And the result of this unique exercise was the collection of 84 fascinating tales of animals and birds, built around simple values, called Panchatantra. For centuries, these fables have been entertaining, guiding and inspiring generations of readers, both young and old, across the world.

According to Vijay Bedekar, President, Institute for Oriental Study, Thane, there is hardly any other secular work in the world which has penetrated so deeply in many cultures encompassing practically every continent. During the last 1500 years, there have been at least 200 translations of *Panchatantra* in about 60 languages of the world. Aesop fables, Arabian Nights, Sindbad and many Western nursery rhymes and Ballads are said to have been influenced by *Panchatantra*.

Panchatantra migrated to Iran in the 6th century. The most important translation of *Panchatantra* was done two centuries later, in Baghdad by Abdallah ibn al-Moquaffa an Arabic scholar. His translation enjoyed great popularity and is considered as a masterpiece of Arabic narrative literature. Almost all pre-modern translations of *Panchatantra* in Europe have their roots in this Arabic translation. From Arabic it got again translated to Syrian, Greek, Hebrew, Latin and German. In fact, the German translation was the first Indian and probably the second book after Bible published by Gutenberg press in 1483. *Panchatantra* had earlier migrated to Tibet, China and Mongolia and almost all South Eastern countries.

The message of *Panchatantra* is loud and clear and its appeal universal. Even today, hundreds of years since the tales were first told, they remain equally captivating and charming and their values just as relevant. In modern times, we talk about the need of a value based society, Vishnu Sharma emphasized this ethos 1500 years ago and helped in creating an order that valued knowledge more than lineage or wealth or position.

The Transcreation and Transition of the *Ramayana*

"As long as hills and rivers remain on earth so long will the story of Rama prevail among men," Maharishi Valmiki on *Ramayana*.

The great sage most likely had little idea how prophetic his words would turn out to be. "Probably no work of world literature, secular in origin, has ever produced as profound in influence on the life and thought of the people as the *Ramayana*. For at least the last two and a half millennia, the tale of Rama and Sita, has entertained, moved, enchanted and uplifted untold millions of people. If the *Ramayana* has dominated the cultures of India and south East Asia, it I has also fascinated a whole tradition of modern scholarship both in India and the west. This corpus includes an extraordinary variety of works ranging from editions, translations, and serious research into the language, metrics and text history of the poem to bizarre retellings traditionalist apologia and wishful fantasies about air-borne monkeys, Indian pharaohs and long tailed tribal people," says Robert P. Goldman.

These words of Goldman eloquently exemplify how *Ramayana* has transgressed the boundaries of time and space and occupied a place in the minds and hearts of people across religious divides, age groups and value systems.

Ramayana has acceptability and a proven track record in several countries worldwide, including Iran, France, USA, United Kingdom, Italy, Russia, Germany, Bhutan, Cambodia, Fiji, Guyana, India, Indonesia, Japan, Laos, Malaysia, Mauritius, Mongolia, Myanmar, Nepal, Philippines, Singapore, Sri Lanka, Surinam, Thailand, Trinidad Tobago and Vietnam.

Rama's story seems to have travelled along three routes, according to well-known social commentator, Santosh Desai. "By land, the northern route took the story from the Punjab and Kashmir into China, Tibet and East Turkestan; by sea, the southern route carried the story from Gujarat and South India into Java, Sumatra and Malaya; and again by land, the eastern route delivered the story from Bengal into Burma, Thailand and Laos. Vietnam and Cambodia obtained their stories partly from Java and partly from India via the eastern route."

Versions Galore

There are thousands of versions of *Ramayana* available in different countries, continents and cultures. Some of these include Cambodia—*Ramakirti*, Thailand—*Ramakien*, Laos—*Phra Lak Phra Lam*, Myanmar—*Yama Zatdaw*, Malaysia—*Hikayat Seri Rama*, Indonesia—*Kakawin Ramayana*, Japan—*Hobutsushu* and China—*Tun-huang*.

In Java, Indonesia reenactments and retellings of *Ramayana* continue to this day even though this is a predominantly Muslim island. In the Hindu island of Bali the epic forms a central part of the religious identity and worship. In Malaysia even today shadow puppet reenactments are prevalent in the deeply conservative Muslim states of Kelantan and Terengganu. In Thailand these stories play a role in the lives of Thai Theravada Buddhists from incorporation in architecture to traditional dancing. In the rather mysterious Kingdom of Cambodia and the communist state of Laos too this Hindu epic continues to form a central part of the many diverse cultures one encounters there.

I bring you two popular versions. In Jain telling the Rama story no longer carries Hindu values. In these versions, Ravana is a great man undone by a passion that he has vowed against but that he cannot resist. In another tradition of the Jain *Ramayanas*, Sita is Ravana's daughter although he does not know it. In that sense his story is further complicated by an oedipal situation. Thus according to the Jains, Ravana is a tragic figure to be admired and pitied rather than feared and hated.

When we go outside India to South-east Asia, we meet with a variety of tellings of the Rama story in Tibet, Thailand, Burma, Laos, Cambodia, Malaysia, Java and Indonesia. Here we shall look at only one example, the Thai *Ramakien*.

Rama is seen as a human hero and the *Ramakien* is not regarded as a religious work or even as an exemplary work. The Thais enjoy most the sections about the abduction of Sita and the war. Partings and reunions, which are the heart of the Hindu *Ramayanas*, are not as important as the excitement and the details of war, the techniques, the fabulous weapons. Desai says this Thai emphasis on war is significant: early Thai history is full of wars; their concern was survival. The focus in the *Ramakien* is not on family values and spirituality. Thai audiences are more fond of Hanuman than of Rama. Neither celibate nor devout, as in the Hindu *Ramayana*, here Hanuman is quite a ladies' man who does not at all mind looking into the bedrooms of Lanka and does not consider seeing another man's sleeping wife anything immoral, as Valmiki's Hanuman does.

Ravana too is different here. The *Ramakirti* admires Ravana's resourcefulness and learning. His abduction of Sita is seen as an act of love and is viewed with sympathy. The Thais are moved by Ravana's sacrifice of family, kingdom and life itself for the sake of a woman. Unlike Valmiki's characters, which are either black or white the Thai ones have shades of grey. The fall of Ravana here makes one sad. It is not an occasion for unadulterated rejoicing, as it is in Valmiki.

Patterns of Difference

A.K. Ramanujan's take on this aspect makes for riveting reading, "Now, is there a common core to the different versions of the Ramayana? Or is it like Aristotle's jackknife? When the philosopher asked an old carpenter how long he had had his knife, the latter said, "Oh, I've had it for thirty years. I've changed the blade a few times and the handle a few times but it's the same knife." On a closer look it seems the various versions are like a collection of people with the same proper name, they make a class in name alone.

Genres of *Ramayana*

The *Ramayana* has fascinated and inspired poets, writers, sculptors, painters, musicians, dancers, puppeteers and singers all over Asia. I shall be discussing in brief a few of the most important genres:

Kohn Ramayana (Thailand)

In Thailand, the Kohn Ramayana, a masked dance, is performed only on special occasions. The performers are required to switch into different modes in order to express emotion and to further the plot. An important factor *of* Kohn is that the performers do not speak. A narrator directs the dancers in the story.

Kecak (Indonesia)

The Kecak dance dates from the 1920s and is a creation of the famous German artist Walter Spies in coordination with Balinese priests. About 60 men sit on the ground in concentric circles to perform the dance. In the middle of the inner circle, burning torches are placed and in their light, the dancers perform episodes from the *Ramayana*. The men in the outer circles use their voices and postures to support the performers. The dance attracts many tourists.

Wayang Kulit (Indonesia)

An important form of indigenous theater is puppetry, of which the most celebrated is the Wayang Kulit, a shadow play of Java. These plays are magical and mysterious. The puppeteer (dalang) uses leather puppets to narrate *Ramayana* episodes. The play is performed against a white screen while a lantern in the background casts the shadows of the characters on the screen. The audience sits in front to watch the shadow figures, but it is possible to sit behind the screen and watch the dalang (puppeteer) at work.

Values in *Ramayana*

As far as children's fiction is concerned possibly *Ramayana* offers a complete package without transgressing the boundaries of correctness. It combines the elements of folk lore, fantasy, realistic fiction, inspirational stories, anthromorphic tales to create a collage which is unrivalled in the world.

Almost every character, every situation has a tale to tell. And most of these stories are as relevant today as they were when they were penned thousands of years ago.

Apart from the main story of Rama and Sita there are many other tales interwoven in the epic—each more delectable than the other.

I have tried to list some of the values so beautifully brought out in this great epic.

1. Family values: The bonding between Rama and Sita, Rama and Lakshmana.
2. Loyalty and faith: Rama's loyalty to Dasratha and Bharata's loyalty to Rama.
3. Devotion and dedication: Hanuman's devotion to Rama.
4. Team spirit and team work: The way a rather assorted army of humans, monkeys, bears and other creatures takes on the mighty Lankan king in his lair and trounces him exemplifies the triumph of team work.

5. Resilience/will to win: Rama and Lakshmana pursue the search for Sita against all odds and then attack the all powerful Ravana speaks volumes for their resilience.
6. Ends and means: Rama kills Bali by deception because he has wronged Sugriva—classic case of end justifying the means.
7. Triumph of good over evil: Ravana who personifies evil, despite his power, is vanquished and killed by Rama who epitomizes good.

These values are universal and eternal. Modern children's writers can use these values in contemporary settings to create a literature which is endearing, enduring and everlasting.

Thus, *Ramayana* can be transplanted and transposed not only in terms of its story line but also in terms of its core values, not only in terms of its style but also in terms of its substance, not only in terms of its form but also in terms of its content.

Case Study

I am taking here the liberty of using my novel *Now or Never* to illustrate how children's writers can achieve synergy between the ethos of the *Ramayana* and modern day sensibilities and compulsions and create fiction which is hopefully inspiring and enriching.

Now or Never is a tale of the relationship between a father and a son. Shiva puts at stake his boxing career to save his son, Rajat. In the process he all but destroys himself. When Rajat grows up he decides to resurrect his papa's career and life, with the help of his friends. The novel describes how Rajat helps Shiva foil the machinations of a match-fixing syndicate to win the most important fight of his life.

The book, which is set in the 'Here and Now' has all the values which define *Ramayana*: Family values, loyalty, faith, determination, team spirit, resilience and finally the triumph of good over evil.

The main characters are ordinary people who face extraordinary situations, not with magic wands and potions but with their intrinsic weapons of courage and conviction, guts and gumption. The solutions to the conflicts are entirely in the realm of pragmatism. The denouement is convincing and the novel ends on a note of optimism and hope.

Kamishibai

Finally, I would like to end with my own experience of adaptation and transition. A Santhali folk tale written by me in English has been adapted as *Kamishibai.* The traditional form of storytelling in Japan. The story entitled 'The Wise Kanhu' is being performed by the artists of International Kamishibai Association of Japan (TKAJA) in different countries and various languages including Spanish, Basque and of course Japanese.

In the process of adaptation, the folk tale has added cultural nuances of its own. It has also acquired its very own character, syntax and idiom while at the same time retaining its intrinsic value and ethos. As a product of two different cultures and the seamless blending of two mediums, the Kamishibai is a vibrant example of adaptation and transition of tales.

Conclusion

Great literature can never be confined in the boundaries of time, space and genre. Tales for children can be adapted to transcend boundaries of time, space, culture and genre. The creators of children's literature should make every attempt to draw from the reservoirs of their own culture as well as look beyond and help create a body of literature which is eternal.

By adapting, transcreating and transposing tales they should craft a universe of creativity, imagination and human values that can provide succor and sustenance, wisdom and learning and above all hope and healing to humankind.

REFERENCES

Bedekar Vijay, "History of Migration of Panchatantra and What It can Teach Us", presented at the Seminar on "Suhbashita, Panchatantra & Gnomic Literature in Ancient & Medievel India", 27 December 2008.

Goldman, Robert P., "The Ramayana of Valmiki: Introduction and Translation", Princter Univerity Press, 1984.

Desai, Santosh N. "*Ramayana:* An Instrument of Historical Contact and Cultural Transmission between India and Asia." *Journal of Asian Studies* 30, No. 1 (November 1970): 5-20.

Ramanujan, A.K. "Three Hundred Ramayanas: Five Examples and Three Thoughts on Translation." In *Many Ramayanas: The Diversity of a Narrative Tradition in South Asia*, edited by Paula Richman, pp. 22-49. Berkeley: University of California Press, 1991.

Welcome Address, Professor Umashankar Joshi, *Variations in Ramayana in Asia: Their Cultural, Social and Anthropological Significance*, Conference: New Delhi, January 8-10, 1981, pp. 21-28.

Sinha, D.P. and Sachchidanand Sahai. *Ramayana Tradition and National Cultures in Asia.* Government of Uttar Pradesh, Lucknow: Directorate of Cultural Affairs, 1989, p. 26.

Sarkar, H.B. "The Ramayana in South East Asia: A General Survey." *Variations in Ramayana in Asia: Their Cultural, Social and Anthropological Significance.* Madras: Diocesan Press, 1983, pp. 206-20.

Kumar, Ramendra, *Now or Never*, Ponytale Books, New Delhi, 2010.

The Wise Kanhu, original story: Ramendra Kumar, translation and adaptation: Etsuko Nozaka, illustrated by Seizo Tashima, published by Doshinsha Publishing Co., Ltd., 2007.

16

Vijay Tendulkar's Children's Plays: A Synthesis of Children's Fantasy and Social Commitment

Beena Agarwal

Children's literature as a literature with distinctive identity and paradigms, has been a subject of debates and arguments. Beyond the rigid convention of aesthetics, children's literature aims at fantasy and consequently it diverts in the comfort zone of human consciousness sacrificing the commitments of aesthetics and social realism. For its focus on amusement and fantasy, it is often supposed to be lacking in high academic standards and the essential requisites of artistic canons. Isabel Jan reinforces the point "On Children's Literature". To quote:

> Critics—always ready to distribute either good or bad marks—are prepared to judge this 'by product' by academic standards and to declare that one of its productions is or is not 'literature' or is not 'well written' and that stands or does not stand a chance of becoming a classic scholastic disputes on this order only disguise the truth, which is that such works exist in their own right and not as rungs on the ladder to adult reading or that of middle class citizens reared on the humanities. To say that a book is a 'first-step' or that an author is an 'imitator' is to subscribe to a preposterous belief in a formidable staircase negotiated easily by some —who take it merrily two steps at a time—while others

> puff and plod or simply settle down contentedly on the first flight. (Jan., 142-43)

It is evident that literature meant for children flourishes on the poetics of the flights of imagination and enjoyment. However in the process of enjoyment, it often pokes at that recess of unrevealed human consciousness that moves in the direction of 'awareness' and 'self-growth'. It is not only 'art' not only meant to 'instruct and delight', not only just "imitation" but also consists of "all works of imagination which are transmitted primarily by means of the written word or spoken narrative. That is in the main novels, stories and poetry—with the addition of those works of non-fiction which by their qualities of style or insight may be said to offer experience of a literary nature" (Townsend, 1971). In spite of the abundance of fantasy, children's books have strong impressions on child's psyche and they prove to be instrumental in deciding the direction of their consciousness in the totality of human experiences. Such books are "culturally formative and of massive importance educationally, intellectually and socially. Perhaps more than any other text, they reflect society as it wishes to be, as it wishes to be seen as it unconsciously reveals itself to be" (Anderson, 47). Fantasy, anti-ethical, anti-intellectual parameters determine the quality of children's literature but in the celebration of the autonomy of fantasy, it helps a child to develop the resistance of horrors or reality that he is likely to fall in the days of maturity and unconsciously in Freudian terms it satisfies the instincts that are dominated by pleasure principle. Hence, the fantasy and amusement in children's literature help to restore a balance of human personality. It is said:

> This elementary wonder however is not a mere fancy derived from the fairy tales. On the contrary all the fire of fairy tales is derived from this. Just as we all like love tales because there is an instinct of sex, we like astonishing tales because they touch the nerve of the ancient instinct of astonishment. This is proved by the fact that when we are very young children, we do not

> need fairy tales, we only tales. Mere life is interesting enough. (Chesterton, 79)

Beyond the canons of philosophy and religion, children are fascinated by the Concept of wonder, Nature, Ghost, Death, Mimicry, Ridicule and Astonishment.

Vijay Tendulkar, the pillar of Marathi Theatre, explored new horizons in the realm of Indian English drama with his six children's plays that are translated by Dr. Ajay Joshi and have appeared under the title *Vijay Tendulkar: Five Plays for Children* in the year 2008. Sulbha Deshpande, the pioneer of the Experimental Theatre Movement in Maharashtra urged Tendulkar to write some plays for his school boys. In an interview in 2006, Sulbha Deshpande revealed that she saw in Tendulkar's children's plays all the things that she felt essential in the plays for children. The situation, the language, the paraphernalia and stage mechanism are appropriate to cope up children's world of fantasy and imagination. It is said:

> Tendulkar wrote with surprising gentleness and innocence, with no lecturing on values or forced judgements. The plays were kept open-ended for the children to interpret. He stressed movement and body language rather than the spoken language. The characters were real and children could identify with them. Most importantly, the plays raised many questions for reader and viewer.

Besides of amusement and fantasy in Tendulkar plays, the synthesis of social concern and the awareness of personal relationship imparts an exceptional sublimity to Indian Theatrical History. The child-like sensibility hidden in the consciousness of the dramatist makes the fabric of children's plays of Tendulkar, fit for enduring popularity.

> Each of these plays is distinct in form and content. Yet the common thread that runs through them all is the fact that they present themes pertinent to children to children and their waved, their thinking, their relationships at home, in school and with their friends. (Joshi, "Introduction")

The very first play in the volume of Tendulkar's Children plays, *Missing: A Father* abounds in all fanciful situations that can stir the consciousness and sensibility of children. Tendulkar makes experiment with the negotiations of animate and inanimate objects. The five non-living objects like Pole, Tree, Letterbox, Crow and Dancer are presented as living characters making reflections on their own conditions. The Pole makes a pathetic confession, "standing here all night, drenched in the rain, lashed by the down pour from the sky, holding on for dear life to lamp...it's unbearable" (3). Tree reveals its anguish, "Whenever it rains, I think of that night. It sends a shiver down my back" (3). Similarly, letter box reveals his agony, "so what if I am a letter box—that doesn't mean, I don't get bored standing in one place all the time" (6). These innocent confessions in children's play provide opportunity for children to identify themselves with the objects of nature. As a foil to the innocence of these objects, Tendulkar presents the kidnapper who has already kidnapped an innocent girl. The idea of kidnapping children arose fear and pity fit for the imagination of children. However even kidnapper instead of any horrible intentions makes an honest confession of his hunger and it is appropriate to introduce amusement fit for children's imagination. He said, "My stomach is ready bothering me." His innocent idea of leaving the girl unprotected for the sake of hunger prepares a dramatic situation appropriate for a children's play. In absence of kidnapper, the short repartee of Letterbox, Tree and Pole is interesting as well as indicative of emerging human apathy in contemporary society. Tree is determined, "I say, we can't let this happen" and simultaneously asserts, "There could be nothing more wicked than kidnapping small children" (9). Such observation suggests that Tendulkar uses fanciful situation to expose his social concern. In the later part of the play *Missing: A Father*, the dramatist successfully projects the psychology of child in absence of the parents. As soon as the girl gets consciousness, she hysterically cries out, "Where is my house, where is my father? Where is my mother? Where am I" (10). Amusement paves a way to suspense and mystery. However from dramatic point of view to reduce the dramatic tension, Tendulkar presents the idea how letterbox walks and talks. Girls fancy blooms with these ideas and there appears an "endless flow of people". The innocence of the girl becomes a mechanism to manipulate the desired dramatic situation. Girl even does not know the name of the street and the name of her father. This innocence of girl contributes to enhance dramatic tension. The anxiety of Pole, Tree and Letterbox is appealing. However, their fantastic suggestions to provide protection to the girl are fantastic but they are powerful enough to retain the undertone of human sympathy. The consolation provided by them help the girl to overcome her extreme fear. Such conversion of children's emotions provides dramatic relief. The fear and insecurity of man is a mockery of the whole situation. It generates fun and amusement fit for children's fancy.

The play *Bobby's Story* is also a suggestive play with the child as the protagonist. Here Tendulkar with all tenderness tries to reconstruct the inner world of child consciousness. It is a dramatic account of the agony of a child, who inherits the pain of gender discrimination and survives in the atmosphere of isolation and insecurity. The play begins with a long self-narrative dialogue of Bobby the protagonist who makes a confession, "I am Bobby, actually I'm Bobby but parents wanted a baba, so I became Bobby. Now everyone calls me Bobby. I have boy's clothes and boy's games" (25). She also makes a confession of her impassioned longing for her parents who all the time remain busy in their works, "I get the keys from the neighbours, open the door and play on my own. But I get on bored playing alone. Then I go and stand in the balcony, climb on to the windows and sing songs at the top of my voice but Ma doesn't come" (25). Such an emotional beginning of drama is quite conducive to grip the sensibility of children. Sympathy exercises a deep impact on the sensibility of children. As a foil to her personal suffering, the idea of Birbal and Akbar is quite amusing. The idea of Akbar and Birbal coming to school with their attendants among children fires the imagination of children. Akbar behaves as an innocent school boy and Bobby becomes their teacher. Akbar's imploring, 'M-m-miss, may come in" and Bobby's assertion of authority,

"Hold your toes and stand" is quite amusing. Bobby in her role as history teacher assumes an authentic role and her imitation suggests Wordsworth's thesis that a child's life is "limitless imitation". After these two dimensions, the entry of Micky with its urge, "I'm hungry" contributes to another dimension of child consciousness. Bobby's idea of sharing biscuit with Mickey is quite suggestive to expose the sensibility of child. Bobby innocently confesses, "There's only one biscuit, okay, this is what we'll do. You take half, and I will take other half" (29). The dialogue of Bobby and Mickey regarding the poor quality of ration inside ration shops is funny but instructive. In between these, two dimensions, the image of moon is delicate and suggestive. Moon, Mickey and Emperor Akbar all collectively suggests the images to give an insight into the consciousness of child. As a subtext of the play, in Bobby's loneliness born out of the professional engagement of mothers is suggestive of Tendulkar's obsessive concern of the disintegration of families in the wake of post Industrial social structure. Birbal almost becomes the spokesmen of Tendulkar, "If you want my wise opinion, ever since mothers have started going to work, this has been the state of small children like Bobby" (25). Shivaji's suggestion of breaking down such offices is quite fantastical. However behind this fantasy Birbal has a realization of the horror of reality that has robbed children of their paternal protection and home comforts, "No, no, if the offices are broken down, where will the money come from? If there's no money, how will Bobby's mother and father get all these nice toys clothes and food? If there is no money, you can't even get ration and milk, you know" (35). The shadows of gloom hovers but soon Akbar's suggestion of ensuring the distribution of money from ration shops converts the situation and the clouds of gloom dispels. Horse Laughs and connects, "If money is given in the ration, people will mix it in their rice and dal and gabble-gabble it all up. Or they'll put it in their tea and stir it" (36). Gradually, the play moves in the direction of a conclusion where each of them is anxious regarding the safety and recue of Bobby. The dialogues are witty. Birbal advises, "Whatever we have, we must share it equally" (38). Shivaji immediately retorts, "you think Bobby's a kingdom, to be divided and shared" (39). Finally, they ask Bobby about her choice of going, she wakes of her dream and in all innocence sings:

> Underneath the ocean, mossy stoles
> Draped over them, are creepers of jewes
> within that a kingdom, where fairies stay
> There, Oh, there I want
> to go today. (40)

It provides a dream-like and fairy-like quality on the play that is quite appropriate to expose child's sensibility. All the images constructed in the play seem to be a projection of the unconscious fantasies existing in the consciousness of Bobby. The confession of the parents of their going to see a movie in contrast to the anguish of Bobby is quite touching. Bobby still remains in illusion and pours out the very core of her consciousness in the form of her longing to be lulled in the hands of her parents. Bobby's stay no longer remains a drama of personal anguish but the confession of human apathy. The last speech in the play is the suggestive exposition of the inner world of child's consciousness. Her innocence is praiseworthy when she confesses:

> I am not really asleep. I'm awake. But don't tell them, Okay! Otherwise, Ma and Papa of will get busy with their work and forget to pamper me. Then what? I like to cuddle into my Ma's arms. And its such fun sitting on my Papa's shoulders. Now they will find, the boy. Then Ma and Papa will open the door and come in. I'll pretend to be asleep. Mama'll wake me up gently. Papa will pat me, he'll say, "Bobby Sweetie Pie" and make a fuss of me, he will pick me up and take me upon on his shoulders. Once Ma feeds me all the tasty food. I'll burp loudly and with papa on one side and Ma on the other, and me in the middle, we'll all to sleep. (42)

In this play, Tendulkar employs child, innocent sensibility as the focal point to expose the structure of drama. The sensibility coupled with sentimentality becomes a significant mechanism to suit the atmosphere of child's play. The idea of parental care corresponding with the sensibility of child is suggestive of the serious social purpose of the dramatist.

Absurdity, incongruity of human behaviour and the flight of fantasy constitutes the cardinal core of child sensibility. The play *The Play of Nosey Parker* is designed on the lines of such fantastic situations. These situations are significant to manipulate strong dramatic content full of mirth and laughter but it often lacks in serious socio-philosophical concern. It is based on the favourite Indian myth of *Andhernagri Chopat Raja, Taka Ser Bhaji, Taka Ser Khaja*. The basic structure of the plot is designed on the requisites of child's sensibility. It begins with the crying of prince. The Doctor, Queen, King and Prime Minister are perplexed on the cause of the pain and cry of the child prince. King is irritated on his failure to find out appropriate remedy for the crying of the prince. King in his snobbery is busy not only in finding out the appropriate meaning of the words but is also restless to find out the meaning of the word 'Son'. From the word 'Son', the imagination shifts to the image of 'Sun' with scorching heat. King without giving any second thought to the whole scenario admits:

> Something must be alone quickly about this. This new sun which has been scorching my son's I mean my boy's feet, has to be dealt with. (50)

He immediately summons all his ministers to find out a plan to obstruct the heat of Sun. Prime Minister to appease the King comes out with a fantastic suggestion, "I'll tell you what! Put a canopy across the sky so the Sun's rays will fall on it and not heat up the ground" (52). King immediately subscribes the view and gives a fanciful suggestions, "Tell the construction in-charge to employ as many as workmen as he needs, buy as much as sackcloth as possible and prepare a large canopy right across the sky" (52). The idea of the canopy of sackcloth to cover the heat of sun is improbable and it brings lot of fun. The second suggestion of spraying cool water around the sun is also amazing. It also ends in foolhardiness. Finally the Prime Minister advises, "Use up all the ammunition in the kingdom, if you have to but destroy the sun" (53). Amid this chaos, the appearance of Sidhwa in rags makes King to doubt his identity as spy. They arrest him and make design to wipe him out putting on the mouth of canons. The misery born out of his chaos makes the position of the stranger pathetic. They do not permit him to speak out. First soldier without caring for his words orders, "Didn't I tell you to shut up, stupid? Why do you keep poking your nose in and asking these pointless questions" (59). Like other characters Sidhwa also comes forward with a suggestion. In spite of his wretched condition, he directs all of them to shut their eyes and then from his sack, he takes out a pair of old tattered slippers and with all confidence asserts, "This is the solution to the problem of the sun" (6). Prince bears the slippers and in all gaiety plays in the light of sun. Prince jumping up and down sings, "The sun is defeated, the sun is defeated! Now my feet don't burn anymore. Now I can play as much as I want, now I can have lots of fun" (62). King in all joy cries out, "Incredible! What an Idea! What intelligence, Wah! Wah! Wah! Wah! Wah! Wah!" (62). King considers him the most intelligent person and the real Prime Minister is dismissed and he is appointed as a Prime Minister. Sidhwa putting on the airs of the Prime Minister order Army Chief, "from today anyone who pokes his nose into other people's affairs will be given the title of 'Nosey Parker' and every one will bow to him. I was made the Prime Minister because I poked my nose and asked pointless questions" (63). In this play, Vijay Tendulkar with the manipulation of improbable situations considerably creates atmosphere to fit for the imagination of children.

The play *The King and Queen Want Sweet* is a humorous and instructive dramatic rendering of the concept of the 'dignity of labour'. The plot of the play is constructed on the ignorance of the king who in his luxury remains unmindful of the value of hard labour in human life. The setting of the play is like that of a puppet play where the King and Queen come on the stage in dancing followed by attendants. Here the word play is used as a major theatrical device and it proves quite effective to inspire children. Ring Leader in the beginning asks about the identity of King and King innocently remarks, "I am the King of this kingdom" (68). Ring Leader in rhytimical mode hints at their luxurious life:

They've sackful of money in their home
They have milk and honey every day.
They sing and dance their days away.
For them everyday's a holiday. (48)

The King and Queen possess and strange desire to have sweat. It seems an strange desire and King feels himself humiliated on the realty "Sweat only drips when you toil and perspire" (68). The King and the Brahmin in their own way try to sort out the problem of the King. However without any seriousness of purpose, in their own way, like a wooden character, they join the chorus and reflect on the condition of the King and Queen. In their chorus, they make a criticism how luxury is not the basis of human pleasure:

How pleased the King will get,
If that works, that swear!
Human sweat
Real sweat
The king hardwork begets. (75)

Even businessman who only worships money fails to get the pleasure of real human sweat in life. Businessman is confused on the demand of sweat and makes an innocent confession, "I don't have sweat of that kind. I never sweat. Ask for jewellery—of gold or silver, of pearls or rubies" (77). Finally they caught hold of a worker and a farmer. Worker makes search in all directions but they were not in a position to reveal the real secret of sweat. However King looking at the condition of different professional in his state concludes, "In this kingdom no one works." In the meanwhile Ring Leader declares, "The post for hanging will be erected, Sampat Sampaji will be selected. However King comes to the realization that his own lethargy is responsible for the dearth of production and prosperity in the town. King's sudden decision to offer himself for sacrifice, so that he can sweat and the laziness can be removed from their land:

I became lazy
So many subjects got lazy

I shunned hardwork
My subjects did too.
I laid the rules
They followed them
I am very, very unhappy today
Nothing can atone for my sing,
No matter what, I won't he happy again.
Therefore, Today I am going to hang.
At least, after I'm gone,
my people will work
hard, toil hard and bring
glory to the kingdom and
grace to mankind. This is my last wish. (90)

As the play ends, the Ring Leader and Attendants enter singing. They move as if in preparation to go. The King also joins them. The hectic movements in preparation for work, accompanied by music, beats and rhythmic work activity (91).

The situations in the play are also quite appropriate both for amusement and enlightenment. King's fortitudes become quite effective for the imagination and fun of children.

The play *The Wedding of the Village Headman's Daughter*, is an humorous dramatic rendering of the persistent conflict of the native life and city life. The selection of names and situations are quite appropriate to cater the innocent imagination of children. Dhondu, is the protagonist of the play and he performs the role of a drummer. The combination of Dhondu, the Drummer helps to instruct fun for children. In all ego, Dhondu introduces himself, "I am Dhondu, the drummer. No one for miles around plays the drum like I do" (95) and at the outset, he declares to beat the drum at "headman's daughter". In consonance with folk theatre tradition, he uses hyperbole with the implied suggestions the beats of drum, "with these very hands, I played the kettle drum—kad kad kad kad dhum...kadhum...kadhum. That was when Ganpat the grocer became deaf" (5). The initial dialogues between Nahray and Dhondu furnish ample information about the state affairs in the state in the village. Dhondu is informed that there will be a city band in the marriage. Dhondu is disgusted to listen it and admits, "The drum doesn't have the same sound as the band...none of the sparkle of colourful satin clothes, none of those foreign tunes, of that style" (102). A feeling of inferiority grips his consciousness, "I won't go for the procession. I won't even go for the wedding. From now on I will not play the drum at any wedding" (102). For introducing ample fun, Tendulkar introduces the character of Bajaya, the stammer. Dhondu, the drummer becomes a spokesmen of Tendulkar when he points out the difference of rural and urban life. "Everyone wants the band. No one wants the drum. They wear colourful, satinlaced dresses, they're loud, and they play foreign songs. Besides, they're from the city. Our work is crude, unsophisticated, they are many, am one" (104). Bajaya with with his stammering voice makes fun that often appeal the young audience inside the theatre. In Bajaya handicapped, Tendulkar expresses his sympathy for these physically handicapped character. Dhondu forgetting his own misery, expresses his sympathy for the wretched existence of Dhondu, "Poor chap he's a cripple a stanner and also stupid. He's good nurtured but what's the use? The whole village makes fun of him. They shoo him away. People say, ask Bajaya a question and then go and have your dinner, take a nap and come back to hear his answer..." (107). In this play, Bandwals appear with their numeral identity without any definite, name identity but their observations on rural life are witty and acute. They ridicule rural life for the lack of elements and the lack of motor cars. First Bandwala remarks, "Man, these village people...just too backward" (108). Second comments, "...And we play foreign songs, what will your ignorant public and his villagers understand anyway?" (108). There occurs lot of a chaos in the band because there was all pervasive darkness. In the darkness, there are the fears of moving images of ghosts, jackals, Tigers. Everyone is frightened and a chaos is created in the band. Such situations are quite conducive in children's plays because the chaos of human intelligence provides enough opportunity for mirth and laughter.

REFERENCES

Anderson, Nancy, *Elementary Children's Literature*, Boston: Pearson Education, 2006.

Chesterton, G.K. "The Ethics of Elfland", *Orthodoxy* (1908) Reprinted from G.K. Chesterton: A Selection of his non-fictional prose selected by W.H. Auden, Faber and Faber, 1970.

Jan, Isabel. *On Children's Literature*, Allen Lave, 1969.

Joshi, Ajay. "Introduction", *Vijay Tendulkar: Five Plays for Children*, New York: Scholarastic India Pvt. Limited, 2008.

Townsend John Rowe. "Standards of Criticism for Children's Literature" from ALA Children's Services Division, Top of News, 1971.

17

In Love with Fantasy: The Fleeting and Seductive World in/of Lewis Carroll's Fiction for Children

Anirban Gupta

One of the greatest verities of history is that the Germans and the English have always been at loggerheads. Professor Southerland Orr, during one of his classic renditions of Shakespeare's *The Tempest,*[1] almost in a sort of musical digression, suggested that the Germans have taught the English two words, 'bastard' and 'bloody'. He was, in fact, fantasizing a reality—ignoring, denigrating and taking by the scruff of the neck the German culture that had not given the world a Bach or an Einstein, but also the crucial literary concept of *Zeitgeist*[2] (in German, "time-spirit"). The whole tradition of European literature, as T.S. Eliot suggested, from Homer downwards, is united in a single line of continuous developing tradition and the vital thread of connection, as (Richard) Shusterman suggested, is provided by the *Zeitgeist.*

The concept of *Zeitgeist* relates a connection between 'Time' and 'Space' which has been held/advocated by scholars as different from Mikhail Bakhtin to Frank Kermode. Looking back at Professor Orr's denigration of the German culture it is quite possible that indirect nudges and winks which form a part of irony and innuendo are, in fact, an integral part of life, as Thomas Hardy suggests in *Life's Little Ironies* (1894). The Russeauian denigration/deprecation/vilification of traditional education for his imaginary son 'Emile' boiled/boils down to the demand for the element of 'fantasy' in children's curricula. Herodotus' explication of history in terms of poetry and Plato's description of poets as "winged creatures" replace in subtle ways the charm and need for fantasy in literature. If life involves ironies and innuendos, it *also* involves the fantastic and the unreal, for how would ironies operate without fantasy? Take away from Pope's *Epistle to Dr. Arbuthnot* (1735) the element of fantasy, and you have the ugly ludicrousness of bitter and trenchant spite.

Therefore, fantasy *is* a part of life which infiltrates not only the ironies of life but also its philosophies. The Frostian or Keatsian philosophies would pale into insignificance without fantasy, and the beautiful worlds of Marquez and Rushdie would be indented *without* fantasy. When Carroll took up the element of fantasy as a major trope in his fictional world, he was doing nothing new, but simply extending the domain of fantasy, creating a blurred interface between fantasy *and* reality, where one teases and titillates the other in a charming and seductive series of pictures and counter-pictures, parts and counter-parts.

If fantasy as a fictional genre contains/incorporates elements that are barely realistic, and is characterized by a departure from the accepted rules whereby individuals perceive the world around them, it is also heavily reliant/dependent for effect on strangeness of setting (such as other worlds or times) and of characters (such as supernatural or unnatural beings). The entire narrative of *Alice's Adventures in Wonderland* (1865-66) takes place in Alice's dream, which is why the characters and phenomena of the real world mix with elements of Alice's unconscious state. This dream motif succinctly explains the abundance of nonsensical and disparate events in the story.

In fantasy, the chief premise is the protagonist's transition between "chronotopes" or "forms of time"[3] which Bakhtin formulates as "an interdependent unity between space and time in a literary text". Alice believes at a point that even though she exists *in* the middle/centre of a fairytale, all her encounters with the grotesque creatures and incidents over there are *actually* part of reality. The initial setting of fantasy literature is reality: a riverbank in Oxford (as in *Alice's Adventures in Wonderland*), or an armchair at home with her kitten (as in *Through the Looking Glass*), wherefrom (the) characters are transported into some magical realm; and, most often, safely brought back (at the end of her "adventures" Alice finds herself awake on her sister's lap, back at/on the riverbank; or at home holding Kitty at the end of *Through the Looking Glass*).

All literary works function by means of language, or "forms";[4] and since language must invariably choose *which* aspects of the thing it is to discuss, delineate, or focus on and represent, they are always abstract, for something *has* to be left out. 'Realistic' art, therefore, does *not* represent an external reality any more than does 'fantastic' art. Throughout the 'Alice' books, talking animals counteract/interact with Alice in perfect human language, cakes and drinks and mushroom have the magical effect on physical size/height, a deck of playing cards or a gigantic cheeseboard with eccentric chessmen sprout up or engage in funny battles or tussles among each other/themselves to question and challenge Alice's perception of reality, the 'present' is held in suspension *through* an eternity, and so on.

"Never imagine yourself not to be otherwise than what it might appear to others that what you were or might have been was not otherwise than what you had been would have appeared to them to be otherwise."

Chapter IX—The Mock Turtle's Story; *Alice's Adventures in Wonderland*

As it were, what we perceive *as* common sense may be *no* more than the product of our particular cultural prejudices. In *Alice's Adventures in Wonderland*, Alice, in projecting herself as a functional non-entity, appears to have been partially lost in a framework/cauldron of common sense distorted, diluted and reversed amid the topsy-turvy world of Wonderland, whose residents feel unconcerned about the lack of a definite referential frame for belief and rationale whereby to substantiate their eccentric views. As K.C. Cole,[5] in exploring the nature of sine waves, has observed how

> ...Carroll conceived of Alice herself *as* a clock pendulum in her encounter with the opposing forces of gravity during her back-and-forth fall through the *bottomless* rabbit hole....

Within an extremely humorous framework of nonsense and fantasy, the first book of "Alice" uses frequent changes in size as a plot device, and draws on the imagery of playing cards, while in the second book, Carroll plays on frequent shifts in time scale and special directions as a plot device, and draws on the imagery of Chase. Fantasy also allows room for a host of other, minor themes, including (the concept of) opposites, time running backwards, and so on. Likewise, Carroll wields language as a unique tool for amusing children—while also instilling in their minds some of life's elemental aspects of knowledge: the various quotes in both texts may appear or seem at first rather mundane, but *essentially*, on a deeper reading, they turn out to be abundant/ rich in truisms and life's great philosophies. Carroll's prime aim is to produce a shiny surface featuring both text and images, sensible and insensible, civilized and savage, as well as appearance and reality, a panoramic world of exquisite wonder, enough to entertain children across generations and cultures, keeping in mind that they are more receptive than adults to fantasy and imagination—their only viable means of wish-fulfilment, and that to the child's eye fantasy and reality are very close to each other, which leads them quite occasionally to indulge in fantasies.

Wonderland offers glimpses into a space populated by strange creatures and fanatical feats, where man is denied entry except on the vehicle of fantasy and dreams. Things exist there almost "unsubstantially"—and the disappearance of reality/ dissolving of a concrete figure—if any—into some gesture or laughter (like the floating green of the Cheshire Cat) adds to a pervasive sense of make-believe.

Fantasy almost invariably entails/necessitates wish-fulfilment. Towards the opening of *Through the Looking-*

The basic principles, or the "ground rules",[7] of fantasy is evident from the novel's unrealistic setting as well as Carroll's use of anthropomorphic animals (animals who/that can speak, think and act, though not quite sensibly, *like* humans) in obvious realistic terms. In Chapter 1 of *Alice's Adventures in Wonderland,* as the animals get engaged in drying themselves off through a performance of the mysterious/queer 'Caucus-Race', Alice eventually frightens them away, unwittingly, by talking about her cat: birds must find 'various pretexts' to leave her/Alice alone, being fearful of cats as their predators. Even the more abstract characters like the chessmen, the playing cards, or the White Queen, are *made* to follow a version of the real world's rules.

The idea of becoming a *real* queen upon a simple, sportive accomplishment is *too* impressive to be real, but the plot is so painstakingly, delightfully constructed/organized that, appointed/ranked as one of the White Queen's pawns, Alice *can* truly be crowned a queen at the end ("Queen Alice"), moments before she is allowed to wake up. By thus imbuing the narrative and the entire cast of characters with a charming feel of improbability and magic—though occasionally interspersed with the real and the rational—Carroll throws open the gateway to a deeper, more sympathetic understanding of fantasy as a thriving literary genre.

Dreaming, Alice enters the sunny spring garden—in *Through the Looking-Glass, and What Alice Found There* (1871)—upon leaving her house on a cold, snowy, wintry night and delights in meeting live flowers endowed with the power of human speech, who perceive her as being a "flower that can move about". She is impressed with the Red Queen's breathtaking speed, being the most "agile" of the chess pieces. Upon revealing to Alice that the entire countryside is laid out in squares like a gigantic cheeseboard, she offers to make Alice a queen *if* she can move all the way to the eighth rank/row in a chess match, thus tempting her into partaking of the game *in* person. Convinced, Alice embarks on the/her mission *as* one of the White Queen's pawns by boarding a train with a Goat, a Beetle and a man dressed in white paper, all of whom nag her until the train lurches to a halt. The train literally jumps over the third row and directly into the fourth rank, acting on the real-life chase principle that pawns *can* shift two spaces on their first move.

The element of *subjectivity* which is an integral part of Alice's fantastic vision emerges automatically from the novel's quasi-realistic setting and characterization. The subtle interplay between fantasy and reality here in Carroll's work/oeuvre is emblematic of a transition of the Self which refuses to address the "problem of knowing",[8] held by critics as a distinctive feature of fantasy literature. In portraying an extended psychological journey into the dream-like unconscious realm of fantasy, by way of fusing the elements of fantasy and inter-subjectivity, as well as the motifs of identity and non-identity, of the logical and the irrational, of time and timelessness, of innocence and maturity Carroll's literature/fictional world holds for adults and children alike a lasting appeal.

While/If she *does* exist in an eternal moment *out of time,* posing existential questions or issues of identity and confronts problems of maturation, in attending her through all her "adventures", one would feel that she *must* function in a metaphorical world where everyone is 'quite mad' and relationships are paradoxical. In addition to Alice's numerous meta-referential allusions as to her own fairy tale, Carroll delights in introducing a host of portmanteau words (such as 'Jabberwocky', 'brillig', 'gyre', 'mimsy', 'jubjub') with reference to Edward Lear (Carroll's contemporary) and James Joyce (who was 'reared' on the Alice books). Carroll's marvellous images are balanced by John Tenniel's illustrations, which caricatured real-life politicians like Disraeli (the Unicorn) and Gladstone (the Lion). It is in this unique blend/combination of text and image, of fantasy and reality, of the abstract and the concrete, that Alice's dual readership finds meaning and enjoyment.

As with H.G. Wells' *The Island of Dr. Moreau* (1896), with its bizarre and cruel experiments conducted upon imported, exotic animals, *Alice's Adventures in Wonderland* delightfully excites our childhood fancy/imagination by portraying an exotic realm of intrigue and mystery that floats somewhere between reality and the dream-world, where animals speak naturally *as* humans, evolution is tested and reality is *bent* until it *really* breaks—all tinged/furnished with an air of make-believe, which makes the unbelievable seem believable and vice versa, where perceptions and subjectivity are continually blurred and intermingled and hence are relentlessly challenged/thrown into question—only to be realigned for the sake of irony and introspection.

The story of *Alice's Adventures in Wonderland* opens with Alice getting bored, reading over her sister's shoulder and pondering/dwelling on the use of books "without pictures or conversation", something which implies her sleepiness/drowsiness and her subsequent 'fall' into the fantastic world of dreams. Immediately after, she glimpses/sees a White Rabbit is a waistcoat, racing/running close by her, across the field—worried that he might have been late a visible *action mmstbmg* which immediately catches her attention:

> ...it occurred to her that she *ought* to have wondered at this, but...it all seemed quite natural); but when the Rabbit actually TOOK A WATCH OUT OF ITS WAISTCOAT-POCKET, and looked at it, and then hurried on, Alice started to her feet, for it flashed across her mind that she had never before seen a rabbit with either a waistcoat-pocket, or a watch to take out of it, and burning with curiosity, she ran....

Chapter 1: Down the Rabbit-Hole; *Alice's Adventures in Wonderland*

Once in the full grip of fantasy, Alice delves into what turns out to be an eccentric, 'mad' world, where to retain one's innate sense of measure and order and judgement is always in the danger of getting lost and dissolved into the arbitrary set of rules, chaos and conflicts characteristic of the adult human world. Though the narrator concludes that part of his purpose is to portray an "adventure" *with* enough of curiosity and pristine innocence characteristic of childhood, it is also possible to see in the novel's fabric the *necessity* to refine one's views, to realign one's parameter of thinking in effectively functioning through an adult human world. Little Alice reminds us of the elemental need to integrate the childhood fantasies with the social obligations of adulthood, without losing either.

Indeed, fantasy plays havoc on *all* the characters that inhabit or visit the Wonderland or Looking-Glass worlds with a subjective or objective stance on the prevalent social issues there. At the outset of *Through the Looking-Glass,* Alice wonders, getting reflectively into a huge mirror of the drawing room mantelpiece, what the world would look/be like if anything in it was turned around, *like a reflection.* Suddenly the glass turns to silvery mist, and Alice passes through it to the other side. This new world (*same* as her own albeit only *reversed*) is patterned like a giant chessboard, the squares divided by green hedges and brooks. All the world's citizens are part of *this* great game of chase, explains the White Queen, who sends her off on a magical journey across that strange country and all/the entire cast of characters Alice meets during her stay there corresponds in one way or the other to the ancient tradition of myths and fairy tales: the White Knight, Tweedledum and Tweedledee, the Walrus and the Carpenter, the Rocking—Horse Fly—and even Humpty Dumpty himself.

Having gulped down the bottle labeled "DRINK ME" Alice feels startled to find herself extremely large in size compared to her *miniaturized* surroundings, which leaves her fantasizing that she has sufficiently 'grown-up', only to be scaled down through the effect of a cake labeled "EAT ME". Throughout, Alice exists in a double state of reality: she discovers that she exists *in* a fairytale; but then fairy tales are supposed to be fantastic and the unreal like the ones she used to read about. Therefore/Hence, through Alice, the reader would perceive her world of fantasy *as* reality, which conforms to the double-edged aspect/perspective of fiction.

The wish to get/break through the usual constraints of childhood into the mature world of adult authority, to vicariously share the forbidden experiences there with fictional charm and indeterminacy of displaying self-efficacy, is also a death wish, foreshadowing the tragic and inevitable loss of childhood innocence. By calmly accepting the truth that growing up also means giving up and abandoning the world/seclusion of immature wish-fulfilment, Alice *becomes* the text of her narrative herself—with a/her potential *to* imagine and be imagined *as* real, all at once.

Like Bronte's heroine in *Jane Eyre,* Alice continues to *misrepresent* reality as it exists around her.[9] Despite her conviction of being in a fairy tale, all her fantastic encounters with the Queen and the mad Hatter are *actually* part of reality. This streak of confusion hovers about the entire plot: even *in* fiction, *as* "Queen Alice", she cannot be wholly estranged from the thought of being *really* a child, and this, curiously, drives her back to the realm of mundane reality only as/since she's/she has matured enough to realize that the mystic may at times be essentially real and true to one's own perception.

From the moment Alice unwittingly falls down the burrow, many realistic constraints do not apply to her, not even the laws of gravity. Unlike Humpty Dumpty, a great fall brings her *no* harm ("not a bit hurt"); in fact, she has got sufficient time to observe her surroundings while she tumbles. To represent this discombobulating nature of the way children experience life, Carroll creates a "metaphysical void"[10] in which reality appears *slippery,* which again corroborates the seductive potential of the fantastic and the surreal. He intends not only to entertain and satisfy the child's curiosity and wonder, but also to warn him of the perils of encountering the absurdities which underlie much supposedly rational adult behaviours.

By weaving in references to the fairy tale and nursery rhymes (like the 'Tweedle' twins and Humpty Dumpty), imagery and symbols (like the White Rabbit, the 'Caucus-Race', the 'Jabberwocky', the chessboard) as well as with subtle twists in the plot, Carroll broadens the scope of fantasy as a fictional genre to inform the reader of the concealed emotional subtexts in the novel. However, he also potentially advocates that children's books—apart from their spirit of delighting and inspiring the child to a mature future—may not always include a point worthy of analysis, and may not always instruct and look for ethical or moral standpoint on life's oddities and ironies. Furthermore, the incorporation in the

'Alice' books of elements characteristic of fairy tales such as dreams, talking animals, the burrow, the presence of magic and the supernatural, turns out to be a potent force in the fictional realization of Alice's dreams.

Carroll's far-reaching *fantastic* vision catches Alice early in the novel in her journey to Wonderland when, after subsequent 'shrinking' and 'growing up' of her body size, she stands alone, helpless and crying—desperate to enter the attractive garden thereof, her tears form a giant pool at her feet. As she keeps crying, Alice shrinks and falls herself *into* it, and has to tread water; while trying to briefly converse with the mouse in elementary French (thinking he may be a french mouse) Alice offends him, though only in fancy, with her opening gambit, "Ouest ma chatte?" (in English, "Where is my cat?"). She meets other animals gathered on the shore, worried as to how to get themselves dry again. After the mouse delivers a very 'dry' lecture on William the Conqueror—upon Dodo's suggestions—they all perform a certain 'Caucus Race', which consists of nothing but everyone running in a circle with no clear winner:

> ...there was no one, two, three, and away, out they organ running when they liked, and left off *when* they liked, so that it was *not* easy to know *when* the race was over. However, when they had been running half an hour or so, and were *quite* dry again, the Dodo suddenly called out. The race is over! and they an crowded round it, panting, and asking, But *who* has won?
>
> This question the Dodo could not answer without a great deal of thought, and...[at last]...said, EVERYBODY has won, and *all* must have prizes.

Chapter III: A Caucus-Race and a Long Tale; *Alice's Adventures in Wonderland*

Carroll's *ironic* exploitation of his theme of maturation as a complex Wonderland experience necessitates an encounter *with* the adult human world as a means of exploring the hidden flaws and weaknesses prevailing in our own society, and is reflected in the co-existence of nonsense and literary parody in the 'Alice' books, which underscores the dual nature of their child/adult readership—and their author. As the pseudonymous "Lewis Carroll", however, C.L. Dodgson wrote whimsical fiction that challenged the moralizing children's literature of the period. His 'Alice' is in the tradition of the abandoned child heroine, but the Wonderland she *invades* and explores borders on Victorian Gothic horror fiction. Carroll's originality was to combine the two genres. He tempered his allegorical portrait of socio-economic upheaval with humorous doses of thought-provoking paradox. This fresh didacticism made his "love-gift of a fairy-tale" so popular that his books were second only to the Bible in bourgeois Victorian nurseries.

The story of Alice tumbling through the rabbit hole and being unwittingly embroiled in the weird incidents of a silly and nonsense world shorn of thought, justice and any definite purpose, is fairly guileless as a tale. Her dream-like 'fall' is delineated in immaculate, picturesque detail, and Alice's acquaintance/interaction with the bookshelves on either side of the hole perhaps hints at suggests an escape into the fictional world, into literature. And falling so slowly down the dark void underneath takes/carries us beyond the immediate sensory experience, creating in our mind the dream-like images of an *abyss*, an experience/sensation amplified by Alice herself as she "began to get rather sleepy, and went on saying to herself, as if in dreams", "Do cats eat bats?...". This image almost leads us beyond sleep, into a numb, narcotic, *sedative* feeling, a psychedelic kind of fantasy—world where one is falling yet desirous of falling asleep/to sleep.

> ...Down, down, down. Would the fall NEVER come to an end! 'I wonder...' I must be getting somewhere near the centre of the earth...— but then I wonder what Latitude or Longitude I've *got* to?'...

Chapter 1: Down the Rabbit-Hole; *Alice's Adventures in Wonderland*

And, on landing, as she beholds darkness overhead and the passage lying before her, a simile is employed by Carroll, right after a brief jolting irony, "There was *not* a moment to be lost [she *is* lost]: away went Alice *like* a wind".

Upon falling through the rabbit hole, she first tests her knowledge to determine whether she has become another girl:

> ...I wonder if I've been changed in the night? Let me think. Was I the same *when* I got up this morning? ...I can remember feeling a little different. But *if* I'm not the same, the next question is '*Who* in the world am I?' Ah, that's *the* great puzzle!...

Chapter 1: Down the Rabbit-Hole; *Alice's Adventures in Wonderland*

Later on, the White Rabbit mistakes her for his maidservant, Mary Ann; and she cannot offer the caterpillar a credible reply as to *who* she is, for/since she feels that she has changed several times since that morning ("...I can't explain *myself,* I'm afraid, Sir, because I'm *not* myself you see..."). The pigeon mistakes her for a serpent, from her extended neck "above the trees"; the Cheshire cat, on the other hand, questions another vital aspect of her identity: he is concerned/ worried *not* about the girl's name or species, but even more menacingly, he's questioning (and hence, challenging) her sanity, convinced that once in Wonderland, she *must* be 'mad', like everyone else there, as he confirms:

> "But I *don't* want to go among mad people," Alice remarked.
>
> "Oh, you can't help that," said the Cat: "we're *all* mad here. I'm mad. You're mad."
>
> "*How* do you know I'm mad?" said Alice.
>
> "You *must* be," said the Cat, "or you wouldn't have come here."

Chapter VI: Pig and Pepper; *Alice's Adventures in Wonderland*

If Alice suffers from acute identity crisis, a good many other characters, too, are no exceptions: the Duchess' baby turns into a pig, the Cheshire Cat is reduced to a floating grin, and the members of the jury *have* to write their own names or/lest they will forget them. In the sequel, similarly, the concept of identity continues to tease the reader: upon entering the woods Alice promptly forgets her own name and the Fawn does not even recognize her *as* a human being. But this apparent confusion of identity is given here a philosophical perspective: the 'Tweedle' twins maliciously provoke her into believing that *everything* may have, in fact, been *a dream* of the Red King and that Alice might herself be no more than a figment of *his* imagination. At first, Alice refutes them by asserting that she alone has constructed her own fantasy world, but at the end of her first narrative the matter is resolved still not/not yet resolved:

> "...Now Kitty, let's consider *who* it was that *dreamed* it all...it must have been *either* me *or* the Red King. *He* was part of my dream, of course—but then I was part of *his* dream, ...too! Oh Kitty, do help to settle *it!* I'm sure your paw *can* wait!" But the provoking kitten only began on the other paw, and pretended it hadn't heard the question....

Chapter 12: Which Dreamed it?; *Through the Looking-Glass and What Alice Found There*

The use of talking animals with human disposition in brilliant, striking illustrations was a favorite/prevalent 19th century ploy in children's literature. The 'Alice' books, too, are profuse in the funny clothed appearance(es) of animals, birds and even insects with human motives and action (human-like habits/practices), who speak and argue a lot—as reflected in their questioning and counter-questioning Alice—for instance, the clothed talking White Rabbit, *always* in haste, who later mistakes Alice for his maid servant; the blue hookah smoking Caterpillar, the magical mushroom that causes Alice to shrink and grow alternatively; the March Hare, the Mad Hatter and the sleepy Dormouse—all trapped in perpetual tea-time; the Mock Turtle and the Gryphon, who sympathize with Alice's strange experiences. Even the inanimate is invoked with fictional charm/attributes: in the sequel, the chess pieces come to life to inhabit the countryside, laid out in the shape of a giant chessboard, and maintain the social hierarchy by pertaining to the norms of a real-life game of chess, the Queen subtly transforms herself into a talking Sheep, and the Red

King envisages Alice as no more than a figment of *his* imagination, without ever appearing *in* person.

Another intriguing narrative technique of Carroll, that of betraying "ineffectual", "diluted violence"[11]—well exemplified in the fictitious, miniature fights/battles between the Red Knight and the White Knight, between the Lion and the Unicorn, and in the Cook's aggressive poseur towards the Duchess—helps preserve the shadowy, ephemeral quality of both the Wonderland and the Looking-Glass worlds, in a way *such that* the pains and injuries of reality are forever exiled. As the Lion and the Unicorn proceed to fight each other, the Mad Hatter explains, "each of them has been down eighty-seven times", but ironically, without any physical damage, and the moment the fighting stops their attention turns to hunting for food. The reader is thus intrigued into believing that, in the context of a fantasy show battles are but illusory, an amusing, comical, humorous diversion/digression.

The way Alice's attention is almost casually captured or hijacked by a little animal explains/implies her innate curiosity and proneness to fantasize the real. Immediately after, she finds herself groping/roaming through a maze of wonderful and exotic landscape/adventures, meeting a host of strange creatures, many of whom—as Alice observed—barely possess the best of tempers and refuse to help Alice figure out *where* to go and *what* to do. Yet, fantasy holds its sway over the curious little girl as she wanders off from one puzzle to another, undergoing frequent, abrupt 'physical' changes and even the rudest and most impudent behaviour from others. Still, being a stranger to that underground Arcadia/recluse, unstained and untouched/untroubled by the need for logic and rationale, Alice never quite loses her prudence and presence of mind, as when she makes much sense of evidence during a/the trial.

Throughout, Alice struggles to construe the meaning embedded in the reversed, *reflected* version of her own surroundings, and also, the nature of the fantastic dream that has motivated and initiated her "adventures", even when sympathizing with the tragic plight of "flowers" as essentially the lower social class (Bread-and-Butterflies always die because of a food shortage):

> ...it isn't manners for *us* to begin, you know....

Chapter 2: The Garden of Live Flowers; *Through the Looking-Glass and What Alice Found There*

In our mundane/ordinary earthly existence, with expectations and their consequent frustration, the *subjective* mind/self can barely comprehend what constitutes an absolute, inviolable *truth* or *reality*. We can barely escape the multiple, various ways in which our own unique opinions and viewpoints could possibly distort and reshape reality—a reality which alters over an extended period of time and space. Carroll brings *this* element of "personal reality"[12] under close scrutiny, challenging it as vague and inauthentic. As the Looking-Glass world questions, challenges and subverts Alice's innocuous childhood perception of the real, so does it refute the reader's established views—a fact well illustrated by the Hatter's imprisonment:

> ...He is in prison *now*, being punished: and the trial does not even begin *till* next Wednesday: and of course the crime comes *last of all*....

Chapter 5—Wool and Water; *Through the Looking-Glass and What Alice Found There*

Carroll's fantasy world may be conceived or interpreted as an all-inclusive "mindscape"[13]—an externalization of the protagonist's interior life, her spontaneous adaptability to the new ecological and psychological ethos. Alice's intuitive response to the characters and situations of her fantasy shows that she craves a sense of control as she grows up. She relates to the residents of both worlds in the same way she communicates/relates to her pets, assuming the role of a good-natured mother figure, as in her interaction with live flowers, the Turtle and the White Knight, displaying solicitude and deference despite her authority.

It is only towards the close of *Through the Looking-Glass* that Alice, by capturing the Red Queen, unknowingly but ironically puts the Red King, stationary throughout the book, *into* checkmate, and is allowed to *wake up,* suggesting the culmination of the process of her maturation into adolescence, or *womanhood.* She is found holding the black kitten, whom she deduces to have been the Red Queen all along, with the white kitten having been the White Queen, and the story ends with her recalling the speculation of the Tweeddles that she might herself be *no* more than a figment of *his* imagination, for she ceases to exist the instant *he* wakes up. *This* breach of confidentiality in the untroubled poise of fantasy also signals her maturation into adolescence and womanhood.

Being a master storyteller, Carroll uses expressive language to make fiction sound *like* reality. Besides, in each episode, he leaves (a) philosophical message(s) to his readers that are truly inspiring. The Gryphon remarks: "The adventures first... explanations take such a dreadful time..." (Chapter X: The Lobster Quadrille). Likewise, in the second book, the Queen has to admit that "It's a poor sort of memory that only works backward." But he is also an expert at coining mind-boggling phrases and linguistic and etymological juggleries, like puzzles, riddles and even poems, apart from a host of portmanteau words. The 'Alice' books contain the famous nonsense verses "The Walrus and the Carpenter" and "Jabberwocky", the second believed to have introduced two entirely new words in the vernacular: "chortle" and "galumph". His *clinical* fantasy plays with an array of literary tropes, ranging from pun and hyperbole to sarcasm, which dazzles the child's eye to humorous and rhetorical effect, as with the Mock Turtle reminiscencing his school days:

> ..."And how many hours a day did you do lessons?" said Alice, in a hurry to change the subject.
>
> "Ten hours the first day," said the Mock Turtle: "nine the next, and so on.'
>
> "What a curious plan!" exclaimed Alice.
>
> "*That's* the reason they're called lessons," the Gryphon remarked: "because they *lessen* from day to day"....

Chapter 9: The Mock Turtle's Story; *Alice's Adventures in Wonderland*

Not only does perspective vary between individuals, it also changes with age, and with growing up. Upon explaining to Alice that time moves backward in looking-glass world, the White Queen plasters her finger, then screams in pain, and finally pricks her finger on a brooch:

> ... Alice laughed. "There's no use trying," she said, "one can't believe impossible things". "I daresay you haven't had much practice," said the Queen, "when I was *your* age, I always did it for half-an-hour a day. Why, sometimes I've believed as many as six *impossible* things before breakfast. There goes the shawl again...."

Chapter 5: Wool and Water; *Through the Looking-Glass and What Alice Found There*

The Queen's concepts/vision/picture/image of reality includes more and more "impossible things" as she gets older. Alice, being stationed on the *other* side of the mirror changes in the *opposite* direction. As she matures, she comes to see all absurd, nonsensical, "impossible" ideas and things as *sheer* fantasy.

In his perpetual quest/longing to delight children by imaginatively presenting them with the *unreal* and the *impossible* as an *absolute* truth, Carroll makes exhaustive use of literary "frames" and devices that would enable him to create space for childhood interactivity with the fading images and figures of the fantasy realm, while himself remaining relatively discreet of his own work. The first of such frames is introduced in the form a dream into which Alice tumbles. The figure of the White Rabbit serves as an initiation of Alice's maturity—as a/her potential relief into the fluidity of dreams.

It is through fantasising about a world she has never been except through her reading of illustrated texts that Alice gains an essential *truth* about human existence which would inform her *knowledge* of the world and in turn help refine her *vision,* which is an essential element in creating/perusing imaginative literature.

The 'encounters' so painstakingly portrayed, all through Alice's solitary journey, assuming of dream-sequence, reflect the lively and playful imagination of the child. The altered and reversed realities Alice confronts in her acquaintance with the world ruled by whimsies, madness and hypothetical exercise of the *will* are evocative of/reflect the precocious fantastic vision of *their* elusive author/Carroll's elusive literature: however fleeting and transient fantasies (or, the *textual* realities) are, they are seductive enough to shape the child's interior life of/with dissolving forms and evolving patterns.

Through a/the juxtaposition and eventual merging of the Self with Nature, of the ideal with the actual, of fantasy with reality, Carroll brings forth the essential harmony between children's fiction with popular adult literature. Though at one point a frustrated Alice exclaims, "If any of them can explain it, I'll give him sixpence. I don't believe there's an atom of meaning in it", curiously, she *has* explored the world in clinical, mathematical detail—on both vertical ("down the rabbit-hole") and horizontal ("through the glass...into the Looking-glass room") dimensions/levels, and (has) been fostered, informed and enlightened by solitude in the process. The *impenetrability* of her narrative has continued to gain popularity among children and adults alike, a status enjoyed by none except Shakespeare and the Bible—as Humpty Dumpty asserts, concerning "Meaning" of the text:

> We've had *enough* of that subject, and it would be just as well if you mention what you *mean* to do next, as I suppose you *don't* mean to stop here all the rest of your life.
>
> ...I cannot rub the strangeness from my sight I got from looking *through* a pane of glass I skimmed this morning from the drinking trough And held *against* the world of hoary grass....
>
> Robert Frost, *After Apple Picking* (1915)

Even "with lots of nonsense in it"—words with which Alice Liddell begged C.L. Dodgson for a story on the/a boat-trip that initiated the tale—*Alice's Adventures in Wonderland* does make sense *when* viewed without the "pane of glass", without the cameo of fanciful imagining—by Carroll's/its persuading the reader to delve into the self, which mirrors and reflects the essential human condition/his existing social, human condition.

In Carroll's hand, fantasy as a genre becomes the "literature of subversion". Through the wondrous, maturing eye of Alice the reader has perceived her unique world of fantasy *as* reality. Now, as she has begun reshuffling and realigning the parameters of her preconceived ideas relentlessly challenged in an alien sojourn, her reader also delights in the way she would excel in preserving the integrity of both worlds—the realms of fantasy as of reality, in the face of our "willing suspension of disbelief"—in the alembic of imaginative literature; no wonder she ends her adventures as "Queen Alice".

...Lastly, she pictured to herself how this *same* little sister of hers would, in the after-time, be herself a *grown* woman; and how she would keep, through all her riper years, the simple and loving heart of her childhood: and how she would gather about *her* other little children, and make their eyes bright and eager with many a strange tale, perhaps even with the *dream* of Wonderland of long-ago: and how she would *feel* with all their simple sorrows, and find a *pleasure* in all their simple joys, remembering her own child-life, and the *happy* summer days....

NOTES

1. "Casebook Series: *The Tempest*", ed. John Dyson, OUP, New Delhi (1992).
2. Introduced by Johann Gottfried Herder in his critique of the work *Genius seculi* by the philologist Christian Adolph Klotz.
3. "Forms of Time and of the Chronotope in the Novel" by Bakhtin, Mikhail, in "Epic and Novel", *The Dialogic* Imagination.

4. *Fantasy and Realism in Victorian Art* by George P. Landow.
5. K.C. Cole, "On the Shapes of Things", (Discover, July 1983).
6. *Ibid.*
7. "Masterpieces of the Imaginative Mind"; Lectures by Professor Eric S. Rabkin.
8. "Fantasy and Concepts of the Real" by Geoege Landow.
9. "Transformation of Fantasy into Reality in *Alice's Adventures in Wonderland* and *Jane Eyre*" by Jane Sorenson.
10. "Diluted and Ineffectual Violence in the Alice Books" by George Kruglov.
11. "Fantasy or Reality?" by Erin Wells.

18

Portrayal of Children Characters in the Short Stories of Ruskin Bond

Norah Nivedita Shaw

Ruskin Bond has often been addressed as a Children's writer. In fact if one closely looks at the vast panorama of his literature, and in particular, where the children characters are portrayed, one is deeply touched with the varied approaches Bond looks at them one. Most of these children are carefree in complete harmony with their surroundings, independent in solving their personal problems without taking any help from the elders. At times some of them might appear as mature as adults. One of the reasons behind this is the writer's childhood himself.

Bond's lonely and pathetic childhood without motherly love and very short-lived father's love was to play a major role in his writings, though in a different mould. The real glimpse of his lonesome childhood is there yet the pathetic shade has been transformed in an objective way bringing out real work of great art. To have a bird's eye view from his life—a non-serious anglo-Indian mother who was fun-loving and had a serious affair with a Punjabi businessman, a British father, working in royal Air force. There was not only wide age gap between them but also a great gap of temperaments. Mr. Aubrey Bond, the father instead of treating 'his erring wife with an iron rod', chose to suffer in silence. Perhaps his love for the child (Ruskin), forbid him to take any risk, trying to be both mother and father to the child. However, destiny had something else in store, for by the time Ruskin was hardly ten, he left for his heavenly abode. Bond could easily have related the realistic elements from his lonely childhood in his art; however he transforms the sad experiences artistically and paints them beautifully and this marks him as a great artist.

The children characters of Bond can be categorized in four groups—lonely boy child under love and care by women who are in fact not in reality the child's mother; little girls whose magical presence empower the hero or the narrator of the piece (and at times seem to act as mothers); the child characters bearing a close semblance with Ruskin the child that is depiction of autobiographical elements, and lastly, some children characters who are independent and decide on their own, without any interference of the adults or their parents.

Let us examine the lonesome boy child in a few of his short stories. The very short story that comes to my mind, revolving round the autobiographical frame of Bond's childhood is the well known piece, *My First Love*. As a growing boy aging from five to ten, Ruskin Bond was all the time left alone to the care of nanny (governess). In the above mentioned piece, the little boy's (reminding us of Bond), entire world comprises of nanny's gossips, fairy tales, magical world of fantasies. Nowhere does one find the child apparently craving for his mother. However this might be lying at the inner conscience of the child, and therefore the boy seems to be all the more engrossed in his surroundings, its inhabitants. In fact the very beginning of the short story immensely touches us deeply—

She was thirty and I six....

For a child of six who should have been completely embossed in the cozy motherly warmth of love and care, however has instead the surrogate mother, who loves him as her own child and naturally becomes the child's beloved. As a result when she is being called ugly by his parents' guests the child's reaction is outright and bold.

No, she is beautiful!

It is very interesting to note that living in a pre-independent set up, the little boy not only enjoys sharing secrets and things forbidden and unexpected of an English or an anglo-Indian child. The child takes full liberty with his nanny when his parents are out-enjoying bathing with her 'magnificent build, colourful personality' in the same bath tub.

'We would wallow together in the long marble tub: I small pink and podgy; and ayah like a benevolent hippopotamus, causing the bath tub to overflow. She scrubbed and soaped me, while I relaxed and enjoyed the sensation of her rough hands moving over my back and tummy. And then before she could heave herself out of the tub, I would leap from the water and charge out of the bathroom without my clothes. Ayah would come flapping after me, a sheet tied hurriedly about her waist and we would race through the rooms until finally she caught up with me, gave me several resounding slaps, watched me burst into tears, and then broke down herself and took me to her comfortable bosom.'

The other cord of bond between the two becomes folk tales or unique stories about snakes, where the snake is declared harmless. The ayah's emphasis is 'that they would not harm' anyone provided 'we left them alone'. The child's passion is intense with envy when he suddenly sees his ayah embracing the Tonga driver and finally her declaration of her intention of marrying him. The boy feels it as an act of treachery, and acts rebelliously 'refusing to speak to ayah no matter how much she coxed and petted' him.

The other important story, where yet the same character with her angelic warmth and love becomes a soothing balm for the lonesome little boy of eight, is none other than the well-known story *The Room of Many Colours*. The nanny seems to be the same character present in *My First Love*. In fact this repetition of same characters in different stories or novellas of Bond again and again forms an important feature; which might have turned his stories into monotony, however it is just the other way round with Ruskin as pointed out by Dr. Meena G. Khorana in *The Life and Works of Ruskin Bond*. In *The Room of Many Colours* the ayah does not simply narrate the snake story, visible in the garden but goes on to relate the snake with Dukhi the gardener and his love, apparently the mad Rani. Here Bond presents a romantic charmed view of childhood, the child protagonist being brought up in the loving, nurturing arms of his father, ayah and the gardener. The mad Rani exiled in the palace tower becomes the archetypal figure of life force—a world of fantasy and magic for the young child. The room having many coloured glass windows mentioned in *My First Love* again here is shown by the mad Rani to the little boy. These coloured glass windows become symbolic of the mysteries of the world. And this is being shown to the child through the eyes of the Rani.

The motherly glow embosses the little boy, instills powerful warmth of passion and touches one deeply in yet another remarkable short story, *The Women on Platform No. 8*. One can very well imagine the trauma of a little boy (boarder) left alone on a station to reach his home. The story as Bond himself states was written recalling his days as a boarder when he used to change train at Ambala station all by himself while his friends were always with their parents. The little boy child Arun embarking upon his journey all alone comes across a stranger, a motherly figure, who though poor and simple, instantly takes the little boy under her safe arms and not only feeds him, but magically embalms his loneliness erasing out his fear completely. In fact the beauty of stranger woman is so magically powerful that the boy does not deny her as his mother when his friend's mother inquires about her identity. Arun's friend Satish is with his mother at the platform. The way Bond gives a unique and charming touch to the whole episode is indeed very touching—

> We shook hands and then he turned to his mother and said: 'This is Arun, Mother. He is one of my friends, and the best bowler in the class.
>
> 'I am glad to know that,' said his mother, a large imposing woman who wore spectacles. She looked at the woman who held my hand and said: 'And I suppose you're Arun's mother.'
>
> I opened my mouth to make some explanation, but before I could say anything the woman replied: 'Yes, I am Arun's mother.'

> I was unable to speak a word. I looked quickly up at the woman, but she did not appear to be at all embarrassed, and was smiling at Satish's mother.

One comes across number of such examples of the child protagonist who is lonesome, left alone, deprived of motherly love and care, but often under the care of some angel becoming his surrogate mother and empowering the child protagonist for the time.

On the other hand there are such children characters in the works of Bond, who are highly empowered and become life force for the narrator/hero cum protagonist. All of these are young and growing girls, who meet the narrator by chance and shower the whole atmosphere with their magical fragrance which lingers long even after they disappear. Some of them appear in short stories like *The Coral Tree, The Story of Madhu, The Window, The Night Train at Deoli,* or *Binya Passes by*. Of these, the two most attractive characters appear in *The Window* and *The Coral Tree;* little girls becoming the centre of attraction not only for the hero-cum-narrator but also the readers. In the short story *The Coral Tree*, the narrator hero, about to leave for abroad is enchanted by a little girl's presence asking for flowers from his coral tree. The hero who then is very lonely and sad nostalgic in leaving his native place behind, becomes only too excited and happily showers the flowers from the tree on the little girl—

> The tree was easy to climb, and I made myself comfortable on one of the lower branches, smiling down at the serious upturned face of the girl.
>
> 'I'll throw them down to you.' I said.
>
> I bent a branch but the wood was young and green, and I had to twist it several times before it snapped.
>
> 'I'm not sure that I ought to do this,' I said, as I dropped the flowering branch to the girl.
>
> 'Don't worry,' she said.
>
> 'Well, if you're ready to speak up for me—'
>
> 'Don't worry.'

On close examination of such little girls it seems that they are in fact the synonymous with the narrator cum hero who also 'like to do things on' his own. And all such nymphets and the hero have deep desire to go everywhere confident that no one can stop them. In *The Window*, the little girl shares the magical charm of the window with the narrator cum protagonist. The window acts as a screen for the varied world view. The window presents interesting and exciting scenes varying from *an ayah, with a baby in a pram, the postman, the fruit-seller, the toy-seller calling their wares...the rent collector, a posse of cyclists; a long chain of schoolgirls; a lame beggar....* Both the characters watching from far though remain detached from the entire view of the window, however are bonded in a strong hinge of love and friendship

> But the window was more fun than anything else. It gave us the power of detachment: we were deeply interested in the life around us, but we were not involved in it.
>
> 'It is like a cinema,' said Koki. 'The window is the screen, the world is the picture'.

What is remarkable is that instantly the two strangers easily trust each other. Koki herself brings *'a magic of her own'* when she enters the room of the author. When the narrator informs her of the power of the window he owns, Koki without giving a second thought, right away believes the author.

> She said nothing but stared out of the window uncomprehendingly at first, and then with increasing interest. And after some time she turned round and smiled at me, and we were friends....
>
> I didn't need to know any more about her, and she didn't need to know anything about me except that I wasn't really a ghost- not the frightening sort anyway....

Kokoi's excitement is very aptly observed—

> 'It's like a cinema' said Koki 'The window is the screen, the world is the picture.'

The window becomes an image of timelessness. The perpetual aspect of the window resembles the timeless spirit of

Koki and therefore after her departure even the window is shut despite the hindrance of bougainvillea's green shoot.

Although these apparently little girl characters about to blossom into womanhood are in fact more womanly and motherly, empowering not only the narrator or the author but the whole surrounding. Their magical glow alleviate the loneliness of the protagonist and become a great source of inspiration for the hero to pursue his long and endless journey even after they disappear, be it Binya, Koki, Madhu or unnamed basket selling girl (*The Night Train at Deoli*).

The portrayal of a few children characters can be easily traced as autobiographical. The fact that his writings are embroidered with personal experiences cannot be averted and which all the more beautifies his work of art. Ruskin Bond boldly declares in the Introduction to *The Night Train at Deoli and Other Stories*—

> Perhaps there is too much of me in my stories.... It is a weakness, I know. It can't be helped.... In fact I can't really write unless I am in love with my subject....

In fact it is not the presence of autobiographical elements but rather the treatment meted out to such elements that become our prime concern. For literature though a mirror to life is after all an art objectively correlated. Ruskin Bond's father died when he was hardly ten years old and at the time he was in Bishop Cotton School, Shimla. Neither the authorities of the school nor his relatives bothered to make any arrangement for the poor little boy to attend the funeral of his father which left a deep scar of anguish in his mind and heart. This incident has however been modified in an entirely unique mould leading to the concept of reincarnation or rebirth. The short story depicts imaginatively the funeral of his father. The main concern by the relatives is not the feeling of grief for the poor boy but that he should not attend the funeral procession. The way Bond beautifully pictures the whole scene is marvelous—

> The boy said nothing. He sat in the darkest corner of the darkened room, his face revealing nothing of what he thought and felt. His father's coffin lay in the next

> room, the lid fastened forever over the tired, wistful countenance of the man who had meant so much to the boy. Nobody else mattered—neither uncles nor aunts nor fond grandparents. Least of all the mother who was hundreds of miles away with another husband.

The story does not relate to the great loss or the suffering the boy is doomed to. In fact the boy's bold acceptance of the universal truth turns to be very forceful converging with the age old Hindu concept of the cycle of rebirth. The child desires to seek life again and this urge unifies him not only with his father but with mankind.

> Superman did it in comics but his father was a gentle soul who wouldn't fight too hard against the earth and the grass and the roots of tiny trees. Or perhaps he'd grow into a tree and escape that way! 'If ever I am put away like this,' thought the boy, 'I'll get into the root of a plant and then I'll become a flower and then may be a bird will come and carry my seed away.... I'll get out somehow!

The cause of Mr. Aubrey Bond's death was Malaria. He was hospitalized. The fact that Ruskin was not with him at the time as he was in Bishop Cotton School is known from his autobiography, *Scenes from A Writer's Life*. But Ruskin Bond again explores and fictionalizes the situation in a different light in his first short story written at the age of seventeen, *Untouchable*. The child is left alone at home under the care of a sweeper boy and neighbours, when his father is hospitalized being severely attacked by Malaria. The background is that of pre-independent India, the family that of Anglo Indian. Naturally the little boy (anglo Indian) is not expected to mix too freely with his subordinates. However the child not only dislikes his Anglo Indian neighbours, supposed to be his guardian for the time being, but also is not interested in the sweeper boy too much.

> Well I did not intend playing with the sweeper-boy; but neither did I intend playing with her children. I was going to sit on my bed all week and wait for my father to come home.

One can very well imagine the fear and panic of a child whose, whole and sole has been his father—the sensitivity of the whole incident has been captured brilliantly. It is indeed a tribute Ruskin Bond who had had an uncommon childhood, seems to be well versed with child psychology, the fear and fright a child feels in the absence of his only guardian that is father. Naturally the little child longs and deeply craves for his presence but at the same time has wrong notions, negative thoughts in the deadly darkness of the night. The stillness and darkness of the night crowded with varied scary sounds—howling of the jackal, hooting of the owl, bat flying against the window, or running of the centipede, the cracking of the doors, the rattling of the shutters or even the terrifying sound of the thunderstorm. Such sounds but are phobia for the lonesome child. Besides Bond also touches upon the episode humorously, when a mosquito crosses by him singing in his ear, and disappears, the boy reasons 'that mosquito' gave the malaria to' his father. 'And now it was trying to give it to me!' The silence and stillness and dreadful darkness of the night are a terror for the poor lonely boy. After having battled for long with the dreadful night, accompanied with negative presumption, the child straightaway dashes to the sweeper boy's room for security hardly bothering about his status or his class or the reaction of the neighbours. The fear of man knows no bond, so is it with a child particularly when lonely, groping for safety, be it under an untouchable or an outcaste. Bond's description of the episode enchants us immensely—

> But at the next thunderclap. Louder this time, louder than I had ever heard, I leapt from my bed. I could not stand it. I fled, blundering in the sweeper boy's room.
>
> The boy sat on the bare floor.
>
> 'What is happening?' he asked. The lightning flashed, and his teeth and eyes flashed, with it. Then he was a blur in the darkness.
>
> 'I am afraid,' I said.
>
> I moved towards him and my hand touched a cold shoulder.

> 'Stay here,' he said. 'I too am afraid.'
>
> I sat down, my back against the wall; beside the untouchable, the outcaste...and the thunder and lightning ceased, and the rain came, swishing a and drumming on the corrugated roof.

Such and many more autobiographical elements are captured with immense beauty and charm in several other pieces like *My Father's Trees in Dehra, Coming Home to Dehra, Escape from Java.*

As already mentioned the most important point that flashes in almost in almost all the children characters of Bond has been their independent nature, boldness, ability to decide on their own. In fact one finds no interference of the guardian. Most of the time the children seem to be as mature as adults. The best example can be related to the simple ten-year old Garhwali girl, Binya in *The Blue Umbrella.* This has also been made into a feature film by the well-known director, Vishal Bhardwaj in the year 2007 and has been awarded the best National film of Children. She is fascinated by a tourist woman's big blue silky umbrella. It is very interesting to observe how Bond depicts the tactfulness of the little girl in order to possess the big blue umbrella. She exchanges with her precious leopard claw necklace supposed to be a good omen for her. The way Bond depicts the entire episode shows his deep understanding of child psychology. The mere craving for sheer lifeless and apparently simple and non-living thing might appear to one a nonsensical issue but this is what distinguishes Ruskin Bond from other contemporary writers and makes him stand on a much higher pedestal than others. The blue umbrella indeed very beautiful becomes symbolic. It casts magical spell not only upon Binya but the habitants of the entire village, in general and Ram Bharosa the tea shop owner in particular. The story finally embarks upon the common theme of craving or longing after something. Since the time Binya owns the big blue umbrella, her entire world revolves round the big blue silky umbrella. She does not leave the umbrella anywhere—it accompanies her everywhere even when she goes to get her cows grazed or fetch water or deliver milk.

With great difficulty, she shares it with her brother at times. Ram Bharosa, the tea shop owner too longs to own the blue umbrella, and tries all sorts of ways to coax Binya but in vain. Finally his helper who tries to steal it is caught red-handed by Binya's brother and this defames Ram Bharosa in the eyes of the villagers. The villagers stop coming to his shop thereby his business starts to fail. At the outset Binya seems to be a simple village girl, but at once she becomes a woman mature and full of understanding—feeling small and full of guilt for the Ram Bharose's downfall

> But had she loved the umbrella too much? Had it mattered more to her than people mattered? She couldn't help feeling that in a small way she was the cause of the sad look on Ram Bharosa's face...and the ruinous condition of his shop. It was all due to his own greed, no doubt; but she didn't want him to feel bad about herself; and she closed the umbrella whenever she came near the shop, opening it again only when she was out of sight.

—and gives the umbrella as a gift to Ram Bharose. One wonders the unique way Bond delves in inner conflicts of a child such as Binya who calmly discriminates between right and wrong, without any compulsion by her parents, realizing, comprehending that umbrella is but a thing, the beauty of which like any beautiful object would fade away with the passage of time. Like Lord Budha she attains true wisdom—for what matters is not a non-living thing but the love and friendship the eternal relationship which bind people together—

> He wasn't used to running, but he caught up with her, held out the umbrella, saying, "You forgot it—the umbrella!"
>
> In that moment it belonged to both of them.
>
> But Binya didn't take the umbrella. She shook her head and said, "You keep it. I don't need it anymore."
>
> "But it's such a pretty umbrella!" protested Ram Bharosa. "It's the best umbrella in the village."

> "I know," said Binya. "But an umbrella isn't everything."

Prof. Meena G. Khorana rightly summarizes the very crux of story aptly—

> On the one hand, it represents the corrupting influence of the outside world—a recurring theme in Bond's stories—and on the other it emphasizes that this encounter leads to growth and self knowledge for Binya and Ram Bharosa and to the recognition that villagers too have the need to own an aesthetically beautiful object.

The other short story where again children characters seem to develop a true understanding on time and in fact seem to be more mature than adults. They do not involve or depend upon the elderly people to solve their tussle. The story is *The Fight.* Very rightly titled the piece relates to the fight among two teenage boy for the possession of a mere pool 'cold and clean and inviting in the forest and'. Ranji who is new in Rajpur suddenly discovers a pool in the forest and presumes himself to be the sole owner of that pool 'quenching his body in the cool waters of the forest pool till another boy named Suraj claims to be himself the owner of the pool. And both of them take to fighting showing their power and strength on the basis of caste or region.

> And then they were at each other's throats, swaying on the rock, tumbling on the sand, rolling over and over, their legs and arms locked in a desperate, violent struggle. Gasping and cursing, clawing and slapping, they rolled right into the shallows of the pool.
>
> Even in the water the fight continued as, spluttering and covered with mud, they groped for each other's head and throat. But after five minutes of frenzied, unscientific struggle, neither boy had emerged victorious. Their bodies heaving with exhaustion, they stood back from each other, making tremendous efforts to speak.

The fight continues the next day despite the hot climate without any information given to the parents. As they come closer to each other, they get to know about each other's qualities Ranji being apt in diving and Suraj who dreams to be the 'world's champion wrestler'—finally both give up their fight and becoming friendly—

> Be my friend, and I will make you a pahalwan like me! I know—if you teach me to dive and swim underwater, I will make you a pahalwan! That is fair, isn't it?

Thus Bond's theme of friendship and universality encircles round his children characters. Though most of his children are fun loving, carefree but at the same time they are brave and daring and at times prove to be more wise and intellectual than adults or their guardians. Moreover one finds them absolutely independent hardly relying upon the elders for their personal problems. The present paper tries to bring out a bird's eye view of children characters in some of the short stories of the great writer. The literature on the said theme particularly in Bond's works is vast and need to be worked out immensely from varied angles of approach.

REFERENCES

Bond, Ruskin. *Collected Fiction.* Penguin, New Delhi, 1996.

——. *Ruskin Bond's Children's Omnibus.* Rupa & Co., New Delhi, 1995.

——. *The Night Train at Deoli and Other Stories.* Penguin, New Delhi, 1988

——. *Our Trees Still Grow in Dehra.* Penguin, New Delhi, 1991.

——. *Scenes From A Writer's Life,* Penguin, New Delhi, 1997.

Khorana, Meena G. *The Life and Works of Ruskin Bond.* Praeger, London, 2003.

Singh, P.K. (ed.) *The Creative Contours of Ruskin Bond: An Anthology of Creative Writings.* Pencraft, New Delhi, 1995.

19

Folklore as a Genre

Bhaskar Roy Barman

I

In dealing with folklore as a genre we come across some related terms such as folklore, mythology and tell-tale and we must seek a plausible answer to the pertinent question, "How far are these terms related to one another?" Alongside of this question crop up other relevant questions "Does mythology mean the same thing as folklore? What is tell-tale? and how are these three different genres used differently related to one another?" Majority of us have heard of folklore and mythology—and they are often used in different meanings—but very few of us have heard of 'tell-tale'. In all probability the term 'tell-tale' has originated in America. But tell-tale is another form of folktale. I shall touch upon tell-tale later on before dealing with it we must needs acquaint ourselves of folklore and mythology.

By folklore is generally meant the traditions, beliefs, legends, saying stories and customs current among the common people. This meaning has now been universally considered a plausible definition, though a universally acceptable definition of folklore has not yet been settled on. But it appears as difficult for us to premise our discussion on folklore, as it is for other folklorists to premise any discussion, on this postulated definition approved by Oxford and Webster dictionaries. We have seen 'saying stories' mentioned in the definition and these two words serve to relate folklore to tell-tale. The main motif of folklore is 'saying a story' or 'telling a tale', but it is not 'writing a story or tale'. But literature involves writing. The question is whether we should study folklore as an oral literature or as a folk-literature. While oral literature tries to some extent to keep true and faithful to folklore, folk-literature infringes the domain of folklore. If the telling is the tale or, rather, if the saying is the story, it is certainly imperative for the folklore to be considered in a new light and for the study of folktales to go beyond motif tracing and source-hunting and how the complex interaction between tale, teller and audience has been transferred to print. The essence of folklore, as is its nature, is its crudeness and unsophisticatedness. The 'telling' gets polished and sophisticated in print through the jugglery of the pen and it violates the essence of folklore. Folktales are very much older than their name or study. A folktale is a story which has been transmitted orally from generation to generation through the lips of the common people of any land and a true folktale is by nature anonymous, for no one wrote it; it evolved off the nature of man to tell and listen to tales. It is, thus, a widespread tale and appears in different forms in different countries, where in each case the local setting imparts a particular flavour to the tale.

Folktales are in fact the earliest form of traditional imaginative literature, that is, oral literature that has come down to us. They comprise unwritten fiction of early man and unsophisticated people in all parts of the world. They enlighten us on the human imagination in its childhood; the attempts of our ancestors to dress their understanding of the world, their ideas and their beliefs, their customs and manner of living, in the garb of memorable narrative. Although there are other causes having led to their origin or having moulded their form once they originated, folktales, I repeat, owe their birth in great part to the universal desire to listen to stories. 'Tell me a story,' the child cried when we were children, we would ask our mothers, preferably our grandmothers to tell us stories, won't we? When I was a child we had no grandmother or grandfather living with us. We would pester my mother who was really a good storyteller with demands for telling us stories. In the childhood of every society there must have been the same cry, the same pestering, followed by an inspired response from those (in many cases, grandmothers, rarely mothers in homely atmosphere and situation) in whom imagination and the faculty of storytelling were most active.

Yet the importance of recording folktales in print cannot be denied. The more civilization advances the deeper many important folktales and folksongs go into an abyss of oblivion. Nowadays grandmothers do not tell their grandchildren tales of prince and princess, ogre and ogress and so on. Hence, the necessity of gathering together in print folktales in the process of receding into oblivion. It should be remembered in this connexion that earlier folk-literature was confused with folklore. Earlier under the vague term, in folk-literature were included folksong, ballad, fairy tales, drama, proverbs, charms and legends. Since 'folk-literature' in the earlier sense is the creation of primitive and illiterate people and therefore belongs to the oral tradition, we should refrain from calling the oral tradition folk-literature, for literature involves writing. Now that people have started gathering it and writing it down, it has become folk-literature in the correct sense of the word on the heels of printing of folk-literature, the folk-tradition is in decline and it declines quite naturally. No child asks its grandmother or grandfather to tell it a story; so many folktales are available in print. Grandmothers with nothing else to do now become a burden to the nuclear families.

There were few systematic attempts to gather such literature until the 19th century, when, for example, the Brothers Grim made their famous collection of fairy tales, and the great Serbian scholar, Vuk Karadzic collected many of the epic ballads, or narodne pesme, the poems (pesma meaning a poem) belonging to the genre of traditional popular narrative poetry based on historical events and created mainly by individual members of an illiterate or semi-illiterate society and preserved by oral tradition in Yugoslavia. The guslari (singular, guslar who plays the gusle, a one-stringed fiddle) were blind minstrels among the South Slavs and professional and itinerant reciters of national heroic poems of the oral tradition have been reciting and passing the narodne pesme since the 14th century.

I think it worthwhile to dwell upon the modern interpretation of folklore, in which lies a plausible answer to the question as to the relation of folklore to mythology and tall tale. It is advisable for my young readers to skip over the modern interpretation. Many famous folklorists like the Grimm Brothers, Max Muller and Andrew Lang, among others, have said apropos of folktales that they are 'monstrous, irrational and unnatural' both as to the elements they are composed of and as to the plots unifying them. Since a tale is supposed to have a different origin from its elements, two questions propose themselves: what is the origin and meaning of the motifs? What is the origin and meaning of the tales? I should like to discuss in some detail the motifs and the tales one after another and this discussion will help us a great bit in understanding how folklore, mythology and tall tale are inter-related.

First about the morifs. Many of the incidents of the merry tales, jokes, yarns, tall stories and anecdotes are but comical and clever inventions spun out of life and no problem do they offer.

The monstrous, 'irrational and unnatural' incidents, so to say, are of a kind with those of myth and, in my view, with tall tale, inasmuch as, they have been derived from myth (and tall tale in the case of American folktales), they must be explained, as is myth. Then how is myth explained? The reply varies according to the authority.

Euhemerus, a Greek writer of the 4th century B.C., notes that Alexander the Great, close on heels of his death, started appearing in legend as a demi-god, hypothesized the theory that the gods are only great mortals and are deified. In the preface to his Prose Edda, a summary of Odinic mythology, Snurri Sturlason (1178-1241), an Icelandic historian and author of Heimskringla, a history of Norse kings from mythic times to 1177, containing graphic pictures of domestic and adventurous life of the Vikings (Scandinavian adventurers who from the 8th to 9th century who practiced piracy at seas and committed depredations on land as far as the Mediterranean), expounded in the same way the pagan divinities of the Norse. The theory called 'Euhemerism'. The term coined after the name of 'Euhemerus', has [its advocates to this day].

Myths were originally believed, among the philologists during the period of the ascendancy of Max Muller, to be sentimental descriptions of nature. Man half-consciously tended to read the tragedy of his own life in the birth of the sun, its 'kissing of the dew to death', its culmination, descent and disappearance into the arms of night. It was owing to the fact that Indo-European noun is either masculine or feminine that the descriptions tended to personify the objects; and it was also owing to the fact that the language was evolving that, the original references of personifying nouns were presently forgotten with the result that words were finally taken to be personal names. For example, such a metaphysical name for the sun as Kephalos, the 'Head' of light, presently lost its meaning and was thought to refer to a human youth. Correspondingly the fading dew, Prokris, the bride of the 'Head' took on the meaning of a mortal girl of tragical demise. One more step: the names might become confused with those of actual historical heroes, whereupon the myth would be transformed into a legend.

Max Muller made an elaborate attempt to account for the mechanics of personification. Majority of anthropologists opined that savages and poets tend to attribute souls to things and personify. The child-like fantasy of primitive man, his poetic feeling and morbid, dream-ridden imagination, played into his attempts to explain the world around him, thus producing a phantasmagoric counter-world. But there is no denying the fact that the savage's effort at the core aimed to discover the causes of things and control them through spells, prayer, sacrifice and sacrament. Mythology was, therefore, only false aetiology and ceremonial is but a misguided technology. With the gradual unmethodical, but nevertheless restrained recognition of error upon error, man progressed through the labyrinth of wonder to the clearer-headed stand of today. Mythology does not have the antiquity of geologic ages, but is, nevertheless, a very old pattern woven into the terrain over the course of thousands of years. Each continent, except Antarctica, boasts its own mythological antiquity distinct from then mythological antiquity of another continent. Myths are not sown, as are gardens, for they are inherited from the past and will be passed on to the future. Myths, when viewed at a distance, creates a luxuriant configuration that suffers a gradual change from place to place, and, viewed at a close range, reflect the desires and fears of distinct peoples, granting them trusteeship of the land with the consent of the unseen powers.

The third theory, the theory that rather supplemented than contradicted the descriptive-aetiological theory, represented primitive man as terrified by the presence of the grave and, hence, anxious to propitiate them so much so that the roots of the myths and rituals went down to the black sub-soil of the grave-cult and fear of death.

The fourth theory was put forward by the French sociologist, Emile Durkheim by arguing that the collective superexcitation (or surexcitation) of clan, tribal and intertribal gatherings was experienced by every participating member of the group as an impersonal, infectious power (mana) which would be thought to emanate out of the clan or tribal emblem (totem). This emblem would be set apart from all other objects, as filled with mana. The mana, this first cult object, would then infect with mana all associated things, beliefs and practices relative to sacred things, uniting in a single moral community all believers. This theory, as propounded by Emile Durkheim, represented religion not as a morbid exaggeration, false hypothesis, or unenlightened fear, but as a truth emotionally experienced. The truth the theory insists on is the relationship of the individual to the group.

It is interesting to note that the recognition by Durkheim of a kind of truth residing at the root of the image-world of myth is supported and elaborated by the psychoanalysts by demonstrating that dreams are but precipitations of unconscious desires, ideals and fears, and further that the images of dream resemble often to the detail the motifs of folktale and myth. Through their study of symbol-inventing, myth-motif-producing level of the psyche, this level of psyche construed as a source of all those universal themes which men have read into the phenomena of nature, into the shadows of the tomb, the lives of the heroes and the emblems of the society, the psycho-analysts have doubtlessly touched the central moment of the multifarious problem.

To sum up, the 'monstrous, irrational and unnatural' motifs of folktale and myth are derived from the reservoirs of dream and vision. Such images represent on the dream level the total state of individual dreaming psyche, but, when clarified of personal distortions and propounded, at the same time, by poets, prophets and other visionaries, turns symbolic of the spiritual norm for man the mascrocosm. They are, thus, phrases that have originated from an image-language, suggestive of psychological, metaphysical and sociological truth. This vocabulary, pondered and more or less understood in the primitive, oriental and archaic and mediaeval societies, has suddenly lost its meaning and been pronounced insane in the wake of Enlightenment.

Now let us switch our attention over to the tales (both folk and tales).

In contrast to the myth, the folk tale is a form of entertainment and in proportion to the entertainment or amusement he affords to his listeners, the storyteller fails or succeeds. Though his motifs may be plucked from the tree of myth, his craft is never precisely of the mythological order. His productions have to be judged, not from a scientific, sociological, psychological or metaphysical point of view, but as an individual art discoverable at discoverable periods, in discoverable stages, which often prompt us into asking: What principle of craftsmanship inspired the narrators who gave shape to these stories in the long reaches of the past?

The Indian, Celtic, Arabian and Mediaeval masters of narrative—we owe to them the most exquisite of tales that have come down to us—practised a craft which strove to reveal through mortal things the brilliance of eternal forms. The quality of their work was a spiritual precision and their power was instructive wonder. To us there exists no distinction between their craft and metaphysics, inasmuch as the connotation of the term, 'metaphysical' has been enlarged to include everything untranslatable into positivistic discourse. But the peoples of the pre-modern type, be they gothic, oriental, archaic, totemistic, or primitive, took for granted the operation of a transcendent energy in the form of space and time. It is, thus, imperative of every artist, no matter what the craft, to get his product to show its sign of spirit and to serve its mechanical end. The function of the craft is, on the other hand, to fill the vacant hour with symbolic fare. The fascination of the tale increases in proportion to the richness of its symbolic content, symbolization being one of the main characteristics of the tale.

In this context comes up the tall tale. The moment the tall tale has come up, a pertinent question proposes itself: Is the tall tale synonymous with tall story? But the essence of the tall story is not in a true sense the same as the essence of the tall tale. I have brought up the comparison between the tall story and tall tale, for the reader confuses the two different terms, because we often tend to regard the two terms synonymous. A tall story is usually an extravagant, outlandish or highly improbable story, often regarded as false. Tall stories are of the same family as fantasy or fairy tale. The epic tradition, and especially the primary epic, contains a good many episodes which are classified as tall stories. The tall story has generally flourished in the environments and atmospheres of frontier life, bad lands, pioneering endeavours, among many sporting fraternities, among fishermen and sailors and especially in rural areas. It should be mentioned in this connexions that though tall stories are not in a proper sense folk tales, there are no mean number of folk tales, the product of rural environments, which have all the traditional elements of a good tall story (i.e. Jack the Giant-killer); not a few of the best tall stories belong to the oral tradition, like the famous R.A.F., one (of the Second World War) about the squadron that bombed dummy aeroplane on a German airfield with wooden bombs. Here we have seen that all folktales are not tall stories and all tall stories are not folktales.

Now let us see how the tall tale corresponds to the folklore and this necessitates a brief discussion of the tell tale. Though tall tale is greatly difficult to trace through history, it has been surely around a long time. The Odyssey, a Greek epic poem attributed to Homer, describing the adventures of Odysseus in course of his return from the Trojan War to his kingdom of Ithaka, must have its source in oral yarn spinning and literature from the first century A.D. onwards abounds in tall tales. Considering the constraint on space, we should not saunter around the history of tall tale; we'd rather pass over to the texts of the tall tale.

The telling of any tall tale is a communicative event, as is any folktale. It is, like any folktale, is a complex intertwining of text and context, form and function. To attempt to separate the inseparable becomes enlightening when one can approach it with a sense of humour, proportion and humility, expecting the division to be neither clean nor permanent, but simply and temporarily useful.

European and American folklorists have judged the folktale to be more peculiarly American than any other types of humour. Early visitors to America as well as those who just read the traveller's accounts or imported American plays agreed upon exaggeration and extravagance of American humour which somewhat paralleled the tall tale to the tall story. But the tall tale is, unlike the tall story, a comic fiction disguised as a fact, but intentionally and deliberately exaggerated to the limits of credibility or sometimes beyond the limits with the sole purpose of revealing emotional truths and defining and binding a social group. The most artistically successful tell-tale writers were those who most creatively transformed folklore's subtle functions and meanings into tall literature.

Although neither invented in nor restricted to North America, the tall tale has held a high place of special significance in American life. Almost from the beginning, the incomprehensible vastness of the continent, the extraordinary fertility of the land and the varieties of natural peculiarities stimulated the tall tale with a humour of extravagance and exaggeration, while the American's need to affirm the value of a culture in many ways independent of European refinements, constraints and mores that endangered a humour that was sociable, though exclusive.

The flush time of the American literary tall tale roughly fits into the period 1831 to 1860. The year 1831 witnessed to the first performance of James Kirke Paulding's tall comedy "The Lion of the West" and to the founding of William Trotter Porter's sporting weekly, "The Spirit of the Times". During the next few decades, when any itinerant judge or small-time editor in the Southwest could become a writer of backwoods sketches. Tall-tales written by them were printed in newspapers, almanacs and gift books, and were reprinted and circulated throughout the country. They described eccentrics, old-timers, jokers and hunters who told of huge and clever bears, giant mosquitoes, extraordinary marksmen and vast deserts and boiling springs of the Gar East. Many of the tales purport to be close transcripts of folk tales and others are but purely inventions in imitation of the previously printed versions of American and European folk tales.

In the above short discussion it is evident that tall tale in North America is what we call folk tale outside North America.

II

Before we touch on the folklore of North-East India which is the part of folklore of India, let us roam through the folklore of India. Anyone, if he or she desires to study the culture of India, requires himself or herself to study not only its written classics, but its oral tradition of which folklore is an important part. Folklore spreads through childhoods, families and communities as the symbolic parts of the non-literate parts of the people and the culture. Even in large modern cities, and even in Western-style nuclear families folklore is only a suburb or grandmother away and flourishes in the back streets of a city like Chennai. Wherever people live, folklore grows. New jokes, proverbs (like the new campus proverb. 'To xerox is to know'), rhymes, tales and songs circulate in the folk tradition. Verbal folklore, in the sense of a largely oral tradition with specific genres (such as proverb, riddle, lullaby, tale, ballad, prose narrative, song), non-verbal modes (such as dances, games, floor or oral designs, artifacts from toys to outdoor clay horses particularly in villages) and composite performing arts (such as street magic and street theatre, which combine prose, verse, song, dance, various local objects, costume and so on), is woven in and out of every aspect of city, village and small-town life.

Whoever speaks of India or Indian cannot help adding that India contains many Indias. In this connexion I quote A.K. Ramanujan as saying in his Introduction to *Folktales from India*, published by Penguin Books, India in 1994, "Over a hundred languages, ten major script systems and several minor ones, many old religions with innumerable sects and cults, racial mixture over millennia, a variety of landscapes and so on have contributed to an incredibly complex braiding of traditions and countertraditions" (xv).

Let us examine two traditions: Great Tradition and Little Tradition. It is commonly held that Great Traditions are pan-Indian and the Little Traditions are not. Sanskrit and Pakrit, despite their having pan-Indian distributions, still originate in regions, Sanskrit, translocal and ageographic though it is, has a variety of pronunciations identifiable in Bengali, Malayali or Benaras. It should be noted at the same time that the so-called Little Traditions do not of necessity confine themselves to small localities or dialects, for proverbs, riddles, and stories and tunes, motifs and genres of songs and dances are not, though embodied in the non-literate dialects, confined to a region. They seem to be enclosed in those mythic entities which are called self-sufficient village communities. It is often said of folklore pieces that they are autotelic, their purpose being to travel by themselves without any movement of populations. The moment a folklore piece is told, it starts travelling by itself, delighting in crossing linguistic boundaries. Though folklore pieces or items arise or are current in apparently narrow incommunicable dialects and localized dialects, they do not confine themselves to travelling within the country or culture, they become part of international network.

III

The seven states of which the North-Easter region comprises have for long shared certain features in terms of their social and cultural history. The shared tradition in history, linguistics, demography and sociology stresses the fact of two or three broad streams of culture flowing through the region to evolve a kind of synthesis still today judged as a continuous and unifying process. There is attached to each tradition certain distinctiveness in relation to the tribes who inhabit the region.

The tribal societies in the North-Eastern region are not all of a piece, but the point of ethnicity and the physical conditions of living give unto them certain common features amidst their diversities in modes of thought and social behaviour. Most studies, centred on rites and rituals in conformity with the known scales of social anthropology, seem to have missed out on such aspects as could have been brought into focus if the range of studies had been enlarged to include those aspects.

Although the relation of the creation myths and the primitive rituals with their vegetation and cultivation cults to the agriculture system obtaining in the tribal societies, their intricate bearing on the evolution of tribal language and folklore has yet to be explored. Yet the studies carried on of the folklore systems, particularly of the myths and the folk tales shed light on the meaningful difference in the perception and conceptualization of thoughts and ideas between the food-gathering and food-producing societies on one hand and the food-producing societies growing paddy and other crops through jum cultivation (shifting cultivation) and wet cultivation. The custom like head hunting and the corresponding rituals acquire, as they grow, a mythical dimension in tribes which have stuck on to the food-gathering stage. When some of them move over to the food-production level, new myths emerge and are interpreted in a new light. The actual physical conditions underlying these differences effect the change in the oral tradition.

The earliest stage here, as in other parts of the world, was that of food-gathering, when tribes took up hunting as their major occupation; then magic dominated the oral tradition. The second stage was the stage of food-production which was still at primitive level which continued up to the second millennium BC when the use of iron was not known. Then we come to an intermediate stage when D.D. Kosambi is quoted by Lalit Kumar Barua in his book, *Oral Tradition and Folk Heritage of North-East India* on page 93 as saying, "farming remained a supplement to food-gathering." Imitative magic intruded into the folklore as a dominant motif when agriculture replaced the food-gathering and inaugurated the cults of vegetation myths or fertility rituals. Since before plough was invented, the breakthrough had achieved in cultivation by woman, there was born the cult of the Mother Goddess. In the north-eastern part of India, the intermediate stage in which food-production remained a supplement to food-gathering can be seen in the life and lore of major tribes, such as the Nagas for instance. The vestiges of the cult of the Mother Goddess can be traced back to the original mythologies of the Austric-speaking Khasi and Jaintia tribes; both the tribes are matrimonial and women enjoy a dominant position. The village gods and deities, mostly adaptations of tribal gods and deities, underwent a gradual change to acquire a symbolic significance and to cope with the demands of changing times.

Ecology greatly determines the condition of living and influences the pattern of thought and behaviour in a tribal society and accounts for the differences that exist between one group and another. It ushers in, as is its nature, occasional changes in the response of each group to the set of notions and beliefs that wield a sceptre over them. Tribes living on a parched dry land differ with other tribes living in a cold mountainous region or in luxuriant forests or river valleys on ritual status of certain ceremonies performed during their traditional festivals common to all the tribes.

Many tribal groups in North-East India have still adhered to the jum cultivation or shifting cultivation. What is significant is the fact that the gathering mode still imposes upon them a severe restriction and keeps them in the areas where it is dominant, language itself function at the rudimentary level of magic and incantation. There is also a wider implication. I have to bang on the door of the book, *Oral Tradition and Folk Heritage of North-East India* to see D.D. Kosambi quoted by Lalit Kumar Barua as saying, "In the gathering mode societies depend almost exclusively on human muscle power and wood fuels as sources of energy, and on naturally available plants, animals and stones to fulfill their material requirements. Their knowledge base is fairly limited and nature is viewed as almost totally capricious, as something not subject to human control" (95). Their ability to store food and other materials was limited, as was their ability to transport over a long distance.

The ability for storing food grains gave a special status to food-sharing and concentration upon one type of food, be it an animal, a fish, a bird, or an insect or a fruit, laid the cornerstone of totemism in the primitive tribal societies. The attitude vis-à-vis food-gathering was associated with a special ritual.

When we pass on to the second stage when agriculture developed, we will see that women occupied dominant position. Thus, the folklore abounds in myths of mother goddess, among others, and the rituals and ceremonies pertaining to various fertility cults. Since the women enjoyed a dominant position, there was a tendency on the part of women to domineer over men folk, resulting in conflicts between men and women which got embedded deep in the myths and the rituals. It is clearly seen in the societies in which transition from one stage to another was more or less swift. In this connexion it is worth reproducing the comment of Sujit Chaudhury (enshrined in his book, *Folklore and History*, 1997, 31) as follows:

> Precisely the end of [the] female domination and the emergence of patriarchy were not devoid of conflict and contradiction in this country. The matricide committed by Parusaram was but a remnant of this phase of transition. In the legend of Savitri, traces of this phase are completely erased out, but in the ritual the indication of social conflict is still discernible. The implement that was instrumental in depriving women of their age-old status of supremacy became an object of disdain and hatred. The plough thus became (a symbol) of bondage to the (sic) women. The tremor of that old conflict still persists. Thus any substance which is a product of plough cultivation is considered a taboo in the Savitri Vrata. (Lalit Kumar Barua has quoted the comment in his book *Oral Tradition and Folk Heritage of North-East India*, 95-96)

In my introductions to the seven parts, each part assigned to each state of North-East India, I have very briefly dealt with the geographical status and the folklore of each state. It would be cumbersome and boring for the readers, my dealing with the folklore of North-East India in further detail. An opportunity arising, I would write a comprehensive book on different aspects of the folklore of North-East India, including Tripura and Nepal. Very unfortunately, the authors of the two books, i.e. *Oral Tradition and Folk Heritage of North-East India* and *Essays on the Folklore and Culture of North-Eastern India*, have omitted discussing in some detail the folklore of Tripura, despite the titles, I could not resist the urge to bring in a short discussion on the folklore of Tripura.

IV

Since time immemorial Tripura has been known as the conflux, I would rather say, watersmeet, of different cultures and the tribal people of the states have been living in communion with different races, particularly Bengali race. The culture of the original tribal people and those of other races who came over to settle in Tripura have intermingled and created a uniform tradition so much so that one cannot separate one culture from another out of this intermingling.

The folklore is the heritage of this tradition. But I shall categorize the folklore of Tripura as the Tribal folklore, since it existed much before other races intruded into this territory.

The tribal folklore owes its source to the tribal people's imagination, their ideas and thought, and particularly, their social consciousness, and bears the distinct evidence of heroism and immortal love. The folktale abounds in numerous tales about kings and princes, about religious rites and rituals and about natural calamities and the tales were embellished with attitude of the ancient tribal people to life in relation to nature.

The jum cultivation (shifting cultivation) has commingled with the tribal life and it has come down to the present day from time immemorial, riding on the shoulder of the tribal folklore. All religious ceremonies were centered on the jum cultivation and the people, irrespective of men and women, busied themselves in jum cultivation and their jum-related thoughts naturally permeated the folklore.

Animism is one of the important aspects of the Tribal folklore. Unable to explain the causes of thunderbolt and other natural calamities, they imagined them as gods and goddesses and put their death down to their anger. Even they deified snakes and trees and worshipped them to propitiate them, as they did the thunderbolt and other natural calamities. There is no dearth of folktales which portray vivid pictures of sufferings, injustice and other social ills and there are no mean number of traditional tales and ither tales that carry the stamp of real life.

The motif of the tribal folklore is oral tradition. The ancient tribal people had no written language and literature to embalm their tales and the tales used to pass from lips to lips and were transmitted trough lips to next generations. In the tribal folklore we taste the savour of the tales that percolated to the tribal tales from outside and this percolation serves to enrich the folklore of every state, every country, for human mind is attuned to the same thought, the same idea relating to life and the way of living and as all human beings pass through the same stage of social development. The gregariousness of human beings enhances the process of percolation.

Even today the tribal community has adhered to the ancient social system. The tribal people live in a composite and congenial community guided by common interests. They are gregarious by nature, though nowadays owing to the spread of education, individualism had made itself felt among the educated youths.

In ancient times people formed communities with a view to saving themselves from the wrath of nature, from the attacks of ferocious animals. Then nature dominated the life of the people. Even people belonging to one community used to regard people belonging to another community as their enemies and this enmity gave rise to communal fights and there are so many tales recording these fights. We even read tales of their struggle against human and divine tyrants and of how even gods themselves courted defeat to their unified struggles.

In the tribal folktale there is an excessive use of totemism, mana and taboo. They were but the natural consequences of the fear of the ancient people, unable to explain the causes of natural calamities and different aspects of nature.

REFERENCES

Ramanujan, A.K., *Folktales from India* (1994).

Barua, Lalit Kumar, *Oral Tradition and Folk Heritage of North-East India* (1999).

Goswami, Prafulladatta, *Essays on the Folklore and Culture of North-Eastern India* (1983).

Bierhorst, John, *The Mythology of North America* (1985).

Brown, Carolyn S., *The Tall Tale in American Folklore and Literature* (1988).

Roy, Arundhati, Tripurar Upajati Lokakatha, Samaj O Ruptattwa (2000).

20

"In Essence Divided"—The Border as a Metaphor in the World of Harry Potter

Shampa Ghosh

In creating the world of Harry Potter, J.K. Rowling has in essence created a dichotomy—a space where the real and the magical coexist harmoniously and the protagonist flits between one and the other effortlessly. The duality exists at several levels providing images of a tangible border as well as the symbolic duality of felt experiences. On the surface the Harry Potter series is the conventional and eternal conflict between the opposing forces of good and evil, moral and immoral, right and wrong symbolized in the person of Harry and Voldemort. But is this all that there is to it? Is there not a blurring of the rigid boundaries between the opposing forces? Are Harry and Voldemort really so very different? Rowling is quick to point out the similarities for the readers—both born to one Muggle parent, both brought up among muggles, both orphans and brought to Hogwarts to be trained as wizards. What Rowling is essentially out to prove is that there are no rigid borders between opposing forces. Just as Harry is joined to Voldemort through his cursed scar so evil is linked to goodness, cruelty linked to magnanimity and morality to immorality but, they are, as Dumbledore points out in *The Order of the Phoenix*, 'in essence divided'.

How do children relate to this dichotomy and where does the appeal of the Harry Potter series lie? What is amazing is how connected Rowling is to the world of children—a world she has never really left behind. Younger readers sense that she knows their world and what they want. She knows their tastes, how they care for brands—the Nimbus 2000 is the best broom there is until the Firebolt comes along to oust it from its place and the young wizards crowd around the display window to stare at it longingly. Adult readers are tickled to solve her puzzles. The love to see that Diagon Alley—the wizard mall is laid out, well diagonally. Readers, young and old, identify with a character who moves from being powerless to magical to having power over adults. Harry's being an orphan makes him both more vulnerable and independent than most boys his age. He had to invent himself because his spirit was not likely to be nurtured by the mean spirited Dursleys and he had to look out for himself and save himself from Dudley and his gang of bullies. This fostered a strong sense of independence, a slight disregard for rules and a precocious ability to make moral choices.

The Harry Potter series is definitely not the first of its kind. There were already a lot of books with unicorn and wizards in them before Harry came along, certainly lots of books about orphans searching for roots and adolescents coming of age in boarding schools. Rowling was carrying forward a literary tradition of novels like the Earthsea series by Ursula Le Guin, in the first volume of which the leading character Ged becomes an apprentice to a senior magician and then goes to attend a school for wizards. Monica Furlong's book *Wild Child* about a young girl living in 8th century Mull and learning to be a 'dòran'—a kind of witch who works closely with the powers of nature deal with a similar theme. The closest similarity to the works of Rowling are to be found in Jill Murphy's 'Worst Witch' books and Anthony Horowitz's Groosham Grange' both of which deal with witches and wizards and are set in boarding schools.

The image of the border as a leit motif in fiction written for children has a long tradition. In myths, fairy tales and more recent literary works we come face to face with the thin dividing line between the everyday world of harsh reality and the magical universe where the protagonist lives out the fantasy of the readers. The border is mundane, sometimes obscure almost always within the grasp of the protagonist. It may be an ordinary wardrobe through which siblings, living in a country house to escape the horrors of wartime England, slip into the magical world of Narnia. Here the conflict of the forces of good and evil symbolized by the Snow Queen vs Asian mirror the conflict raging in the world outside. The rabbit hole through which Alice slips into the terribly confusing world of the Red Queen and the March Hare or the Middle Kingdom of J.R.R. Tolkien all reflect the paradoxical world of reality and magic, magnified and fine tuned into the fantastic and heroic. Platform number 9-3/4 from where Harry makes his leap of faith into the world where he was born and where he was to take his rightful place when it was time for him to claim his inheritance. The platform is a place full of ordinary grownups with little time to spare for a boy with a trunk load of magical artifacts and a snowy owl in a cage. It is a witch who shows him the entrance to the world of magic and the way to step into it. Not only that Molly Weasley is the surrogate mother who takes Harry Potter into the bosom of her family and provides him with a home in the world of magic.

Harry is a link in the long line of heroes whose beginning lies within their heritage. Like the others it may appear at first sight that Harry has been catapulted to heroic stature for a life shattering incident which he does not even seem to remember but the physical manifestation of which—the lightening shaped scar on his forehead is his only link to the past. In creating his character Rowling does not move too far away from the formulaic delineation of the classic hero. Biologically, genetically and embryonically, the hero is likely to come from appropriately strong roots, good DNA. Mythologically, he is the scion of earlier heroes whose qualities are enhanced by the fresh rigors and opportunities of a new environment. Thus, although a boy of ten only, when the first book opens, Harry walks in a line that extends for thousands of years and through numerous narrative structures—a line including figures as seemingly disparate as Gilgamesh (the son of Uruk's King

Lugalbanda), Arthur (the son of Britain's King Uther Pendragon), Kal-El (the son of Krypton's greatest scientist Jor-El), and Luke Skywalker (the son of Jedi knight Anakin Skywalker). It is a manifestation of the boundless interest which is innate in humanity for heroes—a interest both universal and individual. Joseph Campbell describes this interest in *The Hero with a Thousand Faces* as the heroic monomyth "through which the inexhaustible energies of the cosmos pour into the human cultural manifestation". The manifestation of such energies may emerge in the form of a hero who represents the intense human struggle for both power and wisdom, recognition and introspection, grandeur and honour. Few achieve the rigorous balance of such dualities.

The characters and events of the Harry Potter novels match up to the patterns set up with the Arthurian legends, Lord of the Rings, the Chronicles of Narnia, etc. There is a marked similarity between Dumbledore and Gandalf. Both are extremely old, both have a twinkle in their eyes, both set heroes on a quest, both seem to know more than they let on and both die but come back into the story. The duality which exists in the world of Harry Potter is more of a series of parallels drawn between co-existing worlds rather than a border or dividing line between two diametrically opposed worlds. The parallel is rather obvious in the opening pages of *The Half Blood Prince* when the Muggle Prime Minister confronts his magical counterpart and blames him for not using magic to resolve the difficulties plaguing the magical world which are replicated in the muggle world.

Rowling explores the reflexive relationship between childhood and adulthood, heightening the various tensions which coalesce around the issue of duality. Age and youth, good and evil, innocence and corruption heighten the normative structure of the narratology. Rowling reveals Alrays in which evil can be masqueraded as goodness, demonstrating corruption as represented in adults who are deceitful and malevolent. One of the first characters to embody the maxim that appearances are deceptive is Gilderoy Lockhart whose handsome visage is a front for a vicious and depraved personality. Similarly the Veela—hypnotic and beautiful creatures appear ugly and unattractive when viewed closely. The Mirror of Erised is the finest example of the duality of appearance and reality. Reflecting the innermost desires of the viewer's heart, it induces insanity and disconnect from reality. What is displayed is shadowy, unsubstantial from which there is no escape.

The sense of ambiguity, of no clear answers grows stronger with each book as Harry grows older and sees more and farther. The school teachers—benevolent as well as the malevolent ones—are marked by this duality. The most obvious example of which is Professor Snape, inimical towards Harry, unattractive both in physical appearance and disposition, carrying forward a long nursed grudge from father to son, driven by jealousy of Harry yet willing to protect him when he must. Similarly Professor Lupin—distrusted by most wizards, yet truly noble and selfless when it comes to opposing the forces of evil.

In *The Prisoner of Azkaban* we meet the Dementors—hideously telepathic creatures, capable of sucking a victim's sanity away by draining him of all hope and happy memory leaving only despair and hopelessness behind. Yet they are used by the good side as guards of Azkaban, the prison where rogue wizards are incarcerated The Border as a Metaphor in the World of Harry Potter although they are pure evil personified. The dichotomy persists. Rowling constructs the reflexive nature of time and the reflexive relationship between adulthood and childhood in adult characters who exhibit child-like characteristics. Those adult characters who tend to be more positively represented in Rowling's work are those who capture the essence of childhood and remain child-like in some respects. Sirius Black is described as having lines on his young face. Professor Albus Dumbledore though very old "always gave an impression of great energy" (*The Prisoner of Azkaban*, p. 71). Arthur Weasely attending the Quidditch World Cup "Looked as excited as any of the children". (*The Goblet of Fire*, p. 86). The paradoxical relationship between youth and age is encapsulated by Dumbledore's remark that "youth cannot know how age thinks and feels. But old men are guilty if they forget what it was to be young" (*The Order of the Phoenix*, p. 728). However, the most interesting case of duality which Rowling presents in the Harry Potter series is in the presentation of the mythical creatures. The non-human creature who inhabit this world have their own duality. Some of them are imaginary like the Hippogrif which clearly transcends the border between bird and animal. Fluffy—the three headed dog is obviously linked to Cerebrus, guarding the gates of the underworld.

Rowling's whole approach to mythological creature as well as the mythic story she wrote was to turn a prototypical tale of a heroic journey on its head. She tends to take stereotypes and present them differently blurring the boundaries between the felt and the acquired knowledge. Mythological creature from all cultures abound, living unseen by the muggles in their midst, like the goblins, or inhabiting the hallways and classrooms of Hogwarts, or the sinister depths of Hagrid's charmed forest. There are merpeople in the lake and hags in the village. Professor Lupin in his Defence against the Dark Arts classes introduces the students to a variety of creatures like the Kappas, the Hinkypunks and the Grindylow. There is also the Boggart, a shape shifting creature of Irish legend that takes on the form of its victim's deepest fears. Characteristically, it is defeated by laughter, reminiscent of Golux's charge, "Remember laughter, you'll need it even in the blessed isle of Ever After".

Thus, her giant tends to be maternal instead of vicious though beyond the influence of the wizard world they retain their violent and querulous nature. Her spider was innocent of the crime attributed to it and loyal to its keeper and it was also male as opposed to the Jungian and Freudian spiders which are always female. Her dragons though fierce are under the domination of man/wizard and are sometimes victimized. The Forbidden forest contains centaurs and unicorns. Of course, her centaurs are still presented as virile. There is debauchery implied in what happened to Umbridge in the forest and in her PTSD reaction after Dumbledore fetches her back. Her

Unicorns however retain their innocence whereas the centaurs are the wise ones more interested in studying the movement of the stars and what they predict rather than events which take place under their very nose.

One of the most amazing and unusual creatures introduced in the fifth book of the series is the Thestral. Thestrals are fictional creature with no pre-existing history in mythological tradition. They are unusual in the fact that they are visible only to those who have experienced tragedy. So Harry, Luna and Neville are the only ones to whom they are visible. Thestrals blur the physical divide between the visible and the invisible. The characteristics of the Thestral must be inferred from similar horse like creatures in myth and legend and from the context of the new mythology created by J.K. Rowling. Most folktales portray horses as extending the physical ability of their riders so aiding the hero on his journey. In *The Order of the Phoenix* it is the thestrals who carry Harry and his friends to the Ministry of Magic and to the direct confrontation with Voldemort Horse like flying creatures of legend transport the rider from earthly terrain into the internal mindscape of the hero's self—so aiding in his self-dicovery, insight and transformation. Horses that allow humans to ride them are often brave, selfless and loyal to their riders. The relationship between Shadow fax and Gandalf comes to mind. Perhaps the same relationship exists between Harry and Firenze who was kicked out of the magical forest by Bane and the other centaurs for meddling in the affairs of the humans. By crossing over to the other side he overrides the boundaries between man and animal and attains human attributes ultimately taking on the role of a teacher at Hogwarts. Stubborn yet willing, forever wild but sometimes willing to be tamed, sensitive yet strong these horse like creatures are a contradiction. Their best interaction is with those humans-wizard or muggle who are willing to treat them as equals like Dumbledore or Harry or Hagrid.

Harry's world is chock full of fantastic others, creatures fundamentally different from those found in the mundane world of facts—creatures that almost always participate in one way or another in the testing process. The Potter series has dragons—mighty creatures, quite capable of testing any hero. Of more consequence, however, is that Hogwarts itself is a locus for magical creatures of every degree of sentience and significance. The empirical knowledge imparted to the hero by his encounters with these creatures is vital if he is to grow in wisdom as well as strength.

The duality in the Harry Potter universe is best exemplified in Hogwarts. Forever changing shape, leading the hero to new challenges, it is a mystery which is only partly unravelled by the Marauders Map. More than a fairy tale backdrop for the witches and wizards of the Potter universe Hogwarts is the nexus between the agony of their past and the uncertainty of their futures—and not even the Headmaster knows all its secrets. For Harry, Hogwarts is the place for tests—some academic, some practical and some moral. Many of these tests include adventure, danger and choice—heady stuff that forces Harry and his friends to grow up before their time or fail and failure in the magical world is nearly always fatal.

The final duality as represented by Rowling in the Harry Potter books is her delineation of the character of Voldemort—drawn along the lines of the classical Dark Lord and yet for all his similarity to other villains, Voldemort embodies Rowling's own definition of evil. In his search for immortality he embodies the visions of life and death and the ultimate quest. In every culture immortality, though desirable is against the laws of nature. Things must die so that other things may be born. So the border between these two realities fade away in the half life to which the villain is condemned to exist before his final defeat in the massive struggle between the forces of good and evil.

REFERENCES

Rowling, J.K. The Harry Potter series.

——. *The Sorcerer's Stone* (1998).

——. *The Chamber of Secrets.* (1998).

——. *The Prisoner of Azkaban.* (1999).

——. *The Goblet of Fire.* (2000).

——. *The Order of the Phoenix* (2003).

——. *The Half Blood Prince*. (2005).

——. *The Deathly Hallows*. (2007) (Bloomsbury).

Colbert, David. *The Magical World of "Harry Potter*. Puffin books. London. 2001.

Iyer, Pico. *The Playing Fields of Hogwarts*. The New York Times. 10th October, 1999.

Clute, John. *The Encyclopedia of Fantasy*. St. Martins. New York. 1999.

Contributors

Joyashri Choudhury. Associate Professor, Department of English, Khagarijan College, Nagaon, Assam.

George Papantonakis. Assistant Professor, University of the Aegean, Rhodes, Greece.

Sihem Arfaoui Abidi. Ph.D. Jendouba University, Tunisia.

Amber Dinquel. M.A. English, Illinois State University, United States.

Enkelena Shockett (Qafleshi). PhD, University of Tirana, Albania.

Kelvin N. Toh. Ph.D, University of Yaounde 1, Cameroon.

Elena Xeni. Department of Education, University of Cyprus, Nicosia.

Devika. Assistant Professor, BITS Pilani, Rajasthan.

Sushila Rathore. Assistant Professor, BITS Pilani, Rajasthan.

Virendra Singh Nirban. Assistant Professor, BITS Pilani, Rajasthan.

Sushmita Bhattacharya. Associate Professor, Department of English, D D U Gorakhpur University, Gorakhpur.

Saurav Das Thakur. Department of English & OMEL Visva-Bharati, Santiniketan, West Bengal.

Saurabh Kumar Singh. Assistant Professor of English, Vasanta College for Women, Banaras Hindu University, Varanasi.

Vandana Singh. Assistant Professor, Chandragupt Institute of Management, Patna.

Saloni Prasad (Mrs. Kumar). Associate Professor, Department of English, College of Commerce, Patna.

Reena Mitra. Professor in English, Amity School of Languages, Amity University, U.P. Lucknow.

Ramendra Kumar. Chief of Communications & DGM (PR), Rourkela Steel Plant, Rourkela.

Beena Agarwal. Associate Professor, Department of English, D.S. College, Aligarh.

Anirban Gupta. Assistant Teacher, Barrackpore, A.B. Model High School (H.S.), 24 Pargana, Kolkata.

Norah Nivedita Shaw. Associate Professor, Department of English, Sri Arvind Mahila College, Patna.

Bhasker Roy Barman. Indian English Writer, Poet, Critic Translator, Editor and Folklorist, Agartala.

Shampa Ghosh. Associate Professor, Department of English, College of Commerce, Patna.